The Words and Music of Neil Young

THE PRAEGER SINGER-SONGWRITER COLLECTION

The Words and Music of Neil Young

Ken Bielen

James E. Perone, Series Editor

PRAEGER

Westport, Connecticut
London

Library of Congress Cataloging-in-Publication Data

Bielen, Kenneth G.
    The words and music of Neil Young / Ken Bielen.
        p. cm.—(The Praeger singer-songwriter collection, ISSN 1553-3484)
    Includes bibliographical references and index.
    ISBN 978-0-275-99902-5 (alk. paper)
    1. Young, Neil, 1945-   2. Rock musicians—Canada—Biography.   I. Title.
ML420.Y75B54 2008
782.42166092—dc22   2008005330

British Library Cataloguing in Publication Data is available.

Library of Congress Catalog Card Number: 2008005330
ISBN: 978-0-275-99902-5
ISBN: 978-1-4408-3643-5 (pbk.)
ISSN: 1553-3484

First published in 2008

Praeger Publishers, 88 Post Road West, Westport, CT 06881
An imprint of Greenwood Publishing Group, Inc.
www.praeger.com

Printed in the United States of America

The paper used in this book complies with the
Permanent Paper Standard issued by the National
Information Standards Organization (Z39.48-1984).

10 9   8   7   6   5   4   3   2   1

I dedicate this work to my wife Mary: Thanks, honey, my "Heart of Gold," for everything. You were my "Cinnamon Girl" and my "New Mama" and everything else I could have dreamed of. This note's for you.

Contents

Series Foreword

Although the term, *Singer-Songwriters,* might most frequently be associated with a cadre of musicians of the early 1970s such as Paul Simon, James Taylor, Carly Simon, Joni Mitchell, Cat Stevens, and Carole King, the Praeger Singer-Songwriter Collection defines singer-songwriters more broadly, both in terms of style and in terms of time period. The series includes volumes on musicians who have been active from approximately the 1960s through the present. Musicians who write and record in folk, rock, soul, hip-hop, country, and various hybrids of these styles will be represented. Therefore, some of the early 1970s introspective singer-songwriters named above will be included, but not exclusively.

What do the individuals included in this series have in common? Some have never collaborated as writers. But, while some have done so, all have written and recorded commercially successful and/or historically important music *and* lyrics at some point in their careers.

The authors who contribute to the series also exhibit diversity. Some are scholars who are trained primarily as musicians, while others have such areas of specialization as American studies, history, sociology, popular culture studies, literature, and rhetoric. The authors share a high level of scholarship, accessibility in their writing, and a true insight into the work of the artists they study. The authors are also focused on the output of their subjects and how it relates to their subject's biography and the society around them; however, biography in and of itself is not a major focus of the books in this series.

Given the diversity of the musicians who are the subject of books in this series, and given the diversity of viewpoint of the authors, volumes in the series will differ from book to book. All, however, will be organized chronologically around the compositions and recorded performances of their subjects. All of the books in the series should also serve as listeners' guides to the music of their subjects, making them companions to the artists' recorded output.

James E. Perone
Series Editor

Acknowledgments

To Allison Krause, Bill Schroeder, Jeff Miller, and Sandy Scheuer of Kent State University: The world needed you more than it needed "Ohio." And if you had had the chance to live your lives and contribute to society, perhaps we would not be "living with war" today.

To Bill Schurk of the Sound Recording Archives at Bowling Green State University—thanks for building such a great collection—and to the window students for finding the vinyl, the video, the compact discs, and the books.

To the staff members of the Wood County Public Library in Bowling Green, Ohio, the Maumee, Ohio Branch of the Toledo-Lucas County Public Library, and the Jackson Library on the Indiana Wesleyan University campus in Marion, Indiana—thanks for helping to get compacts discs, books, videos, and DVDs through the interlibrary loan.

To Wessels 3rd Floor at Rutgers in New Brunswick, especially Dave Springer, Joe Ossi, Bob Myers, and Dave Twitchell: it all began when I brought Buffalo Springfield *Again* back to the dorm after winter break 1967–68.

In memory of Elvis Presley (1935–1977), Rick Nelson (1940–1985), and Carl Wilson (1946–1998), the heart and soul of the Beach Boys. Without their presence, Neil's music wouldn't have been the same.

To Ben Urish, super friend and colleague in relating music and culture.

To Allyn Beekman and Amber Simos of Indiana Wesleyan University, for friendship and encouragement.

To my parents, Stan and Fran Bielen, for unfailing love and teaching me to imagine.

To Neil, we share the same birthday, our daughters went to the same college together, and we were together the night Nixon announced his resignation: there must be some connection in this cosmic soup.

To Mary Cotofan and the staff at Apex CoVantage on the production side and Dan Harmon on the acquisitions side for assistance in making this book a reality.

To Duane Heck, thanks for the loan of the vinyl.

To Linda Ronstadt, Emmylou Harris, and the late Nicolette Larson, thanks for adding harmony to Neil and to the world.

To my sisters, Joyce Bielen McNally and Judy Bielen Smith, for being, well, sisterly.

To Neocles and Vassiliki Leontis for always being there.

To Kelly, Alex, and Dylan Bielen: Thanks for keeping me young(er).

Introduction

Neil Percival Young was born in Toronto, Ontario several months after the curtain fell on World War II. After the breakup of his parents' marriage, he moved to Winnipeg in western Canada where he spent his formative years. How do you describe the height and width and depth and breadth of Neil Young's musical output? Young has been all over the musical map in his long, successful career. As a young musician, he tried to eke out a living as a folksinger in the coffeehouses of Toronto. He joined a rock band called the Mynah Birds that featured future Motown funkster Rick James. He made a legendary trip in an old black hearse across the United States with bassist Bruce Palmer in tow. The trip ended in Los Angeles in a serendipitous encounter with Stephen Stills and Richie Furay.

Young was a founding member of Buffalo Springfield, a band that was turning heads on the Sunset Strip within two weeks of its formation. Young was restless and quit the band several times. On his first sabbatical, he created the dreamy "Expecting to Fly." He came back to the band with that track. Within months of the release of the second album (*Again*), however, Young split again. The third album, *Last Time Around,* was put together in a piecemeal manner.

Young's eponymous solo album was issued in the winter of 1968–69. In less than six months, he followed that with a totally different album, an electric album titled *Everybody Knows This Is Nowhere,* featuring his collaboration with Crazy Horse in loose, primitive jams. Before the dust could settle, Young became a full partner in the firm of Crosby, Stills, Nash, and Young, appearing with the band at their second gig at Woodstock. Young contributed two songs to the supergroup's *Déjà vu* album.

Young's next issue, *After the Gold Rush*, released in 1970, featured members of both Crazy Horse and Crosby, Stills, and Nash. It captured the spirit of the fertile Topanga Canyon arts scene. He followed that in early 1972 with his contribution to the early 1970s singer-songwriter genre, *Harvest*, his most successful album. The collection contained two hit singles, "Old Man" and "Heart of Gold." But after the worldwide success of *Harvest*, Young took a sharp turn, as he put it, toward the ditch. This was partially in response to the drug-related deaths of colleagues and friends. He responded by creating and recording the bleak *Tonight's the Night* album; however, his record company would not release it. Instead, he issued a live album of new songs (*Time Fades Away*). Sung in a strained voice, it was guaranteed to alienate those who embraced *Harvest* and were looking forward to *Harvest II*. *On the Beach* contained a couple of pop-friendly tunes but again lacked the commercial potential that had developed from his debut through the *Harvest* album. *Tonight's the Night* was finally issued (with a black label). Although the critics acclaimed it, the public did not understand.

With *Zuma*, Young began to make inroads back into the popular music market. *Comes a Time* was the *Harvest II* that fans expected half a decade earlier. From the quiet character of the release, Young veered off into the distortion-drenched side two of *Rust Never Sleeps*. Both critics and fans embraced the late 1970s model of Neil Young. He stumbled on his next two releases, *Hawks & Doves* and *Re*ac*tor*, and, dissatisfied with his record company, he went looking for a better deal. The 1980s was a maddening period, not only for Young's new employer (Geffen Records), but for fans as well. Young dabbled in electronica (*Trans*) and rockabilly (*Everybody's Rockin'*) and traditional country (*Old Ways*) and roadhouse blues (*This Note's for You*). He even tried synth pop rock (*Landing on Water*). His experiments often failed, but Young continued to develop his modus operandi of never doing what was expected of him.

Evidence of Young dropping off the musical radar is on the cover of the paperback edition of journalist Bill Flanagan's *Written in My Soul*, published in 1987. The cover lists 11 of "rock's great songwriters" including Elvis Costello and Sting, but Young is relegated to the "and 18 others" not listed on the jacket. Keeping a promise to David Crosby regarding cleaning himself up from drug abuse, Young returned to the studio with Crosby, Stills, and Nash for 1988s *American Dream*. Young wrote the title cut. Young redeemed himself with *Freedom*, a well-thought out, eclectic album that, in the long run, came to cement Young's reputation as a formidable musical force in the history of popular music.

Young began a roll of strong, well-received albums. Crazy Horse returned for *Ragged Glory* and followed with the live *Weld* from the tour in support of the studio album. In the early 1990s, Young returned to the acoustic side with *Harvest Moon* and the live *Unplugged* from an MTV telecast. In 1994, Young responded to the tragic death of Nirvana's Kurt Cobain with *Sleeps with Angels.* The next year he partnered with Seattle grunge band Pearl Jam on *Mirror Ball.* Crazy Horse regrouped in the studio again for 1996s *Broken Arrow.* The band followed with a tour that resulted in the *Year of the Horse* live set as well as a film of the same name by Jim Jarmusch. Young again contributed the title cut to a Crosby, Stills, Nash, and Young album, *Looking Forward,* in 1999. Young turned acoustic again for *Silver & Gold* in 2000. Young had been tinkering with the title track for more than a decade. He also issued *Road Rock,* a live compendium with some of his favorite collaborators in attendance. *Greendale* was an elaborate concept album with backing by old stalwarts Crazy Horse.

After being diagnosed with a brain aneurysm, Young quickly recorded the quiet *Prairie Wind,* which was steeped in autobiographical overtones, as he reflected on his life. In response to the Iraq invasion, Young, along with Rick Rosas and Chad Cromwell in a power trio, recorded the raucous, antiwar *Living with War.* Rumors abounded of the release of the first part of Young's *Archives* retrospective in 2007. These were supported by the issue of two concerts, one with Crazy Horse from the Fillmore East in 1970, and the other a solo set from Toronto in 1971. As 2007 ebbed, it was announced that the retrospective would be held up again. *Chrome Dreams II* was issued in fall 2007. The album combines older unreleased tracks with more recent compositions.

Not growing up in Los Angeles, southern California, or the United States for that matter gave Neil Young a fresh perspective that Americans are desensitized to from spending their formative years couched in a celebrity-driven popular culture. Just as the French geographer Jean Gottmann was able to identify a "megalopolis" that stretched from Boston to Washington, something that went unnoticed by native geographers,[1] Young was able from his first recordings to observe the U.S. pop culture from a distance, from having grown up in the prairies that surround Winnipeg.

Young has been and continues to be a prolific songwriter. The focus of this book is on recordings that have had an authorized issue, and not on those available only on bootleg recordings.

With Buffalo Springfield, 1966–1968

BUFFALO SPRINGFIELD (DEBUT ALBUM)

Buffalo Springfield formed in early 1966. Soon they developed a reputation for energetic, musically powerful shows on the Sunset Strip, where locals affectionately referred to the band as the Herd. Record company executives courted the band and the group signed with Atlantic, which placed the musicians on its ATCO label. The self-titled debut was issued in January 1967. Shortly after its issue, the band enjoyed a Top-10 hit single with the Stephen Stills-penned "For What It's Worth," a track not included on the recording. The album was reconfigured to add the hit single. Another Stills-composed track, "Baby Don't Scold Me," was dropped from the album to make room for the bestseller.

Young wrote five tracks on the Buffalo Springfield debut. He sang lead on two of them. Bandmate Richie Furay had the lead vocal duties on the other three. On two of the debut compositions, Young contributed piano.

"Nowadays Clancy Can't Even Sing," with vocal by Richie Furay, was issued as a single but did not chart. The recording has some fine guitar lines and first-rate harmonies by Young, Stephen Stills, and Furay. The meaning of the song is obscure. The listener wonders who Clancy is. Young described Clancy as "just an image, a guy who gets come down on all the time" for being "beautiful."[1] At one point the lyric breaks the theatrical fourth wall. The singer remarks that he "should be sleepin'" instead of "writing this song." Before the band formed, Furay and Stills had heard Young's composition. In California, the duo developed their own arrangement, without the knowledge of Young.[2]

The flip side of Buffalo Springfield's most well-known song, Stills's "For What It's Worth," was Young's "Do I Have to Come Right Out and Say It" with vocal again by Richie Furay. The track is mid-tempo, with drummer Dewey Martin prominently setting the time with a stick to the edge of the snare. The lyric speaks to how love can "crowd" all other thought from the mind and how hard it is to risk entering a relationship after losing at love. Young played piano on the track.

The third Young song sung by Furay on the debut is "Flying on the Ground Is Wrong." Like the other two Furay-vocalized tracks, it is mid-tempo in its timing. Again Buffalo Springfield harmonies add a unique touch to the production. The narrator speaks to a love interest about acceptance. Although he may have bad habits, she needs to accept him since they are of a piece from the same neighborhood. The protagonist may have a drug problem, as the opening lines seem to describe a psychedelic trip. In the end, though, it is a song of unrequited love.

Neil Young sang lead on the uptempo "Burned" and the ballad "Out of My Mind." In "Burned," the narrator may have been swindled. He may be feeling the effects of bad dope. Or he may be suffering from withdrawal symptoms. Fellow Canadian Bruce Palmer's bass line is in the forefront of the instrumental breaks in the recording. Young contributed a rocking, upright piano line to the instrumentation.

Buffalo Springfield is only the first album Young appeared on, but already he showed a keen awareness of the California celebrity culture in "Out of My Mind" and its effects on a young person. The song opens with a processional drum beat underlined by a reverbed electric guitar. Young sings of how fame ensnares and traps. The only sounds heard by the narrator are the "screams from outside the limousine." Not only does this affect his mental health, but also these sounds crowd out the opportunity to create new music, placing more stress on the psyche. Young did something interesting with the lyric structure. The first line of the second verse is a continuation of a phrase begun at the end of the first verse, as well as the beginning of a phrase that goes into the second line of the second verse. In the second verse, Young hints at his ambivalence at being part of a group (and this is only his first album with the band). The protagonist is "tired of hanging on" and he may be "gone." In the third and final verse, he even wonders if he has chosen the right career. He is "left behind by…what (he's) living for."

AGAIN

"Mr. Soul" is the opening track on the Buffalo Springfield *Again* album. The disc debuted on the *Billboard* Top Album charts in November 1967 and peaked at Number 44.[3] The production successfully translated the excitement of the band's dual lead guitar attack. The track opens with a flourish of electric guitar chords that set a fast pace for the performance. The guitar riff is borrowed from the Rolling Stones' "(I Can't Get No) Satisfaction."[4] Young again focuses on celebrity and fandom. He speaks of the expectations of fans and how they think they know the person of the artist because they know the music. He also addresses the perils of fan worship. Young's narrator speaks of his "head" being the "event of the season." And he underlines the danger of selling out to the celebrity image when he wonders if his "smile" will "turn to plaster." He notes the rush of life going by when you are in the spotlight. Ironically, he ends the track by suggesting the listener ask the fan if she is concerned with how he is changing (his image or his music). "Mr. Soul" was the B-side of the band's "Bluebird" single, which reached Number 58 in the summer of 1967 (the Summer of Love).

The string-filled ballad "Expecting to Fly" underscored the diverse musical interests of Young and Buffalo Springfield. The recording was the first in a long line of collaborations between Young and Jack Nitzsche. Nitzsche was part of Phil Spector's studio team in the early 1960s, a group popularly known as the "wrecking crew."[5] Nitzsche's part in the development of Spector's "wall of sound" production technique is evident in Young's recording, which Nitzsche and Young co-produced and co-arranged. At the time, Nitzsche was working with the Everly Brothers, and Young considered giving the song to the duo to record.[6]

The track opens with swirling strings increasing in volume to where the tension breaks and the listener feels that he/she is in the bright blue sky above the clouds. The song continues with an ethereal, dreamlike character that seems to defy gravity. The lyrics follow this notion by painting a picture of someone standing on the "edge" of a "feather." The overall tone is one of melancholy as two lovers part. The narrator grasps for an unreachable love, as though he is in a bad dream where he cannot stand up. At the same time, though, he declares that to survive he has to live without her. Richie Furay sings along with Young on the recording. The production ends with a coda of beautifully sad strings. The song is used to great effect in the film *Coming Home* (1978) in the scene when the characters played by Jane Fonda and John Voight consummate their relationship. "Expecting to Fly" was issued as a single but barely broke into the Top 100 in early 1968.

The *Again* album closes with Young's ambitious track "Broken Arrow." It is a multipart pastiche featuring a number of ensembles. The track could have been created only in the studio. The cut opens with a portion of a live performance of "Mr. Soul." The lead vocal is by drummer Dewey Martin, who flavors the tune with a touch of Memphis soul. The audience, full of screaming, female fans, roars along in appreciation of the stage performance.[7] The live bit segues into a quiet, acoustic guitar and Young begins the first verse.

And, again, Young addresses the music scene and fandom and celebrity. The scene is the end of a concert. The curtain falls, fans wait at the stage door, and so does a "black limousine." As the song moves to the first chorus, the piano line by Don Randi becomes more assertive and picks up the tempo.

The chorus lyric describes a riverside setting. A group waves from the river. (Young experimented with a similar scene involving only one person at the river in the opening words of his demo of "Down Down Down.") In a scene symbolizing peace, a Native American holds a broken arrow. It conjures a western image that complements the Young persona, which also included his trademark leather fringe jacket.

After the chorus, the listener is presented with crowd sounds as though the setting is a midway or a circus ring. We hear booing, as a pump organ enters the mix and then becomes loud and distorted. The second verse opens with the piano alone and a change of scene in the lyric. The opening line, "Eighteen years of American dream," could mean that the character is now eligible for the draft. Young adds psychedelic imagery, noting that the same character "hung up his eyelids." As the second chorus ends, we hear the sound of martial drum rolls. The effect conjures up an image of a military funeral, which would tie in with the draft eligibility and the symbol of the broken arrow for peace. Like the organ in the prior interlude, the drum rolls increase in volume until they become just noise.

With the third verse, there is another change of scene. There is an Old World flavor with a description of royalty at a wedding parade. The singer notes "they married for peace," which is the only connection to the remainder of the composition. After the last chorus, we are presented with the sound of a jazz combo, first with a clarinet up front and then with the piano up front. As the jazz music fades, a heartbeat enters the mix for the final 20 seconds to the final fade.

With only three songs on the album, Young showed that he was interested in a wide variety of music styles. Each song had a completely different character, and the final, six-plus minutes "Broken Arrow" evidenced his wide-ranging ambitions.

A notable contribution that Young made to the *Again* album was his lead guitar work on Richie Furay's "Sad Memory." In this quiet love song, which Furay sings accompanied by his acoustic guitar, Young adds a wonderfully sad lead guitar line that mimics a muted trumpet.

LAST TIME AROUND

Just as a Neil Young song opened *Again,* a Young composition opens the final Buffalo Springfield album *Last Time Around.* "On the Way Home" is a breezy, pop confection that the record label hoped would be a hit as it was released as a single. It had the ingredients to be a hit including strong vocal harmonies, horns, and a driving rhythm, but the track struggled on its way up to only Number 82 in fall 1968. The lead vocal duties on the recording were handed over to Richie Furay. It is a love song sung to a lover who is far away. Young equates nonsensical imagery ("a smoke ring day when the wind blows") to the rush of a fresh love that turns a person upside down.

Over the course of his career, Young has taken on several different personas through his narrative voice, including that of a woman. In "I Am a Child," he takes on the character of an innocent youth. The song opens with Young's harmonica. Over a shuffling beat held down by Dewey Martin, Young's lyrics present the inquisitiveness of a child ("What is the color when black is burned?"), as well as the child's perspective in regard to the actions of the parent. The adult "hold(s) (his) hand" and "rough(s) up (his) hair." The child perceives the boundaries and limitations the parent sets to make her feel secure ("You make the rules, you say what's fair"). The song closes with the realization of and the resignation to the eternal generation gap. Young sings that the parent cannot "conceive of the pleasure in (the child's) smile."

BUFFALO SPRINGFIELD OUTTAKES

Young's 1977 retrospective *Decade* includes the first release of the Buffalo Springfield track "Down to the Wire." The recording sounds like a typical production of a mid-1960s rock-pop outfit. According to Young, the track was to be included in the unreleased *Stampede* album that was the scheduled follow-up to the band's debut.[8] Young's voice is overproduced over a heavy beat. There are some interesting guitar lines and harmonies. The hook in the track is an extended chord progression line with the electric guitar. The lyric is about a romantic relationship that is difficult for the protagonist. The phrase "down to the wire" has a double meaning in the song. It refers to the fact that the relationship has run its course. It is finished. Young also presents the image of the losing fellow "hang(ing) on" even though "touch(ing) her sets (his) hands on fire," suggesting that the heat of the heartache of the relationship burns through the insulation to the core. The track also appears on the Buffalo Springfield *Box Set* (1998). In the latter release, Stephen Stills sang the lead vocal. Einarson and Furay suggest that there never was a planned *Stampede* album, although the record label assigned it a catalog number and prepared an album cover.[9]

The box set also includes Young's demo of "The Rent Is Always Due." It features Young alone with his acoustic guitar. The lyric is full of obscure images. The theme of the song is that reality always sets in no matter what the situation. Another demo of Young's, "There Goes My Babe," presents his narrator singing from the female point of view. In this song about a lover who has left, Young sings, "He was the only one" in the first verse and "I'd long to hold him near" in the second.

Harvest, 1969–1972

NEIL YOUNG (SOLO DEBUT)

After the hard rock of "Mr. Soul," the swirling strings of "Expecting to Fly," the infectious pop of "On the Way Home," the celebrity-culture-contemplating "Out of My Mind," and the ambitious multipart "Broken Arrow," how did Neil Young kick off his solo career? His self-titled debut album, *Neil Young* (1969), opens with a breezy, countrified instrumental titled "The Emperor of Wyoming." A country and western electric guitar plays the melody over a backdrop of upbeat strings. A pedal steel guitar adds to the country effect. The song is one of the few self-contained instrumentals recorded by Young in his career. Of course, Young has recorded many extended jams with long instrumental passages, but this song is rare in his body of work. In the context of the album, the song serves as an appropriate introduction to the country pop flavor of the collection. The emperor of the title is David Briggs, the producer, who began a long collaboration with Young on this debut album. "Falcon Lake (Ash on the Floor)," an instrumental recorded by Young in 1968, is the progenitor of "The Emperor of Wyoming." On the former song, Young played guitar, piano, and harmonica. Buddy Miles added percussion. Although the songs are not similar in melody, they feel as though they are drawn from the same lineage.

The first vocal on the album is "The Loner." The mid-tempo track opens with an organ and an electric guitar with a sound similar to Young's guitar work on the *Last Time Around* album. The theme of the song is the loss of love of the protagonist. But the song acts more to solidify the image of Young as a "loner." Just as on the cover photo of the final Buffalo Springfield album, where Young was turned away from the rest of the group, the song underscores the persona of the artist as one on his own who either can do it alone or cannot find a partner. The instrumental break after the first verse and chorus borrows from the style of former bandmate Stephen Stills in both the organ part and the guitar figure, which is reminiscent of Stills's "Uno Mundo" from the final album. The instrumental breaks after the second and third choruses slow the tempo of the song and feature both acoustic and electric guitars.

"If I Could Have Her Tonight" is about the pain of yearning for a love in life. The track is taken at a slower tempo than the prior cut. The song, like several others on the album ("Here We Are in the Years," "What Did You Do to My Life?"), has an understated, pretty melody. The vocal is mixed so low that it is obscured by the instrumental track. Shortly after the initial release, a version was released with the vocals more in the forefront. Young's record label used an untested mastering process on the album that "muffled the dynamics" of the first pressing.[1] Like much of the album, this song is unlike anything Young would compose or record as the years went on. In a way, the album is Young's version of the Beach Boys' *Pet Sounds* project. Most of the tracks have a melancholy feel supported by pleasant melodies. Young evidenced an affinity for the Beach Boys in his career. He told Jimmy McDonough, "I loved The Beach Boys" and "Dennis (drummer Dennis Wilson) and I were real tight."[2] Before this album was released, he considered signing with the Beach Boys' Brother Records label.[3] The soundtrack of his 1972 film project *Journey through the Past* closes with the Beach Boys' "Let's Go Away for Awhile," one of the two instrumentals on the *Pet Sounds* release. In his mid-1970s song "Long May You Run," Young mentions the song "Caroline No," a vocal track from *Pet Sounds*.

"I've Been Waiting for You" is a mid-tempo, slow-burning rocker that features a sinuous, fuzz-tone guitar solo that moves from one speaker to the other. In this love song, the protagonist seeks a woman who will empathize with the pain of the loss of love.

A centerpiece of the album is "The Old Laughing Lady." The beginnings of the song date back to summer 1967 when Young recorded a demo while still a member of Buffalo Springfield. The demo consists of only his vocal with an acoustic guitar accompaniment. He also recorded a live version of the song for his *Unplugged* album in the mid-1990s. The song is about a mysterious character (death? a ghost?) who interacts with and changes the lives of those she encounters. The song opens with a bass drum beat and adds an electric piano, creating a mid-tempo foundation. Young enters with a quiet, muffled vocal. It is an ambitious track but unpretentious in its construction.

The song consists of four verses with no chorus. After the third verse, female, gospel-tinged background singers enter singing and repeating a wordless phrase that sounds like, "Oh-hi-oo." Reaching the last two lines of the song, the tempo slows to a crawl and Young describes a supernatural scene that heralds the "old laughing lady's" entrance. The song closes with an understated piano figure, and thus ends side one of Young's debut album.

Like side one, side two opens with an instrumental. Unlike the side one instrumental, however, the "String Quartet from Whiskey Boot Hill" is not composed by Young. It was written by Jack Nitzsche, who co-produced and co-arranged Young's "Expecting to Fly" track on the Buffalo Springfield *Again* longplayer. The track is indeed performed by a classical string quartet. It is unlike anything else on the album. It serves as an interlude, balancing the two sides of the album. Its only clear connection to the album is the frontier connotation of the song's title, which connects to the western image of Young's persona plus the country elements of the album.

Nitzsche also contributed guitar and keyboard work on the album. Buffalo Springfield member Jim Messina played bass on the album. Except for "The Old Laughing Lady," "String Quartet from Whiskey Boot Hill" and "I've Loved Her So Long," which were produced and arranged by Nitzsche, Ryland Cooder, and Young, the album was produced by David Briggs and Young.

"Here We Are in the Years" and "What Did You Do to My Life?" are similar in their music arrangements to "If I Could Have Her Tonight" and underline the album's *Pet Sounds* character. The former track begins with comfort images, including the "holidays" and rural scenes, such as gleefully watching "farmers feeding hogs," but then turns to a nostalgic look at the loss of the countryside to urban and suburban sprawl and the sadness of the work-a-day life. It is a song about growing up and growing old. The elderly, who provide the primary point of view in the lyric, can rest in what they have accomplished in life. But at the same time, development "claim(s) a quiet country lane." And we participate in "games" to avert the "fear of growing old." The song looks back regretfully to how "lives become careers." The protagonists, in the winter of their lives, realize they are at the place "where the showman shifts the gears." At the same time, the younger generation wants to flee the rut that their elders gravitated toward. The song ends with percussion mimicking the sound of a heartbeat, signaling that life goes on. Young repeats the same effect that he used to end his Buffalo Springfield song "Broken Arrow." The composition uses the melody of Young's Buffalo Springfield instrumental "Falcon Lake."[4]

The protagonist sings of his love exiting his life in "What Did You Do to My Life?" The song addresses the illusions contained in the emotions of love. The narrator strived to "pretend we could make it." He sings of how nothing else matters in the face of love, especially when love departs.

In "I've Loved Her So Long," the narrator pictures himself as the one who can redeem the female protagonist from the issues that plague her by giving her his love. The gospel-tinged female voices that provided backing vocals for "The Old Laughing Lady" also appear on this track. The five singers include

Merry Clayton, who dueted with Mick Jagger on the Rolling Stones' "Gimme Shelter," and Brenda Holloway, the successful Motown recording artist.

The album closes with a long track unlike anything else either on the debut or anything Young had recorded with Buffalo Springfield. "The Last Trip to Tulsa" is a long, wordy, Dylanesque story-song. The song features Young alone with his acoustic guitar. At some points the narrator is male; at others, she is female. Young wore different personas on other occasions as well. On the Buffalo Springfield *Last Time Around* album, he took on the persona of a young child for "I Am a Child."

The song opens at a slow tempo with a few guitar chords and a soft vocal delivery. The narrator starts piling on images that could be from a dream or a psychedelic trip. In the opening scene, he says he "fell into a dream." He speaks of people "eating pennies" and young women hysterical over an apocalyptic event ("the West Coast is falling") or an earthquake. Young turns his focus to uncover one of his wry comments about the church and religion. When the "preacher" sees the "congregation running," he escapes, too. Evidencing a loss of faith, the man of the cloth figures there is no point carrying on when danger is imminent.

In the second verse, the narrator takes on the role of the female protagonist. She speaks of how she let her man have her way with her, both sexually ("I let you fly my airplane") and mentally ("you're the kind of man...who likes what he says"). The verse closes with an image of oral sex at a wedding ceremony. Young makes one of his pointed comments about the music business in the third verse. He speaks of being a "folk singer keeping managers alive." The female narrator returns in the fourth verse. Found dead, she relates a nonsensical couplet, "The coroner was friendly, and I liked him"

The tempo picks up as Young strums faster into the fifth verse. The scene seems to come from a nightmare or a bad drug trip. Having run out of fuel, he is afraid to seek assistance because the "servicemen were yellow" and the "gasoline was green." Reminiscent of nightmares, the narrator relates how he wants to scream but cannot. The song ends with the narrator felling a "palm tree" that falls on his Cadillac-wielding friend. The song is full of images that within themselves make sense, but as a whole, it is difficult to decipher a clear message. The song was a harbinger for later material that Young would produce.

Everybody Knows This Is Nowhere

For his next album, also released in 1969, Young took a turn away from the musical styles he experimented with on the debut. *Everybody Knows This Is Nowhere* began a long association with the trio Crazy Horse (originally Danny Whitten, guitar; Billy Talbot, bass; and Ralph Molina, drums). The centerpieces of the album were two long jams, "Down by the River" and "Cowgirl in the Sand." Young stretches out his guitar solos over the rhythm foundation of Crazy Horse. The trio provides a foil to draw out guitar lines from him that other ensembles he has worked with over the years do not or cannot. The two jams plus the opening track, "Cinnamon Girl," contain the seeds of the grunge music form.

The opening cut, "Cinnamon Girl" was released as a single and received a modest amount of radio airplay. The narrator yearns and daydreams for a love he can call his own. He describes himself as a "dreamer of pictures" as he visualizes himself with a romantic companion. And Young, again, through his narrator, observes the music scene. He sets the scene of a musician waiting "between shows" for his sweet love and creates another scene of a hopeful musician calling home for funds because he is "gonna make it somehow." The backing track is energetic with an engaging hook. Young closes the song with a one-note solo that breaks down into an attack of staccato notes to the end. Young comments that he wrote the song for a "city girl...playing finger cymbals," a reference to Jean Ray of the 1960s folk-rock duo Jim and Jean.[5]

"Everybody Knows This Is Nowhere" has a country-rock flavor complete with a country-effect staccato guitar break. The lyric talks about being caught up in the rat race and yearning for the old homestead. What the narrator thought would be nice to have (fame? success in the music business?) is in the end "nowhere." Young recorded a version of the song solo for his debut album, but the song did not see the light of day until Young clicked with Crazy Horse.[6] The track has gained in currency over the years. Contemporary folk artist Dar Williams sings a cover version on her 2005 release *My Better Self*.

"Round & Round (It Won't Be Long)" has a lilting, ethereal spin to it. Musically, the number is unlike anything else on the album and reveals Young's rapidly growing musical maturity. Robin Lane duets with Young on the track. She and her band, the Chartbusters, recorded several albums of new wave music in the early 1980s. The lyric speaks of how it takes a long time to recover from the hurt and pain of lost love. Young sang a demo of the song with a plaintive vocal (the working title was "Round and Round and Round") in 1967 while still part of Buffalo Springfield.

Side one of the album closes with the first of two long jams that would define Young's collaborations with Crazy Horse over the decades. The nine-minute "Down by the River" tells the story of a fellow who shoots his lover dead. The tale follows the theme of the contemporary "Hey Joe" popularized in a 45-rpm single version by the Leaves in 1966 and by the Byrds and Jimi Hendrix in album tracks in 1966 and 1967, respectively. Even though he entices the female to come along with him, the protagonist sings that the woman takes him to such emotional heights that he cannot go on, so he survives by killing her.

The song opens with electric rhythm and lead guitars followed by the introduction of the electric bass guitar and the snare drum. The music shuffles along slowly, as Young unfolds his tale of tragic love. After the first and second choruses, the musicians enter into two long instrumental breaks, with Young playing short, staccato notes and occasionally using a fuzz effect on the guitar.

"Losing End (When You're On)" is a crying-in-your-beer song that you can imagine hearing on the jukebox of a sawdust-floor country-and-western saloon. Young affects a lead vocal that goes along with the character of this tale of the heartbreak of romance. Before the final chorus, Young belts out a phrase in a Daffy Duck voice that leads into a Buck Owens and the Buckaroos-style instrumental break.

Like "Round & Round (It Won't Be Long)," the track "Running Dry (Requiem for the Rockets)" evidences Young's musical development. The recording has a funereal character that underscores Young's remorseful vocal delivery. The performance opens with Young's electric guitar and violin by Bobby Notkoff. Young softly offers his plea for "someone to comfort" him. He confesses his failures and regrets letting his love go (following the similar theme of Dylan's "I Threw It All Away" from *Nashville Skyline,* which was released only a month earlier in 1969). The singer wonders what is left after love is tossed aside. The song is carried along on a foreboding rhythm that brings Young's confessional vocal into sharp focus. The words never define who the "Rockets" are. Whitten, Talbot, and Molina were in the band the Rockets before Young encountered them and changed the group's name to Crazy Horse. In the album liner notes, Young offers "Extra thanks to the Rockets." Notkoff's violin aids in giving the song its ominous tone, particularly near the closing when he moves to a higher register.

The album finale is its second long jam, the 10-minute "Cowgirl in the Sand." Opening with a finger-picked electric guitar that moves into a fuzz tone, the introduction adds drums, cymbals, and bass as the lead guitar moves into staccato fuzz notes. The "cowgirl" image fits neatly with the frontier persona that Young was championing. A cowgirl "in the sand" could refer to the migration of young people to California and its beaches. The woman of the first verse could be Young in disguise. He made his way from Canada to California. In the first line of the chorus, he sings "Old enough . . . to change your name," which may be a reference to breaking off from the Buffalo Springfield and going solo. He continues by asking, "When so many love you is it the same?" reflecting Young's ambivalent attitude to the spotlight.

In the second verse, the narrator asks, "Has your band begun to rust?" Again, this appears to be a reference to Young's acrimonious relationship with Buffalo Springfield. In the final line of the chorus, he says, "It's the woman in you" that causes her or him to "play this game." Despite the harassment of the media and fans, there is an addiction to fame that may be rooted in the narrator's feminine side. Young uses much fuzz-tone effect in the extended breaks that follow each of the three choruses. After the first chorus, he plays low fuzz-tone notes; after the second, he works from an extended fuzz note to a jam led by fluid fuzz tones; from the final chorus to the fade, he uses an extended, reverbed fuzz tone on his guitar.

"Sugar Mountain"

Recorded live in Toronto in 1969, the nonalbum track "Sugar Mountain" is a coming of age song.[7] Young paints scenes of nostalgia and the naiveté and curiosity and innocent romance of youth. Delivering a somber vocal full of resignation, he expresses the reality that we all have to break away from the nest. Choruses that set a scene at a midway or arcade with "colored balloons" couch the verses. Through half a dozen choruses, he affirms that you cannot remain and grow old at the scene of your youth as much as the feeling to stay tries to hold you back. Young's only instrumental accompaniment is his acoustic guitar. The track first appeared on record as the flip side of the "Cinnamon Girl" single. It was reprised as the B-side for one single release from each of Young's next two solo albums.

Crosby, Stills, Nash, and Young: "Sea of Madness"

In the summer of 1969, Young joined the supergroup Crosby, Stills, and Nash. In the early morning hours of Monday, August 18, 1969, the band played before a sea of faces at the Woodstock Music and Arts Fair. Young's performance of his composition "Sea of Madness" was included on the three-disc *Woodstock* compilation issued in 1970. He sings lead and plays organ on the performance. The song has a rhythm-and-blues feel to it that Young would not return to too often in his career. The lyric is an unabashed pledge of love by the narrator to his paramour. This is the only official release of the song.

Crosby, Stills, Nash, and Young: *Déjà vu*

The first Crosby, Stills, Nash, and Young studio album was *Déjà vu*. Released in early 1970, it soon climbed to the top of the bestseller charts. Young contributed two compositions to the collection. "Helpless" begins with an odd, little, extended-note guitar opening. The lyric looks back at the past. Young is nostalgic for the geography of his homeland and the clear, rural skies. In describing the area where he came of age, he creatively strings words together ("dream comfort memory to spare") while looking back at the scene. The supporting background vocals by Crosby, Stills, and Nash add a warm sheen to the track that would not be possible in a solo effort. Reminiscing about the occasion that the trio visited Young to ask him to join the group, David Crosby said, "He played 'Helpless,' and by the time he finished, we were asking him if we could join *his* band."[8]

A year later fellow Canadian Buffy Sainte-Marie covered "Helpless" on her *She Used to Wanna Be a Ballerina* album. Both Young and Crazy Horse provide backing on the track. The album was co-produced by Young collaborator Jack Nitzsche. He also provided the musical arrangement of Sainte-Marie's cover version. Young also performed "Helpless" at the Band's goodbye concert in San Francisco on Thanksgiving 1976. His performance is included on the soundtrack of *The Last Waltz*, as well as in Martin Scorsese's film.

The ambitious "Country Girl" is made up of three parts titled "Whiskey Boot Hill," "Down Down Down," and "Country Girl (I Think You're Pretty)." The conception of the "Down Down Down" segment goes back to the mid-1960s. Buffalo Springfield recorded a full-band version of "Down Down Down" in 1966 during the sessions for the band's debut album. "Country Girl" has an elegant production feel in the vein of "Expecting to Fly" and "Broken Arrow" from the second Buffalo Springfield album.

Part one consists of two verses and two choruses. In the opening and before the choruses, a keyboard is prominent in the mix. The lyrics are somewhat obscure, although the setting seems to be a bar or café and the focus appears to be on a waitress or waitresses. The narrator observes "stars" sitting "in bars," reprising Young's fascination with the culture of celebrity. The title of this segment, "Whiskey Boot Hill," may relate to the drinking establishment setting. It does not have any connection to the instrumental track "String Quartet from Whiskey Boot Hill" on Young's solo debut.

From the wall-of-sound style of the closing of part one, a production that includes crying Crosby, Stills, and Nash harmonies and a forte organ line, the music quiets down for part two, "Down Down Down," which consists of two verses. Young and Stephen Stills duet on the first verse, perhaps in a nod to the two being founding members of Buffalo Springfield, the group Young was attached to when he composed this part. Crosby and Nash join in for the second verse of "Down Down Down" as the music crescendos. The tension breaks into part three, where Young delivers the vocal release in a loud, yearning voice. The song closes with a loud, echoed harmonica that takes the track to its fade.

Young also co-wrote the album closer "Everybody I Love You" with Stephen Stills, but Stills is most prominent in the song's production. Although Crosby, Stills, Nash, and Young would regroup periodically for performances and various combinations in the studio, *Déjà vu* would be the ensemble's only studio album for almost the next two decades.

Live at the Fillmore East

Backed by Crazy Horse (Danny Whitten, Billy Talbot, Ralph Molina, and Jack Nitzsche on electric piano), Young's early 1970 New York shows were recorded for a possible live album. A portion of the electric set was released 36 years later at the end of 2006. The release features four short songs and two long jams. The two long tracks are "Down by the River" and "Cowgirl in the Sand," both from the *Everybody Knows This Is Nowhere* package. Similar in style to their studio counterparts, both tracks provide evidence of Young and Whitten's guitar talents at an early stage in Young and Crazy Horse's development. The song "Everybody Knows This Is Nowhere" is punchier in both vocals and instrumentation than the studio version. "Winterlong" is similar in arrangement to the studio version that appears on *Decade,* but the vocals are rawer on the Fillmore set.

Young introduces "Wonderin'" by saying it would be on the next album, but the track did not see the light of day until the release of Young's rockabilly album *Everybody's Rockin'* in 1983. "Wonderin'" is a country-rock shuffle sung by Young with vocal support by rhythm guitarist Danny Whitten. Whitten sings lead on his own, "Come on Baby Let's Go Downtown." This version was included on Young's *Tonight's the Night* album from 1975. The six tracks clock in at 42 minutes total. It would have been interesting if more of the electric set had been included and, for that matter, the acoustic set as well.

CROSBY, STILLS, NASH, AND YOUNG: "OHIO"

While *Déjà vu* was being played in dorm rooms across the college campuses of the United States, something shocking, but not unexpected, happened in the country. Shortly after President Nixon announced the expansion of military operations in Cambodia, there was an increase in campus unrest. On May 4, 1970, Sandy Scheuer, Allison Krause, Bill Schroeder, and Jeff Miller were shot dead and another nine were injured by Ohio National Guardsmen during a protest rally at Kent State University in northeast Ohio.[9] The unspeakable tragedy sparked a nationwide, negative reaction to this horror. Young's response was to convene his supergroup bandmates and record his journalistic impression. What the song lacks in the studio finesse of *Deja vu,* "Ohio" more than makes up for in its urgency, immediacy, and vitality.

In a guitar-based rocker, all four singers deliver a vocal seething with anger. Young marshals the listener to not be complacent and to not depend on a government that kills its young. He sings, "We're on our own" and "Gotta get down to it" and wonders "How can you run?" His question about finding a victim "dead on the ground" brings to fore the iconic image from the Kent State massacre of the young Mary Ann Vecchio kneeling helplessly and crying out over the dead body of Jeffrey Miller. After the final verse, Young's bandmate David Crosby starts spitting out numbers wondering "how many more" will be shot dead in the struggle to bring the war to an end.

AFTER THE GOLD RUSH

Young's exposure through the releases of Crosby, Stills, Nash, and Young helped to catapult his third solo release, *After the Gold Rush,* into the Top 10.

The first single release from the album was a bouncy song about the heart-break of romance titled "Only Love Can Break Your Heart." The song is about our complicated selves that keep us from being all we can. In the second verse, Young talks about a "friend (he's) never seen." This friend "hides...inside a dream." The singer urges "someone" to draw this friend out "to lose the down...he's found." The friend is one of those personal demons that causes the self to be afraid to risk opening up and being vulnerable to the complexities of love and romance. Introducing the song at a concert in 1977, Young said it was written for sometimes bandmate, the lovelorn Graham Nash.[10] It would have been fascinating to hear the Carl Wilson-led Beach Boys of the early 1970s execute a cover version of this song. Their harmonies would have provided an appealing interpretation.

The liner notes state that the inspiration for the bulk of the songs was a screenplay by Dean Stockwell and Herb Berman titled "After the Gold Rush."[11] This seems to be most apparent in the title track. The vision unfolded by the narrator is akin to that of a proclamation of an Old Testament prophet. The lyrics describe a medieval scene and sling ahead to a science fiction future of "silver space ships flying." The medieval setting (in verse one) includes "knights in armor" and "peasants" and an "archer" and a "fanfare." In Young's Buffalo Springfield track "Broken Arrow," one of the song settings was a medieval wedding ceremony. The second verse is set in the present. In a night scene, the narrator finds himself in the middle of the floor of a basement that is all that remains of a home. He gazes at the sky above until sunrise. The third verse details an escape of "chosen ones" from the earth to a "new home in the sun." In this vision, there is crying as though an apocalypse or extinction is on the horizon for those who remain.

The only instrumentation on the cut is Young's piano and Bill Peterson's flugelhorn.[12] Although the song dates itself by referencing the 1970s, it has a timeless character. Linda Ronstadt and Emmylou Harris recorded a cover version for their 1999 release *Western Wall: The Tucson Sessions*.

The album contains a number of ballad and mid-tempo pop songs, two hard rockers, and a couple of partially realized pieces. "Tell Me Why" is an appropriate album opener. The melody is light and upbeat. Opening with a strumming acoustic guitar, the mid-tempo track deals with the longing for love. The background vocals are reminiscent of Crosby, Stills, and Nash, although, of the three, only Stephen Stills appears on the album. The lyric offers some intriguing images of the lonely seeker of romance. The song opens with the line "Sailing heart-ships through broken waters" and continues by describing the seeker of companionship as riding a "dark horse, racing alone in...fright." The lonely narrator will be satisfied even if the love is temporal or not genuine. He offers a companion an out: "tell me lies later."

The summer before *After the Gold Rush*'s release, Young introduced a new song at Crosby, Stills, Nash, and Young performances that he told audiences was "guaranteed to bring you right down."[13] "Don't Let It Bring You Down" is set across the waters in England. The setting contains "lorries" and "castles." The lyric describes a fatal accident. Young uses a cinematic flashback technique to unfold his tale.

The first verse opens with the victim "lying" along the edge of the pavement as trucks barrel by. The new day dawns, but it is not a new beginning. Young's lyrics detail the harsh, hopeless atmosphere: a bitter wind blows through an "alley" and discarded newspapers are carried along by the wind. We will learn in a flashback in verse two that the deceased male has been lying helpless and undiscovered since the night before. The victim is blind, yet ironically, in death, he now has "daylight in his eyes."

The second verse opens with the flashback. A "blind man" is moving through the "light of the night." The image ties in with the later scene described previously in which the victim's eyes are filled with daylight. The lyric suggests that the blind man is moving about because he seeks a healing. He is urged to approach the "river of sight." But then there is an accident. Young's lyric then jumps ahead to the present. The victim has been found along the roadway, as an emergency vehicle enters the picture. The lyric notes the flashing "red lights" and "sirens." The description of a "cane lying in the gutter" at the close of the verse affirms that the victim is the blind man.

The choruses contain an image of "castles burning." As if not bleak enough in its story line, the words add another coat of desolation to the mood of the story. As Young indicated in his stage introduction, it is not a happy song.

"Birds" and "I Believe in You" are slow love songs. The former is about the end of a relationship; the latter is about the beginning of a romance. The only instrumental accompaniment to Young's voice on "Birds" is a piano. The narrator assures his lover that someone will come along after he is gone. The lyric uses bird imagery. The protagonist will "fly away" and someone else will "hover" over the one left behind. When he flies away, "feathers" will "fall." In "I Believe in You," the narrator is hesitant to enter into a relationship. He cannot quickly embrace new love. It is a matter of trust. And he wonders where love fits in his life. Rita Coolidge covered the song effectively on her debut album.

The two rockers on the album are "Southern Man" and "When You Dance I Can Really Love." "Southern Man" addresses the complex racial relationships of the southern United States. There are allusions to the Bible and the Ku Klux Klan in the first verse. Young suggests the "southern man" needs to read his Bible more carefully. In the second verse, he talks about the role of slavery in the South's agricultural economy. He sings, "I saw cotton and I saw black." He follows by juxtaposing the different conditions of the ruling class and laborers: "Tall white mansions and little shacks." And he addresses the corporal punishment put on blacks: "I heard...bullwhips cracking." Added to this setting are the interracial liaisons between the daughters of the plantation owners (in this case, "Lily-Belle" with the "golden" hair) and black workers of the land. Nils Lofgren's relentlessly driving piano helps to convey Young's anger over the injustices he views in the region. Young adds a fluid guitar solo with effects just before the first chorus.

The song touched a nerve. Three years later Southern rock outfit Lynyrd Skynyrd responded to Young in "Sweet Home Alabama" telling him "a southern man don't need him around anyhow."[14]

"When You Dance I Can Really Love" was a single release from *After the Gold Rush,* but it barely cracked the Top 100 in spring 1971. It opens with an electric guitar using an effect similar to that on "Cinnamon Girl." The lyrics are not particularly significant. The song is about how the narrator is attracted to a woman on the dance floor and his assurance that he can "love...really love." The lyric is basically dressing for the melody, the hook and the guitar solos. "Sugar Mountain" made its second appearance as a B-side on the "When You Dance" single.

Young performs one cover version on the record. Side two opens with country and western singer Don Gibson's "Oh, Lonesome Me." The song's lyric helps to solidify the loner persona of the artist. It is a song of self-pity over lost love. The ensemble performs a solid instrumental arrangement. Young opens with a sad harmonica line that sets the mood for the song. Crazy Horse percussionist Ralph Molina keeps the beat with his hi-hat cymbals.

Both album sides end with partially realized tunes. "Till the Morning Comes" and "Cripple Creek Ferry" end side one and side two, respectively. "Till the Morning Comes" has only three lines of lyrics that are repeated over the melody. Piano, bass, and drums support the mid-tempo sing-a-long style, with a trumpet entry near the close of the song, which clocks in at 1 minute and 17 seconds. "Cripple Creek Ferry" is not much longer. It consists of one verse sandwiched between two recitations of the chorus. The chorus is sung in unison as though its members are all gathered around a table at a saloon. The lyric is about a vessel making its way through the waters. There is a brief focus on the "captain" and a "gambler."

The under-construction character of the two side-closing songs is reminiscent of the incomplete creations of the Beach Boys during the 1967 and 1968 period when the California band recorded and issued the *Smiley Smile, Wild Honey,* and *Friends* albums. As noted earlier, Young was fond of the Beach Boys and particularly admired the *Pet Sounds* album.

CROSBY, STILLS, NASH, AND YOUNG: *4 WAY STREET*

Young did not release any solo material in 1971. However, he was still in the spotlight as part of the Crosby, Still, Nash, and Young live project, *4 Way Street,* a Number 1 album in spring 1971. The two-disc set opens with the closing bars of Stephen Stills's "Suite: Judy Blue Eyes." Then, over the applause, Graham Nash shouts out, "We'd like to introduce our friend Neil Young!" Acoustic guitar chords signal the introduction to Young's Buffalo Springfield chestnut "On the Way Home." Unlike the Springfield recording, Young's reading is taken at a slower, more reflective pace. And, of course, the instrumentation is different. His and his band mates' acoustic guitars back Young. (The Buffalo Springfield version featured Richie Furay on lead vocals over a slick, pop production.) The trademark Crosby, Stills, and Nash harmonies add a warm luster to the performance.

A live version of "Cowgirl in the Sand" is also much different than Young's earlier recording. The 1969 collaboration with Crazy Horse was an extended jam. For *4 Way Street,* Young sings the song solo over an acoustic guitar accompaniment with some percussive elements in a more compact rendition of the composition. The 1992 reissue of the album also includes a solo acoustic medley that incorporates "The Loner" from the debut album and two songs from the *Everybody Knows This Is Nowhere* album, "Cinnamon Girl" and "Down by the River." The "Cinnamon Girl" segment is brief and acts as a bridge between the other two compositions. Like "Cowgirl in the Sand," the acoustic "Down by the River" is much shorter than the electric studio jam version.

As noted earlier in the discussion of "Don't Let It Bring You Down," Young performed a version of this song on the summer 1970 tour before the track was issued as part of the *After the Gold Rush* album. On the live-recorded version, Young is accompanied by acoustic guitar rather than by piano as on the studio version.

Two of Young's rockers appear on *4 Way Street.* "Southern Man" is extended into a 13-minute jam with the lead guitarists (Stephen Stills and Young) feeding lines off each other. Young's voice is strained, adding an extra element of emotion as he moves into the final verse about Lily-Belle. After the next chorus and before the final chorus that ends the performance, the song picks up the pace (faster than the studio version) as the instrumentalists move into an extended, galloping jazz groove propelled by Calvin "Fuzzy" Samuels's bass playing and Johnny Barbata at the drum kit.

Recorded less than two months after the shootings at Kent State, the in-concert version of "Ohio" still maintains the urgency of the studio version. Unlike other tracks on this live recording in which the audience applauds in recognition during the opening bars of a song, there is complete silence as "Ohio" begins. It is not a song of celebration. It is a song of mourning. The electric guitar attack after the "How can you run when you know?" line conveys the anger of the performers at the government-sanctioned killings of college students. Drummer Barbata bangs the heck out of the hi-hat and the snare adding to the emotion as the singers repeat the line "four dead in Ohio" over and over. In the closing bars, Crosby sounds even angrier than on the studio track as he counts off how many more martyrs there may be in the battle for peace.

HARVEST

With the solo *After the Gold Rush* album being a bestseller, and his high profile collaborations with Crosby, Stills, and Nash, including two Number 1 albums in two years, Young was primed for success with his next solo release. Released in the halcyon days of the singer-songwriter era, when artists like James Taylor, Carole King, Elton John, and Cat Stevens were at their peaks, *Harvest,* a quintessential singer-songwriter album, climbed to the top of the charts in early 1972. Most of the tracks were recorded with the Stray Gators, a studio group that included Nashville's Kenny Buttrey on drums, Tim Drummond on bass, Ben Keith on pedal steel guitar, and Jack Nitzsche on piano and slide guitar. Nitzsche collaborated with Young on Buffalo Springfield's "Expecting to Fly" and Young's debut disc.

The album includes two Top 40 hits, "Heart of Gold" and "Old Man." Both feature backing vocals by James Taylor and Linda Ronstadt. Taylor was at the peak of his popularity. Ronstadt had yet to achieve the fame that would come in the mid-1970s beginning with the Number 1 smash "You're No Good." Both recording artists were with Young in Nashville for a taping of the Johnny Cash television show. Young asked the two back to the studio to sweeten the two tracks. "Heart of Gold" is a mid-tempo love song about the universal yearning to "give" love. The song features Young's harmonica and Drummond's characteristic bass plucking. Ronstadt's voice is prominent at the end of the song when she goes up in the register to sing the closing line, "I've been a miner for a heart of gold." "Sugar Mountain" made its most prominent appearance as the B-side of "Heart of Gold."

Side two opens with the hit single "Old Man." In performance, Young has stated that an elderly caretaker at his northern California ranch inspired the song. The instrumental trademark of the song is the banjo that appears after the second verse and again after the third verse. The singer meditates on life and love as he considers the experiences of one who has been through it all. Although the narrator is only 24 years old, he sees he has much in common with the seasoned fellow. Young sings that he "live(s) alone in a paradise," which may refer to his Broken Arrow Ranch. But paradise is not enough. The narrator yearns for companionship. The problems, experiences, and situations of life are universal.

The track that has aged best over the decades and has gained the most cachet is the cut on the disc that required the least production effort. "The Needle and the Damage Done" was recorded live in 1971 on the UCLA campus. The performance simply presents Young and his acoustic guitar. The song addresses the horror of addiction to drugs. Young sings the song with a soul full of hurt and the realization that he is powerless to help those in need of healing. Young was face to face with people caught in this downward spiral. He alludes to this in the second verse. He sings, "I lost my band" and suggests that it happened because the "needle (took) another man." Crazy Horse guitarist Danny Whitten died later in 1972 from a drug overdose. The closing words, "every junkie's like a setting sun," warn the listener that there is no future for the drug addict.

"Out on the Weekend," the album opener, is an easy-flowing pop song with a comforting vocal delivery from Young. The recording has a catchy hook, and had it been released as a single, it may have been a smash hit. Again, Young focuses on lonely lovers who cannot seem to connect. The "lonely boy" experiences moments of love and romance but nothing lasts. The lyrics of "Harvest" loosely relate to maturing out of adolescence. It is a guitar-based, slow to mid-tempo track that has well-done pedal steel guitar accents provided by Ben Keith.

"Alabama" could be subtitled "Southern Man, Part II." Young's lyric is a journalistic impression of the conditions in the state. He focuses on the poverty in the region and wonders why federal assistance is not sought. He juxtaposes disparate images of the "devil" in one line of the first verse and "Swing low" in the next line, a reference to the spiritual "Swing Low Sweet Chariot." Showing a keen eye for detail, Young describes a rural scene where there are "banjos playing through ... broken glass." The opening electric guitar is reminiscent of the guitar sound on "Southern Man." The supporting vocals by David Crosby and Stephen Stills further the connection to "Southern Man," in this case, the *4 Way Street* version.

Graham Nash and David Crosby provide the backing vocals on "Are You Ready for the Country?," the side one closer. The song has a punchy melody that complements the sing-a-long vocal character. Nitzsche's slide guitar contributes a rustic, homegrown element to the production. Drummond's bass guitar is more booming and unlike his playing on the rest of the album, but there is not much to the lyric. Young does include a brief glimpse at organized religion with the assurance of a "preacher" followed closely by the reality of death in the person of the "hangman."

"A Man Needs a Maid" is one of two tracks on which Young is accompanied by the London Symphony Orchestra. Jack Nitzsche arranged both this track and "There's a World." Neither track has the feel of "Expecting to Fly," the Buffalo Springfield track that was arranged by Nitzsche and also included strings. "A Man Needs a Maid" opens with just Young and a piano. His vocal is mixed low, similar to some of the vocals on his debut disc. The full orchestra kicks in after Young first sings, "A man needs a maid." Hammered chimes and strings are prominent in the break. In the lyric, the narrator is alone. At first, he suggests he wants the services of a maid to do typical maid duties: clean house, "fix my meals," and "go away." But then he draws up the notion of love and falling in love and sings again, "A man needs a maid." Although he tells the maid to "go away," he also asks when he will see her again. The song has an autobiographical element. Young sings of falling "in love with the actress" in a film he watches. That is how his relationship began with the actress Carrie Snodgress, the mother of Young's first child. The song title was not terribly politically correct during the nascent days of feminist consciousness.[15]

"There's a World" is full of encouragement (for children, perhaps) to find where their place in society lies. The song has a big orchestra opening with timpani, horns, and strings. At various measures, harps and woodwinds are prominent.

Harvest closes with "Words (Between the Lines of Age)." Backed by the Stray Gators, the track features vocals by Stephen Stills and Graham Nash. The words do not make a lot of sense and do not combine into a clear narrative. Perhaps, that is the point of the title and the chorus, "Singing words…words, words." He suggests the verses are just words, glimpses that do not need to coalesce into a meaning. Two characters "by the pond" are labeled "someone and someone." While they are there, the narrator is waiting for water to "boil." In the second verse, he offers a riddle. If the listener's "mind" was in the narrator, what would the listener "wonder"?

Later in 1972, Young released the soundtrack to his first film *Journey through the Past*. The vinyl release includes a sidelong version of "Words." The extended track includes studio chatter at several points when the track is interrupted. The melody on the piano is played ad infinitum in the longest, uninterrupted officially-released version of the song.

LIVE AT MASSEY HALL 1971

About a year before the release of *Harvest*, Young was introducing the songs from the *Harvest* album on a solo acoustic tour. Recorded in Toronto, Young's birthplace, *Live at Massey Hall 1971* (2007) documents a concert from the tour. It is an excellent recording. Young's colleague David Briggs thought the Toronto concert should have been released on vinyl instead of *Harvest*. It would have been interesting to see how that would have changed the trajectory of Young's career.

The concert album is book-ended by "On the Way Home" and "I Am a Child," Young's two vocal contributions to the final Buffalo Springfield album *Last Time Around*. The repertoire was fan-friendly by Young's standards. About half of the tracks were already well known by the audience. The other half were new. Several of the tracks are similar in arrangement to Young's performances captured six months earlier during the *4 Way Street* recordings. The only difference in the arrangement of "On the Way Home" is the lack of background vocals from Crosby, Stills, and Nash. "Cowgirl in the Sand" and "Don't Let It Bring You Down" are identical to the *4 Way Street* arrangements. Although not included on the Crosby, Stills, Nash, and Young live set, "Tell Me Why," originally released on Young's *After the Gold*

Rush, is the same arrangement that Young used during his 1970 shows with the group.

Young's solo reading of "Helpless," accompanied only by his guitar, is a beautiful, naked performance of the song originally issued on *Déjà vu.* Listening to it without the *Déjà vu* production, the listener can imagine what it was like when Crosby, Stills, and Nash went up to Young's home, heard the composition for the first time, and were bowled over. "Down by the River" maintains the same intensity of the *Everybody Knows This Is Nowhere* version, even though Young is without the backing of Crazy Horse.

The reaction to "Ohio" from the audience is much more exuberant than the subdued reaction captured on *4 Way Street.* Eight months and a national boundary removed from the events at Kent State, the song had taken on a more anthemic and universal character as a protest against governments leading their citizens into war. The Crosby, Stills, Nash, and Young recorded electric version was presented to an audience still in the emotional throes of the shootings. It is engaging to hear the opening riff of "Ohio" performed on an acoustic guitar.

The new songs on *Live at Massey Hall 1971* would find their place on Young's next three studio releases, *Harvest, Time Fades Away,* and *On the Beach.* Two songs, "Bad Fog of Loneliness" and "Dance Dance Dance," did not have an official release until the issue of the Toronto concert album in 2007. By early 1971, Young had "Old Man" pretty much worked out. It is very similar in form to the *Harvest* version, albeit without the Nashville production and backing vocals. The Toronto version of "The Needle and the Damage Done" is basically identical to the *Harvest* version, as the latter was also recorded in a live, solo acoustic performance (in Los Angeles).

It is fascinating to hear what Young was doing with "A Man Needs a Maid" and "Heart of Gold" in early 1971. He performed the two compositions as a medley, with "Heart of Gold" nesting within "A Man Needs a Maid." Accompanied only by his piano playing, the bare emotions of Young's reading of his lyric to "A Man Needs a Maid" are not overwhelmed by the London Symphony Orchestra, as they are on the *Harvest* production. It is a wonderful performance that actually carries the song to a higher plane than "Heart of Gold," partially because "Heart of Gold" is wrapped by the other song.

Going back to the idea of what would have happened in Young's career if this concert had been released in the early 1970s instead of *Harvest,* I would hazard a guess that Young would not have had a Number one single in 1972, as he enjoyed with "Heart of Gold." Instead, "Old Man," which peaked at Number 31 on the *Billboard* charts, would have been the bigger hit. The "A Man Needs a Maid/Heart of Gold Suite" would probably not have been issued as a single owing to its length and the fact that it was only Young and his piano. Who knows for sure what would have happened? Perhaps Young would not have headed for the "ditch," as he noted he did as a result of the staggering success of *Harvest.* "There's a World," which was also performed with the London Symphony Orchestra for *Harvest,* appears on the Massey Hall set in a piano version. Although improved without the massive production, the composition is still lacking.

"Bad Fog of Loneliness" is a song of unrequited love with a sunny melody. In his concert introduction, Young noted that he wrote the song for a scheduled performance on the Johnny Cash television show. He said he wanted to perform the song with Carl Perkins and the Tennessee Three. Half of the Toronto audience laughed at the notion, while the other half applauded in appreciation. Young was serious about the proposal, but some of his fans still did not get his wide-ranging musical interests. "Dance Dance Dance" is a hoedown, sing-a-long performance that elicits a lot of hand-clapping on the beat. The track was several years old at the time. In the handwritten lyric sheet included with *After the Gold Rush,* the song title is included in a draft track listing.

JOURNEY THROUGH THE PAST

Journey through the Past (1972) includes several live Buffalo Springfield performances from television broadcasts, including Young's "Mr. Soul" taken from an appearance on *The Hollywood Palace* television variety show. The lead guitar on the track has an Arabian music feel. The soundtrack also includes a different live version of "Ohio" than the one included on *4 Way Street.* The only new song on the album is "Soldier." The song features Young alone with his piano. The words are few but pregnant with meaning. In the first verse, he addresses a soldier noting that his eyes "shine like the sun." This can be an allusion to death on the battlefield. In the second verse, he addresses "Jesus." He witnessed Jesus "walkin' on the river" (the miracle of walking on water), but the narrator does not believe him. He rejects faith. Reflecting the surrounding instant gratification culture, he complains, "You can't deliver right away." The word "deliver" also hearkens back to the Lord's Prayer. Because Jesus cannot "deliver us from evil" promptly, the narrator rejects him.

NEIL YOUNG WITH GRAHAM NASH: "WAR SONG"

Just as Young had reacted swiftly to the shootings at Kent State with "Ohio," he wrote "War Song" in response to the assassination attempt on Alabama Governor George Wallace in May 1972.[16] Young gathered together the Stray Gators for instrumental backup and Graham Nash for vocal support. The song is a mid-tempo rocker with a funky guitar riff in the instrumental breaks. The narrator looks around at the destruction that surrounds him in helplessness and hopelessness. "Mines" are planted in the oceans; "bridges" are blown up; the "jungle" is burned; "Vietnamese" are killed; and George Wallace was shot down. Reprise rush-released the track as a single and it charted modestly in the summer of 1972.

Tonight's the Night, 1973–1979

About the hit single "Heart of Gold" (and the statement could cover the whole of *Harvest* as well), Young said the track placed him "in the middle of the road; travelling [*sic*] there...became a bore so I headed for the ditch."[1] The next three albums, a trilogy of sorts, found Young in that "ditch."

TIME FADES AWAY

The next album Young recorded in the studio was *Tonight's the Night*. Reprise, his record label, however, did not deem it as a worthy follow-up to the Number 1 *Harvest* collection. Instead Young released a batch of new songs recorded live-in-concert at various venues across the United States. Typically, a live-in-concert recording is a stopgap measure used by recording artists to bide the time before they come up with new material. Usually the concert album is a reprise of greatest hits. Young did not take the usual and typical route on *Time Fades Away;* instead, he presented a group of unfamiliar songs to his audiences. Three of the eight tracks feature Young alone. The remaining tracks have him backed by the Stray Gators save for drummer Kenny Buttrey, who is replaced by Johnny Barbata of the Crosby, Stills, Nash, and Young band.

The title track, which is also the opening cut, is founded in the Bob Dylan *Bringing It All Back Home/Highway 61 Revisited* 1965 era. Young sings "Time Fades Away" in a raw strained voice, supported by raw, backing vocals over a driving shuffle reminiscent of the1965 model Dylan. Even the lyrical images and the manner that Young strings the words together in his delivery give the song a Dylan cast. The narrator sings of "thirteen junkies," one of whom is a diamond peddler, "down on Pain Street." He addresses the Nixon administration. Verse two begins with a scene of "presidents" peering "out windows." The image reminds the listener of the post-Watergate President standing insecure in his decisions both domestic and foreign. Young's narrator thinks back (perhaps, autobiographically) to his youth in Canada "riding subways through a haze." That could be a reference to both urban air pollution and the substances that carried him through the time.

The next track could have been the title song of Young's film, the soundtrack of which was released just before *Time Fades Away*. "Journey thru the Past" is performed by Young alone with his piano. He wonders whether his lover or friend will "think" about him as he takes a journey. The journey is one of nostalgia for a remembered geography. He speaks of the "fiddler" and the "drum...keep(ing) good time" on this journey. The line has several levels of meanings. Joni Mitchell composed a song titled "The Fiddle and the Drum," which contains a dialogue between Canada and the United States centering on the neighboring countries' relationship. In the Young lyric the fiddler and the drum agree to negotiate: "I will stay with you if you'll stay with me." So it could be about the United States and Canada. Or Young may use the song title to symbolize the friendship of Young and Mitchell (both are Canadian).[2] Whoever the fiddler and the drum are, they will "keep good time." This could mean they would keep the right beat in the music. Or, in a play on words, it may mean they will have an enjoyable respite together. Young is in much better voice in his rendition of the song in the earlier Massey Hall recording from 1971. As on the *Time Fades Away* version, Young accompanied himself alone on piano. Not surprisingly, there is no reaction from the Oklahoma City audience to the lyric "going back to Canada." The Toronto audience applauded at the phrase.

"Yonder Stands the Sinner" is a rocker that features David Crosby on guitar and supporting vocal. The lyric is not clear, but the song contains some religious imagery. The second verse outlines someone in an "attic window yellin'...through" a "broken pane." This could be a religious icon represented in a stained-glass window. In the chorus, the sinner "calls (the narrator's) name without a sound." Again, Young offers one of his images that do not make sense. How is a name called without a sound? Unless, like the way a statue or an icon can draw someone forth spiritually, the sinner tempts in the same form.

As noted earlier, Young is fascinated with the southern California culture. This is evidenced again in the track simply titled "L.A." In the verses Young runs his words together as he delivers them. But at the chorus, the tempo slows down, and over a pretty melody, he sings affectionately of the "city in the smog." In contrast to the tender chorus, much of the song deals with the threat of destruction through an earthquake in the area that hugs the fault line. He sings of the "ground crack(ing) under you" and "mountains erupt(ing)" and the "valley (being) sucked" under. Though he paraphrases a postcard sentiment in the chorus, "Don't you wish that you could be here," his beckoning is to the listener to join him as a witness of the end times.

Like "Journey thru the Past," "Love in Mind" again only features Young's voice and piano. Young's voice is stronger than on other tracks on the album. His thoughts of the one he loves comfort him while he is away. In the midst of ruminating on love and how it affects a person, he tosses in a verse about religion and how it represses natural sexual attraction. He closes that thought by repeating three times the eternal question: "What am I doing here?" His thoughts about sex and the church draw him into thinking about deeper philosophical issues. The Toronto recording of "Love in Mind" is quite similar in execution.

"Don't Be Denied" is an autobiographical rocker. In the first verse, Young sings about going to Winnipeg after his parents' marriage ended. Later in the song, he sings about the music scene on the Sunset Strip. Record company executives were drawn to "hear the golden sound" of the emerging Buffalo Springfield in the mid-1960s. In the closing verse, he confesses the disillusionment that follows fame and fortune. Beyond the façade of the spotlight, he is a "pauper" who rejects the mask of celebrity. The song was composed shortly after the death of Young's Crazy Horse bandmate Danny Whitten.[3]

"The Bridge" is the third of the three tracks of Young solo with piano. He plays the harmonica as well in the quiet, slow-tempo performance. The words unfold a tale of the restoration of broken love.

The album closes with the electric fuzz and feedback effect-filled rocker "Last Dance." The subject of the song is the rhythm of the work-a-day life that is difficult to escape. There is "Monday morning" and a "coffee cup" and "headlights" and the commute home. The chorus is ironic. With Crosby and Nash singing background vocals, the listener is given the hope that "you can live your own life." But each chorus ends with "no" until the climax of the song, when the singers repeatedly sing "no," affirming that most people cannot really live the life they desire. Someone from the stage yells "Last dance" and so ends *Time Fades Away,* the first of several dark albums that will form a trilogy.

ON THE BEACH

Time Fades Away did not have the commercial legs that Young's previous album *Harvest* had. The album reached Number 22 on the *Billboard* charts in the fall of 1973. As a result, Young's record label may have had some say in the sequencing of his next album *On the Beach*. The two tracks with the most commercial potential kick off the disc. Those two cuts plus a Crosby, Stills, Nash, and Young summer reunion tour across the North American continent through a series of stadiums propelled *On the Beach* to Number 16 in the late summer of 1974.

The leadoff track, "Walk On," was issued as a single. Ben Keith plays slide guitar on the track and the Crazy Horse rhythm section of Billy Talbot on bass and Ralph Molina on drums keeps the tempo upbeat. The lyric suggests that Young is being criticized for the music he has recently released. He opens with the words, "I hear some people been talkin' me down." In a touch of nostalgia as well as regret over being famous, he recalls the "good old days" making music "the best we could" when the "money was not so good." He addresses the seduction of drugs in the chorus. People may get "stoned" but in the end they have to face reality.

"See the Sky about to Rain" is a quiet, emotional track. Young sings the song in a plaintive, restrained voice over a pretty melody. The recording opens with an electric piano (with a vibrato effect) that sets the mood for the performance. The listener feels compelled to listen to Young and his ensemble that includes the Band's Levon Helm keeping the beat. Like the opening track, this cut consists of two verses and two choruses. In this song, however, Young opens with the chorus. The lyric is full of train imagery, including a closely painted detail of "signals curling on an open plain," referring to the smoke from the engine in a land out west, as well as to a Native American form of communication.

The final verse presents another view of the perils of the music business. He sets a scene of playing a "silver fiddle" in the South until "the man broke it down the middle." On one hand, the action is reminiscent of mythical meetings at the crossroads where the musician sells his soul to play his music, or duels musically with the devil to get his soul back. Beginning in 1971, Young's music publishing company was called Silver Fiddle, which brings an autobiographical element to the setting. He takes a swipe at music industry executives, symbolized by "the man" who "broke" the "fiddle." The Massey Hall live recording of "See the Sky about to Rain" stripped the song to its essence as Young sang over his piano accompaniment. The reading was no less serious than the studio version, but it did not have the self-importance that the large studio production seems to cast on the tune.

"Revolution Blues" has a Dylanesque feel to it in part because Dylan's old rhythm section (when he was backed by the Hawks) performs on the track. Rick Danko plays bass and Levon Helm plays drums on the recording. The murderous narrator does not see the incongruity between killing the neighbor's "guard dog" and releasing "doves," a symbol of peace. McDonough suggests the lyric is based on the story of Charles Manson.[4] Young notices the warped logic of those who call for revolution.

The revolutionist narrator has a thirst for death. He has a vision of "bloody fountains." In one way, the narrator is like Young, who lyrically unfolded his distaste for the California celebrity culture on a number of occasions. The narrator promises to "kill" the "famous stars" of "Laurel Canyon."

Young's banjo and Ben Keith's slide guitar provide the only instrumental accompaniment on "For the Turnstiles." The narrative thread is unclear.

Part of the lyric is set along the waterfront, and part is set at a ball field. In a strained voice, Young unfolds a scene of "sailors" drawn to the "siren" calls of prostitutes. He juxtaposes the partying sailors on leave, with a "granite" statue of "explorers," conjuring the image of the Discoverer's Monument along the Tagus River in Lisbon, Portugal. The track closes with the end of a ball game and the hometown "crowd" heading "for the turnstiles."

"Vampire Blues" is an electric blues following an A-A-B structure. The lyric combines horror movie imagery with the concern over the depletion of nonrenewable resources. Young, of course, is fascinated with southern California culture, of which film is a large part, and he is interested in environmental issues. As a "vampire" sucks "blood," barrels of oil are being sucked "from the earth." The relentless "black bat," a symbol of greed, demands its "high octane." Who cares about the impact? In the third verse, Young points out the false optimism of those who see no problem in quenching the thirst of a culture caught up in moving about. Three times he sings, "Good times are comin'," but at the end of the verse, he notes, "they sure comin' slow." After the final verse, he delivers the "Good times are comin'" line one more time, but he does not do it convincingly. The guitar at the end of the performance sounds like a droning airplane in trouble, signifying that the fuel has run out. Good times are gone.

"On the Beach" also follows a blues form, albeit in a different structure than the previous track. The song opens with guitar and Latin percussion and follows an A-A-B-A form in the first three of its four verses. As is wont with Young's lyrics, the song has several meanings. There is the apocalyptic vision of California being destroyed by an earthquake, and there is the fear of the artist losing his audience. The title references the 1959 nuclear holocaust film (based on Nevil Shute's novel) of the same name. The narrator hopes the "world" does not "turn away." This could be from existence or from his music. He appears at a "radio interview" but discovers he is "alone at the microphone." Again, either his audience has gone, or there has been a holocaust. The narrator, whose "pictures are fallin' from the wall" (because of an earthquake) decides to escape and "get out of town." It is music like this that fellow Canadian Michael Timmins, leader and songwriter of the melancholy tunes of Cowboy Junkies, must have listened to in his formative years.

Young's fascination for California and its celebrity industry is again evident in "Motion Pictures." Academy Award-nominated actress Carrie Snodgress and Young lived together at the time. Snodgress shared Young's disdain for the spotlight. After garnering an Oscar nomination for *Diary of a Mad Housewife,* she turned her back on the film industry to live with Young. The narrator of the lyric rejects stardom. He "wouldn't . . . trade anything . . . to be like" a film star. He continues in the next verse, "headlines bore me now." More than once, Young's lyrics revealed his desire to be out of the spotlight.

From a close-up on the film industry, Young turns back to the scene he is most familiar with, the music business, and opines about the problems with that scene. Young talk-sings his way through the album closer, "Ambulance Blues." The track is a long narrative in the spirit of "Last Trip to Tulsa" (from his solo debut), but it has a different feel and a different vocal delivery. The first verse reflects his nostalgia for simpler music times, before the bestsellers. He speaks of the "old folky days" when the "air was magic when we played." Verse five cautions about selling out in the music business, a warning that Rick Nelson provided at the top of the decade in "Garden Party." Young sings of how "easy" it is "to get buried in the past." Rusty Kershaw adds a fiddle line to the track, and at this point in the song, he makes it sound like a bothersome fly. In the next verse, Young has a word for "critics" that attack the path he has taken. He tells them, "You're no better than me." Some of the verses are more obscure, but for sure, Young is not happy with the dynamics of the music industry.

TONIGHT'S THE NIGHT

On the Beach was bleak but not as desolate as his next release. The story goes that Young was previewing an album titled *Homegrown* for his musical friends. Apparently the tape also included the masters for *Tonight's the Night*. The listening guests were impressed with the raw reality of the earlier work and suggested that the *Tonight's the Night* sessions be released. At this point, Young's record company agreed to release Young's dark album. *Tonight's the Night* was so dark that the traditional black letters over a field of orange of the Reprise label on the vinyl was replaced with white letters over a field of black. The liner notes state, "This album was made for Danny Whitten and Bruce Berry who lived and died for rock and roll." Whitten, the Crazy Horse guitarist, and Berry, a road worker (roadie) for the Crosby, Stills, Nash, and Young touring band, both succumbed to drugs. The album opens with the title track and closes with "Tonight's the Night—Part II," a second performance of the same song. Both are electric instruments-based and both include Nils Lofgren on guitar, Ben Keith on slide guitar, and the Crazy Horse rhythm section of Ralph Molina on drums and Billy Talbot on bass. Lofgren played piano on Young's *After the Gold Rush* album. Young plays piano on "Tonight's the Night."

The song opens with piano and guitar and voices quietly chanting the title line over and over. The lyric focuses on the life of Bruce Berry, who was a casualty of heroin. His day job was as a roadie, but Young saw another side of Berry "late at night." In the first verse, he unfolds a scene of Berry taking "my guitar" and "sing(ing) a song in a shaky voice that was real." Berry's art was true to the spirit of rock and roll and he did not need an audience for a stamp of approval. Young reflects on the moment of hearing of Berry's death. It gave him a "chill" when he learned that Berry had "died out on the mainline." The cut ends with an almost a cappella chant of the title phrase. The voices quietly fade as Lofgren plays some spare guitar chords.

"Speakin' Out" is a blues number. The performance is introduced with a blues piano that moves into a slide guitar. Later, in one of the breaks, there is an electric blues guitar solo. The choruses are addressed to a lover, one who is expectant with the narrator's child. The two verses are not connected to the choruses or to each other, except that they both deal with the media, the first with film and the second with television. The second verse is addressed to a TV reporter, one who had a "notebook behind (his) eyes." Young's narrator says he will be "watchin'" as the television watches the reporter.

Young again addresses his disillusion with celebrity in "World on a String." It "doesn't mean a thing" to have fans and music industry people and the media and hangers-on fawning over him. All that matters is how he "feels." The instrumental track is a rocking country shuffle that has an attractive melody line in the second half of each verse. Young's vocal is raw and strained.

Young acknowledges in "Borrowed Tune" that he nicked the melody from a Rolling Stones' song. The tune is borrowed from the mid-1960s track "Lady Jane." The lyric is a number of unrelated, brief impressions. Attempting to sing in a higher register, he is wary of the spotlight (as usual). He is "climbin' this ladder," but "havin' my doubts." He offers a point of view from the stage of the fans in the audience as "an ocean of shakin' hands" grasping "at the sky."

In the midst of the album, Young tosses in a tribute to his late friend Danny Whitten, who lost his life to heroin. "Come on, Baby, Let's Go Downtown" is a live track from 1969 of Neil Young and Crazy Horse recorded at the Fillmore East.[5] The up-tempo track opens with a barrage of electric guitar chords. Whitten sings the lead vocal on the verses. Sadly and ironically, the lyric deals with the drug scene. The chorus sets up a scene where someone is "dealin' with the man" (the pusher), who is "sellin' stuff."

More like *Harvest* in character, at least in the instrumentation and the first part of the vocal, is the love song "Mellow My Mind." The track opens with a wheezing, Dylanesque harmonica bit. Young's vocal begins smoothly, but soon deteriorates to a ragged state (unlike *Harvest*). The words are few. The narrator is alone. Using railroad imagery, he states that the "lonesome whistle" of a locomotive has "nothing" on his "feelings." Nils Lofgren's piano and Ben Keith's pedal steel guitar add an agreeable touch to the track.

Young is purposely off key in the vocal to "Roll Another Number (For the Road)," a track with a country music feeling. The second verse is about the Woodstock Music and Arts Fair specifically and about the culture of the era. He talk-sings the verse about Woodstock, labeling his experience there as "that helicopter day." Logistics required that the musical acts be ferried in and out by choppers. In the same verse, he adds that he will not be "goin' back that away." You cannot relive the past. He cannot go back, but he can stay high. The narrator says his "feet aren't on the ground" and he will keep it that way as he "roll(s) another number."

"Albuquerque" is another driving and smoking song. Again, the narrator "roll(s) a number" before he "rent(s) a car." The opening electric guitar uses an effect similar to that of "Alabama" on *Harvest*. The lyric also deals with escaping fame and places where the narrator is recognized. The narrator is "starvin' to be alone" and away "from the scene." Continuing this theme of discontent with the spotlight, he says he will run until he finds a place "where they don't care who I am."

"New Mama" is a tender song with sparse instrumentation (acoustic guitar, piano, and vibes). The song is about the joy of a newborn. The narrator says he is "livin' in a dreamland" because of the new life that has come.

"Lookout Joe" is an electric rocker with a confusing narrative. The song opens with a street scene of characters that want to seduce "Joe." The second verse is about a groupie named "Millie," and the narrator talks about a "woman" who hustled Joe for his "money and left town." After the second chorus, Young plays a lead guitar break that is reminiscent of the guitar line on the Rolling Stones' "Time Is on My Side." Right after that, Young borrows two lines from the spiritual "Glory, Glory, Hallelujah," which does not seem to connect, unless the narrator is focusing on another street character.

"Tired Eyes" climaxes with a scene of a botched drug deal that left "four men" dead. The lyric is based on an actual incident. Young speaks the verses in a style similar to Frank Zappa. He sings the choruses. The song has a depressing cast as the background unfolds to the fatal scene. Someone is "left...lying in a driveway" (presumably dead), and there are "bullet holes in...mirrors." In the choruses, the singer pleads, "open up the tired eyes." He is asking people to realize that drugs are murderous in so many ways.

Tonight's the Night closes with a reprise of the title song. It was not a fun album.

ZUMA

With *Zuma,* released in fall 1975, Young began to climb out of the funk that shadowed his previous three releases. Crazy Horse was back, with Frank Sampedro replacing the late Danny Whitten on rhythm guitar. The group's collaboration with Young resulted in several ambitious, extended tracks, "Cortez the Killer" and "Danger Bird," and helped improve his lyrical and musical outlook. "Cortez the Killer" is a seven-minutes-plus track taken at a slow tempo. It has a long introduction of electric guitars, bass, and drums and hearkens back to earlier extended jams of Young with Crazy Horse. Although the explorer Hernan Cortez is the title character, the lyric focus is more on life in the Aztec Empire under Montezuma. Young describes a people living in harmony ("hate was just a legend" and "war was never known"). He also addresses the mystical side of the emperor Montezuma ("he...wandered with the secrets of the world"). But, as history books tell us, Cortez came to conquer Mexico for the Spanish crown, and destroyed the Aztec culture that Young paints nostalgically in this track. Near the close of the song, the narrator recalls a woman, possibly Aztec, who "loves" him, but he "lost (his) way." It is not clear how this fits into the context, unless it is one of the Spanish conquerors or an Aztec warrior reflecting about how life was before the conquest.

"Danger Bird" is a trademark Young and Crazy Horse recording in the spirit of "Down by the River" and "Cowgirl in the Sand." The song is taken at a slow tempo. Young sings with a strained voice. The vocal structure is different than the typical Young composition. In two verses, someone else, either Billy Talbot or Ralph Molina sings the primary vocal line, while Young sings a different phrase behind the deeper voice. Again, Young presents an oblique narrative. The "Danger Bird" may be a creature or a person. He has wings of "stone" yet he continues to "fly, fly, fly." The lyric speaks of a "museum" and "rain pounding." One intriguing line the narrator (the Danger Bird) offers is "freedom's just a prison." A theme is how we become comfortable in our complacency. We fear vulnerability.

The album opens with "Don't Cry No Tears." The song draws the listener in with a striking electric guitar hook and a robust melody that Young sings over in a strong voice. Even the background "aaahhs" by Crazy Horse members Talbot and Molina have a touch of Beach Boys' harmony to them. The song has a bit of a country feel to it, but it is too rocking to be considered country rock. The lyric is about lost love. His woman has gone away to another.

"Lookin' for a Love" has a country-and-western-guitar feel in its introduction that spills over into Young's vocals. The melody has an appealing, hopping hook to it. Young's narrator ruminates on finding true love. He recognizes the importance of the eyes in communicating caring and love. He sings, "In her eyes I will discover [a] reason why I want to live." He unfolds a beach scene along the Pacific Coast where he may encounter this love. He knows he cannot plan or force a relationship ("she'll be nothing like I pictured her to be"). When he does find a partner, he hopes not to hurt her when she discovers his "darker side."

"Barstool Blues" opens with heavy, electric guitar chords. The song is not a blues, in the traditional sense of a blues structure. Singing the song in a higher register, Young's lyrics bring up a variety of impressions, as though he is holding court from a barstool. The first verse is primarily about focusing on "one thought." The second verse talks about a film star the narrator watched sitting on a "barstool." Whether it was someone he knew well (the actress Carrie Snodgress) or someone he only viewed from a distance is unclear. Whoever it was, the person was on edge ("You held that glass so tight"). And Young's narrator sees the subject in both his "nightmares" and "dreams." The final verse addresses an issue of celebrity (one of Young's ongoing lyrical topics). Young speaks of someone who was surrounded by "parasites" and faced "idle threats." After the final guitar break, the tempo slows down and Ralph Molina closes the performance with a final tap on his ride cymbal.

"Stupid Girl" appears to be addressed specifically to a well-to-do woman, someone who acts out "self-defense" exercises within the confines of her luxury vehicle. The track has a spare Crazy Horse sound with a marching bass. After the third reading of the tag line, "You're such a stupid girl," the background vocals sing out "Na, Na, Na, Nas" in a 1968 Beach Boys' *Friends*-era style. The listener does not learn why the narrator is angry with the subject. He indicates that she is striving for something else, when she could have what is right in front of her, possibly the narrator himself. She is "lookin' for the wave (she) missed, when another is close at hand."

Young opens "Drive Back" with the words "Whatever gets you through the night, that's all right," closely echoing the words of John Lennon's Number 1 hit single of the year before, "Whatever Gets You through the Night." The song is basically about a one-night stand. The narrator speaks frankly ("I wanna wake up with no one around"). He commands the one he was with to "drive back," or go away. In a twist, though, he tells the person in the final verse that he will be a shelter. He offers to "hide" the person "from yourself and...old friends."

"Pardon My Heart" and "Through My Sails" are not Crazy Horse tracks. On "Pardon My Heart," Young plays all the instruments save for the bass guitar by Tim Drummond. "Through My Sails" is for all intents and purposes a Crosby, Stills, Nash, and Young recording. "Pardon My Heart" is about a relationship that did not meet the narrator's expectations. It is a quiet, mellow song. Molina and Talbot of Crazy Horse contribute to the background vocals. They trade lines with Young on the choruses.

The album closes with "Through My Sails." Young plays guitar; Stephen Stills plays bass; Russ Kunkel plays the congas; and Crosby, Stills, and Nash harmonize with Young on the vocal. The lyrics are light and are basically about leaving the city to be refreshed by the sea. They are simply words for the singers to hang their harmonies on.

THE STILLS-YOUNG BAND: *LONG MAY YOU RUN*

In 1976, Young and Stills collaborated on a recording project. Along with Joe Lala on percussion, Jerry Aiello on keyboards, George "Chocolate" Perry on bass, and Joe Vitale on drums, the Stills-Young Band retired to Criteria Studios in Miami and recorded the album *Long May You Run*. Young contributed five songs to the album and Stills four. The title track has become one of Young's more popular songs over the decades. "Long May You Run" is a car song. As noted earlier, Young has a penchant for the music of the Beach Boys, who were the primary purveyors of car songs in the 1960s. The song is a fond remembrance of a hearse affectionately named "Mort" the singer owned when he was a young driver.[6] The song has a pleasant shuffling beat. It opens with harmonica over acoustic guitar.

The lyrics contain hints that the song is about a car without being specific. Young sings of "*trunks* of memories," "*chrome* heart shining" and "missed that *shift* on the...decline" (emphasis added). Introducing the song in concert, Young reminisces about how he would downshift going downhill to save gas, and he did it one too many times and the car came to its end. He brings the lyric around to the Beach Boys and mentions the song "Caroline No." It is an interesting choice, as "Caroline No" is not about a car, nor would one think of it as a Beach Boys' song remembered from the car radio while cruising along, such as "Fun, Fun, Fun" or "All Summer Long." Plus, in the verse that mentions the Beach Boys, the lyric speaks of "waves" and "surf." "Caroline No" is far from being a surf song. It was the closing moment of *Pet Sounds,* the album that wrested the Beach Boys from the sun-and-fun image (for a spell). Maybe because the track was the end of a new beginning, or maybe because of its bittersweet character, Young saw it as applicable to his fondness for his old car. In the "Caroline No" moment, just after Young sings the title, the background voices (Stills, Perry, Lala, and Vitale) chime in with "Oh, Caroline no" in the style of a Beach Boys harmony.

"Midnight on the Bay" has a sunny, summer, island feel in its arrangement. The vocal is backed with quiet, electric guitar and hand percussion that together create a mellow groove. Young's lyric sets a scene through the Florida Keys with swaying "sailboats" and "ocean breeze(s)." Even in this idyllic setting, however, Young cannot escape being recognized. A woman approaches him and says, "I know your name." Again, Young takes a harsh look at the experience of celebrity.

In addition to "Midnight on the Bay," Young's tracks "Ocean Girl" and "Fontainebleau" also have a south Florida setting. This suggests that the songs were written while the band was in the studio in Miami. "Ocean Girl" is a mid-tempo, mellow song with an Afro-Caribbean influence. The lyric is basically an enticement to a woman the narrator is attracted to. "Fontainebleau" is the name of an old, grand hotel in Miami Beach that had seen its better days by the time the Stills-Young Band sessions were in progress. But the song is not just about the "green exterior" or the "blue-haired ladies" that visit. A theme is change ("Who took everything from where it once was"). Another is the seduction of riches and luxury. The narrator remembers fearfully that he "stayed there (at the landmark hotel) once and...almost fit."

Young has commented on religion in his lyrics a number of times across the decades. "Let It Shine" has a southern gospel feel. It is a shuffle with a country vocal delivery that leaves the listener wondering if the singer is sincere or performing a parody. The narrator addresses the lyric to "my Lord." The gist of the song is that there may be more than one way to find God. He sings of "a light...over (his) head" and adds, "it may not be the only one." There may be several paths to spiritual enlightenment. The second verse is about a car, a "Lincoln," and the point may be that there are other vehicles that would be just as satisfactory on the road to transcendence. Young lays out an airport scene where he gets nabbed by proselytizing Hare Krishna adherents while "waiting." He says it is fine if they "chant" or "dance," but that does not mean they have the only connection to ultimate truth.

AMERICAN STARS 'N' BARS

American Stars 'n' Bars is a patchwork of tracks recorded with various ensemble groupings during November 1974, November 1975, May 1976, and April 1977. Young was about to release his *Decade* compilation at the end of 1976 when he asked his record company to postpone it for a year so that *American Stars 'n' Bars* could be released. He played a copy for the record company and they agreed, but by the time the album was issued, he had changed it from its earlier format. The album was released several months after the last tracks were completed. Two tracks feature just Young and Crazy Horse. One of those is "Like a Hurricane," which has maintained a prominent place in Young's body of work over the years. The lyric makes good use of the violent storm imagery. In comparing the one to whom he is attracted to the storm, he speaks of the "calm in your eye." He is "getting blown away" as if by gale force winds. It is a testimony to the raging power of love. He desires a safe haven "where the feelings stay" and he could "love," but the force is too much. McDonough describes the song as the culmination of a series of "dark, descending minor-chord Del Shannon-style mood pieces" by Young.[7]

"Homegrown" can be considered a life theme of Young's musical career. He records at his Broken Arrow Ranch, his home. The graphics of his album covers and compact disc booklets are full of hand-printed titles and lyrics. Again this track features only Young and the three members of Crazy Horse. "Homegrown" is an off-kilter, jumpy rocker with an agricultural slant. Crops "start jumping...from the ground." Another level of meaning relates to growing one's own marijuana stash. The song closes with three readings of the chorus, first a cappella, then with just the bass guitar, and then accompanied by the whole band. "Homegrown" was to be the title track of an album that was shelved in 1975, so that *Tonight's the Night* could finally see the light of day.

One track, "Will to Love," features Young alone on various instruments including acoustic guitar, vibraphone and percussion, and vocals. It is a long, wordy track (10 verses plus 4 repetitions of the chorus) with an ethereal feel. (Young even sings, "Sometimes I ramble on and on.") The narrator is a fish and Young's vocal is phased to sound as though he is underwater while singing. Robert Christgau describes the song as Young morphing "into a salmon while masturbating in front of the fireplace."[8] The recording opens with vocal "la, la, las," which is rare for Young, as his songs typically begin with an instrumental introduction. The song is about the instinct to love and to continue the chain of life. Love is a mystery he suggests, as he sings in the chorus, "It's like something from up above." It is supernatural; it is spiritual. Young described the creation of the track in detail to Bill Flanagan. He sang only one take of the vocal and used that on the final recording.[9]

On "Star of Bethlehem," Young plays acoustic guitar and harmonica; Emmylou Harris and Ben Keith add vocal support; and Ben Keith plays Dobro. The rhythm section consists of Tim Drummond (bass) and Karl T. Himmel (drums). "Star of Bethlehem" is not a Christmas song, although the narrator may be reflecting on his life on Christmas Eve. He describes the evening as a "cold and chilly night of gloom." He thinks of how not only "lovers," but "dreams," too, betray you and take advantage of you. Yet, he exposes nostalgia for the past, or as he says, he has "memories of happiness." He has come to a place where he has lost faith. He "wonder(s) who (he) can…turn to." The "answer…is nowhere" around him. He is confused. In the final verse, he seems to express both hope and the rejection of faith in the same breath. "A light is shining…down the hall." That "light" may provide direction and lead him on a path out of the abyss in which he resides. But he closes the song contemplating whether the "star of Bethlehem" was really a "star." If it was not a star, if it was not related to the birth of Jesus Christ, then maybe there is no truth to the faith and hope grasped by those who find true meaning in Christmas.

All five tracks on side one of *American Stars 'n' Bars* are credited to Young, Crazy Horse, and the Bullets. Other than Young and Sampedro, Talbot, and Molina of Crazy Horse, the other musicians (the Bullets) in the ensemble are Ben Keith on steel guitar, Carole Mayedo on violin, and Linda Ronstadt and Nicolette Larson on vocals. The opening cut, "The Old Country Waltz," begins, as one would expect, as an old, country waltz. The lyric presents a prototypical crying-in-your-beer style song. The narrator thinks of how he "loved" and "lost" while he is "knock(ing) down tequila and salt." Young connects music and memories. He recalls what the "band" was "playing" when he learned the "news that you set me free."

Studio chatter opens "Saddle up the Palomino," giving the recording an informal cast (like the Beach Boys' *Party* album). It is a country rock song about lust and adultery. The narrator is ambivalent about his desires. He accepts that there is "no reward in your conscience" when you have an affair with the "wife" of "another." Still, it is she he is "after." "Hey Babe" is a country shuffle with a catchy melody line in the chorus. Ben Keith's pedal steel guitar stands out in this promise of love and devotion by the singer. In a Tex-Mex musical vein, "Hold Back the Tears" presents encouraging words directed to someone who lost a love. The narrator does wonder why with the "pain" that love brings on, we keep going back for more. Mayedo plays a melody during the fiddle break that seems familiar, yet difficult to identify.

The side closes with "Bite the Bullet." It is a rousing, ribald, lustful track that sounds like it was recorded in one take, live in the studio by a group of friends having a good time. Adding to the informal character is a grating edge to the mix. (During the sessions, vocalists Linda Ronstadt and Nicolette Larson thought they were only rehearsing the songs in the studio, but Young decided to use the rehearsal takes in the final masters.) The narrator thinks (heatedly) of a woman in Charlotte, North Carolina, with whom he has been intimate. He says frankly in the choruses that his desire is to bring her to orgasm ("I'd like to make her scream"). She attracts men ("good old boys") like syrup draws flies. Other than being a song that extols the romantic qualities of a woman ("a walking love machine") from the Carolinas, the track has nothing in common with Chairmen of the Board's "Carolina Girls" or any other record in the beach music genre.

DECADE

In time for the 1977 holiday shopping season, Reprise released a three-vinyl disc retrospective commemorating Young's 10 years as a recording artist. Young had compiled the album a year earlier, but asked that it be held up until after the release of *American Stars 'n' Bars*. Among the 35 tracks on *Decade* were one unreleased Buffalo Springfield recording ("Down to the Wire"), one track that had never appeared in an album format ("Sugar Mountain"), and four previously unreleased tracks from Young's solo career. Both "Down to the Wire" and "Sugar Mountain" were discussed previously.

"Winterlong" is from the early Crazy Horse days. A live version from 1970 is included in the 2006 *Live at the Fillmore East* release. The track has a big guitar opening like the later power ballads of the 1980s and 1990s. Rhythm guitarist Danny Whitten joins Young on the vocal duties. The narrator is in a romantic relationship that is in jeopardy. Opening with an acoustic guitar, "Deep Forbidden Lake" sets a quiet scene and atmosphere. The imagery is of sailing and nature, but the song has a deeper, spiritual meaning. Although the lyrics are somewhat opaque, Young describes a crowd reacting to the words of a "passerby." Like the waters of the lake, the reaction "ripples" through the hearers, resulting in a race to the lakeside to "cast their doubts" into the waters. The final verse has little relation to the impressions of "turtles" and colorful "banners," yet it seems to bring closure to the narrative.

Linda Ronstadt popularized "Love Is a Rose" on her 1975 Top 5 album *Prisoner in Disguise*. So, in listening to Young's version, it is easy to think something is missing because there is no banjo, like the one that helped define the Ronstadt reading. Young's version is introduced with a standup bass, which moves into a harmonica playing followed by the strumming of an acoustic guitar. The theme of the lyric is that if you try to possess love, it will slip away from you. Young laid down the track while rehearsing with Crosby, Stills, and Nash for the summer 1974 tour.[10]

"Campaigner" has a 1960s folk song aesthetic. The track is presented by Young alone with his acoustic guitar. The theme is politics, although the details are obscure. Each of the four verses ends with phrases about Richard Nixon having "soul." The world would have been a better place if indeed Nixon had "soul."

COMES A TIME

The solid song selection on *Decade* gave Young renewed cachet. He was primed for the Top 10, and *Comes a Time,* an album in the vein of *Harvest,* brought him back there for the first time since *Harvest.* The album peaked at Number 7 in the fall of 1978. Although the album was recorded by 10 engineers at six different studios in London, Nashville, Florida, and California, with oversight by four producers, there is a cohesive quality to the collected tracks.

The title track opens with Rufus Thibodeaux's fiddle, but the track is more folky than country. The instrumental track has a cozy feel that supports the lyrics of domestic bliss, a season of new love and new life. The rhythm has a comfortable, easygoing gait that contributes to the bliss of the recording. In addition to including some of his regular musical collaborators on the album—Ben Keith on steel guitar, Tim Drummond on bass, and Spooner Oldham on piano—Young's Gone with the Wind Orchestra contains 16 string players and 8 acoustic guitarists.

The record kicks off with "Goin' Back." Young's acoustic guitar and Tim Drummond's characteristic bass style (another connection to the *Harvest* album) lead off the track. Nicolette Larson, who is credited in the liner notes for singing harmony vocals, duets with Young in this tale that suggests that just as prehistoric creatures were "driven to the mountains," or "sunken in the cities deep" (a reference to the La Brea tar pits of Los Angeles), the same is happening to humanity. Young likens the lyric to "the debris of the sixties. There's nowhere to stay, nowhere to go and nothin' to do."[11]

Two of the tracks were popularized by two of Young's favorite supporting vocalists. Nicolette Larson had a Top 10 hit with "Lotta Love" around the same time that *Comes a Time* was popular. A little over a year after the album's release, Linda Ronstadt included "Look Out for My Love" on her Top 5 new wave-influenced *Mad Love* album of 1980. Young's versions of these two tracks are backed by the Crazy Horse trio, with producer Tim Mulligan sitting in on saxophone. "Look Out for My Love" has an ominous feel to it. When the narrator addresses his paramour, and says "Look out for my love," the thought is foreboding and dangerous. There is nothing calming about his statement; it is a warning. He predicts that "things" will "change, but (he) can't say (whether the change will be) bad or good." The narrator makes no promises. In several verses in the latter half of the song, he talks about being on a plane or in an airport thinking about his love, but these impressions do not easily dovetail with the rest of the tale. "Lotta Love" features acoustic guitar and upright piano and a lot of "la, la, las" by the vocalists. The song is about overcoming past romantic failures. The narrator warns whoever will take him up on his plea for love that his "heart needs protection."

Larson sings the harmony vocal on "Peace of Mind." Again, there is an acoustic guitar and piano opening. And, again, the lyric deals with romance. It is about the human foibles of love. The narrator observes how a person will hold tight to love, pledging an eternal bond, until "you leave her first." Still, the only time there was "peace of mind" was when the woman was "treated...kind."

When Crosby, Stills, Nash, and Young reunited for their summer tour in 1974, there was talk of a studio album in the works. "Human Highway" was supposed to be the title track of that abandoned project. The performance has a Carter Family influence to it. The song only has two verses, one of which is repeated twice. The song is about the unkindness and cruelty that rear their heads when we join the stream of humanity. At the end of each verse, Young asks, "How could people get so unkind?"

Like "Comes a Time," "Already One" is a song about domestic harmony with a focus on the wonder that a child brings to the life of a couple. Young was already exploring the melody that would become part of "Harvest Moon" almost a decade and a half later. The theme of the couple as "one" echoes the words of the Apostle Paul who wrote, "two shall be as one flesh"[12] and more recently the words of Noel Paul Stookey who sang in "Wedding Song (There Is Love)" that "the two shall be as one." Larson again sings the harmony vocal.

Young affects a country style vocal delivery while singing with Larson on "Field of Opportunity." Young gives Thibodeaux's fiddle a prominent role in the production. The song is about loneliness and the need for companionship. The lyric uses agricultural and rural imagery to make its point. Five times he repeats a couplet about it being time for plowing "in the field of opportunity." As he often does, Young lyrically paints the picture with stunning details. The narrator "borrow(s) seeds of sadness from the ground" as he unfolds the tale of how his "lover" disappointed him. He rests on his "porch" waiting for a love and watching for "headlights comin' down the hill between the stars."

"Motorcycle Mama" is a quirky song in the spirit of "Bite the Bullet." Young seems to record tracks like these every now and then to blow off steam from the tensions of long studio sessions. Similar to "Bite the Bullet," there is a salacious character to the lyric. The lyric is a dialogue between Young and Larson. Larson plays the role of the "motorcycle mama" and Young her suitor. At one point, they sing together, "I see your box is open, and your flag is up" in a thinly veiled sexual allusion.

Ian Tyson's most well-known song, "Four Strong Winds," is given a top-quality reading by Young and Larson. The track exudes Young's appreciation for his fellow Canadian's composition. The introduction has a pleasant, acoustic guitar opening. Thibodeaux's fiddle is up front in the mix in the second verse. The track was issued as a single but failed to crack the Top 60.

RUST NEVER SLEEPS

While Young was mining the country rock vein and dabbling with Crazy Horse and the Stray Gators, the punk scene was emerging in the late 1970s, with British bands the Sex Pistols and the Clash, and American bands like X and the Ramones. Punk threatened the rock music establishment that still embraced a 1960s aesthetic and was making the earlier music its canon. Punk questioned the old school. It was the first time that rock performers were on the defensive. Young and Crazy Horse reacted to the young, defiant sounds on side two of *Rust Never Sleeps*. This must be the album that a young Eddie Vedder, the singer and songwriter of Seattle's Pearl Jam, and the late Kurt Cobain of Nirvana took to heart. *Rust Never Sleeps* is at the core of the mantle bestowed on Young as the godfather of grunge.

Rust Never Sleeps is a schizophrenic record. Side one is acoustic and seems like an extension of his previous release, *Comes a Time*. The side one ensemble includes Nicolette Larson, Joe Osborne, and Karl Himmel. Side two is electric and is performed only by Young and Crazy Horse. The album is book-ended by two versions of the same song. "My My, Hey Hey (Out of the Blue)" is given a folk ballad treatment by Young. In the lyric he mentions Johnny Rotten, lead singer of the Sex Pistols, the archetypal purveyors of punk rock. Young sings, "the king is gone," a reference to the passing of Elvis Presley two years earlier. He comments negatively on the closing years of Presley's career. Young sings, "It's better to burn out than it is to rust," suggesting that it would have been better not to witness the decline of Presley. Recording artists who die when they are young (Buddy Holly, Ritchie Valens, Sam Cooke, Otis Redding, Jimi Hendrix, Janis Joplin) never "rust." They are remembered as they were. They did not sell out on a casino stage.

"Thrasher" is a long, story-song like "Last Trip to Tulsa" and contains a narrative that is as difficult to comprehend. But "Thrasher" has a more pleasant melody and aesthetic to it. Young sings alone backed by one or two acoustic guitars and his harmonica. The song is nostalgic, there are rural images, and there is the sense that things change for the worse. Young acknowledged to Bill Flanagan that the song was partially about breaking away from Crosby, Stills, and Nash.[13] "Ride My Llama," too, has a tale that is hard to follow. The lyrics evoke frontiers such as when he calls the listener to "Remember the Alamo" or when he names the planet "Mars," but they do not seem to have a central place in the story. It is an account of moving on and traveling on.

"Pocahontas" is a classic piece of music in Young's body of work. He opens with a wonderful lyric image that makes you feel the cold breeze whistling by.

He sings, "Aurora borealis, the icy sky at night, paddles cut the water." It is easy to visualize a canoe in an earlier era cutting through a stream. The song is about the plight of Native Americans. He brings forth images of escaping the "white man," of "women" murdered, and the killing off of the "buffalo." He portrays a harrowing scene of motherless "babies cryin' on the ground." The narrator wishes he could go back to a purer time before the European invasion of North America. In the last verse, Young mentions Marlon Brando and Hollywood. This may seem out of place, but here Young makes reference to the 1973 Academy Awards ceremony, which the nominated Marlon Brando refused to attend. He sent a Native American actress, Sacheen Littlefeather, in his place. When he was selected as Best Actor for his portrayal of *The Godfather,* she mounted the stage, refused the award, and explained Brando's distaste for the way Native Americans were portrayed in film.[14]

Rust Never Sleeps, like the album before it, was a Top 10 hit. It reached Number 8 on the *Billboard* charts in the summer of 1979. Side one ends with a pretty song called "Sail Away" that features a Dobro line. Nicolette Larson contributes a pleasing harmony in the chorus. The song is about how things will be fine as long as the couple can escape from the hassles of life when they need to.

On side two Young answered the punk rockers by experimenting with highly distorted fuzz-tone notes on his guitar. This is particularly evident in the closing track, "Hey Hey, My My (Into the Black)," the electric version of the album's opening tune. The electric notes are almost a white noise. When Young sings "rock and roll will never die," he expresses hope. His optimism stems from the fact that the punk rockers are challenging Young's complacent musical peers. Nirvana's Kurt Cobain listened carefully to these lyrics. He included the line about it being "better to burn out 'cause rust never sleeps" in his suicide note in 1994. The opening and closing tracks were both recorded live. The ambient sounds of the audience at the venue are evident on the two tracks. None of the other cuts on the album are live performances.

The second side opens with "Powderfinger," a song from the Young catalog that has remained in high regard over the decades. Like a film noir, the youthful narrator is already dead and gone as he begins to unfold the story of his untimely demise. In the first verse, a hostile military vessel approaches a rural homestead. The theme of the song is the tragic and wasteful loss of youth to the conflicts between countries and their leaders. The 22-year-old protagonist realizes it is his responsibility to defend his family's outlying land against the invader. But the firepower of "Daddy's rifle" is no match for the vessel with "numbers on the side." Gruesomely, the young guardian elucidates his demise ("my face splashed in the sky"). Sorrowfully, he "fade(s) away...with so much left undone."

The production of "Welfare Mothers" is a rambunctious wall of sound stirred up in a messy mix. The members of Crazy Horse members loudly chant "Welfare mothers make better lovers" after every line delivered by Young adding an off-balance quality to the track. It is one of those blowing-off-steam tracks like "Bite the Bullet" and "Motorcycle Mama" from previous albums. The lyrical premise is tongue-in-cheek or sarcastic. The lyrics suggest that low-income women are easier sexually. Part of the setting is a "Laundromat," suggesting a lower-income environment. Each verse ends with a one-word line, as the vocalists extend out the word "Divorcee," suggesting that these women at the center of the song are experienced in the ways of love.

"Sedan Delivery" is characterized by its varying rhythms. The track starts off at a sprint and alternatively slows down and speeds up through its course. Each verse presents a different scene. The narrator may be a drug runner because the only time he actually delivers something it is a package of "chemicals and sacred roots." We view him at a "pool hall," at a dentist office for tooth extractions, and "sleepin' in a hallway." Young's lyrics often only create an atmosphere rather than unfold a linear narrative. He adds a verse about watching a film of "Caesar and Cleo," and, unlike them, he was able to "get away." Another verse is set in a "lab" where an "old man" (a mad scientist) wears "white clothes."

LIVE RUST

In some ways, *Live Rust* is like a live version of the *Decade* retrospective issued two years earlier. Nine of the 16 cuts appear in different versions on *Decade*. Like *Decade*, *Live Rust* was released in time for holiday buying in its year of release. *Live Rust* was Young's second album release of 1979. It complements the *Rust Never Sleeps* album released earlier in the year. The font of the lettering on both jackets is the same. In small letters on the front cover of *Live Rust*, between the two words of the album title, the label "Record 2" is printed. This indicates that *Rust Never Sleeps* was "Record 1." Both album jackets contain photos of Young and Crazy Horse performing on stage in front of oversized amplifiers and microphones. Young was saying that the performance had taken over the music. The musicians are miniaturized in the landscape of the event. The event overshadows the art.

Live Rust is a career-spanning, live-in-concert, two-record set (in its original release) that gave the fans what they wanted. The album includes the best of his acoustic and the best of his electric material. The album opens with Young solo with his acoustic guitar, harmonica, and piano before the band walks on for the electric set that closes the concert. The concert set opens with "Sugar Mountain," a song that appeared on the B-side of several singles and was collected on the *Decade* retrospective. The well-known version of "Sugar Mountain" is also a live recording. The *Live Rust* version is taken at a bit of a faster tempo. After running through acoustic guitar and harmonica accompanied versions of "I Am a Child" (from the Buffalo Springfield years), and the then recent "Comes a Time," Young sits at the piano to play the title track of the *After the Gold Rush* album. When he gets to the line about "getting high," the late 1970s audience cheers. It is a paradoxical moment, as the previous decade had been darkened by the overdose deaths of two of Young's close musical colleagues. Before closing the acoustic set with "My My, Hey Hey (Out of the Blue)," the artist cynically announces to the audience, "When I get big, I'm gonna get an electric guitar." The audience raises up a cheer when he sings the name "Johnny Rotten." The audience response is not as loud, though, as when he sang earlier about "getting high."

The electric set starts with an energetic version of "When You Dance I Can Really Love." Without stopping, Young and Crazy Horse plow into a powerful version of "The Loner." The live version exudes an excitement not contained on the studio version on his debut solo album. Young retreats to his acoustic guitar for a solo version of "The Needle and the Damage Done." Just before he commences strumming, stage announcements from the *Woodstock* soundtrack album are played. The portion played is from Sunday afternoon when the dark clouds rolled in over the Catskills hills. The stage announcers urge the audience to get down from the towers and someone begins a "No rain" chant. So, what is the connection between the Woodstock Music and Arts Fair and "The Needle and the Damage Done"? The ominous clouds that came across the rolling hills of the Catskills can be an allegory for the drug abuse that destroyed artistic potential in the music scene. Or it could relate to Jimi Hendrix, one of the world class musicians who succumbed to drugs. Young and Hendrix hung out together at the 1969 Woodstock gathering waiting for their respective stage appearances. And Young wears a Jimi Hendrix button on his guitar strap on the back cover photo of *Live Rust*. The performance of "The Needle and the Damage Done" highlights the incongruity of the audience's reaction to Young's words about "getting high" in "After the Gold Rush."

Young and Crazy Horse then give a soulful reading of "Lotta Love," which is particularly enhanced by the supporting vocals by the members of Crazy Horse. It comes across as a pretty performance with a pleasurable piano figure thrown in. Then, Young warns, "We're gonna play some rock and roll," and the band vaults into the high-speed attack of "Sedan Delivery." "Powderfinger" follows, with the lead guitar playing higher notes than on the studio version. "Cortez the Killer" brings the energy down by slowing the tempo in a subdued performance of the composition. The band is still very electric, but there is a mournful character to the reading. Toward the end of the song, the band goes into a reggae style groove, as Young sings in an affected delivery, "He come dancing across the water, man, Cortez, Cortez." "Cinnamon Girl" begins with a fuzz-tone electric opening and has a bouncy feel throughout.

After "Like a Hurricane," Young asks the roadies (he pronounces them "road-eyes") to "take a bow." For this tour, with its odd props as mentioned earlier, the road crew wore hooded robes as though they were from a lost tribe on a *Star Wars* set, adding to the surreal and science fiction fantasy character of the presentation. Before the final two tracks, Young also thanks his "research staff" and the "great audience." Young and the Crazy Horse trio launch into the distorted chords of the opening of "Hey Hey, My My (Into the Black)" in a concert version as full of white noise as the one included on the earlier release of the year. Both Record 1 (*Rust Never Sleeps*) and Record 2 (*Live Rust*) of the 1979 Rust set contain live readings of the acoustic "My My, Hey Hey (Out of the Blue)" and the electric "Hey Hey, My My (Into the Black)."

Live Rust closes with "Tonight's the Night." It seems like a downer after the energy and excitement of the earlier portion of the set list, but the events surrounding the creation of the song colored much of the music Young created in the decade. The choice of the song again casts the audience reaction to the phrase "getting high" in a strange light. Despite his calling them a "great audience," did they really understand what he was saying? Young and his band mates grieve over a driving bass line. Toward the end, the vocalists, all of whom were touched by the loss of friends and musical colleagues to drugs, gather together and sing the title phrase over and over in an a cappella chant. Finally, the bass drum kicks in, the full band joins in, and the concert comes to a close.

And so the 1970s ended for Young. It had been quite a decade. He had reached the pinnacles of the bestseller charts and the depths of losing people he cared about to habits that could not be broken. Over the course of the first decade of his solo career, he built an impressive body of musical work. With three well-received, although disparate, albums in a row, *Comes a Time*, *Rust Never Sleeps*, and *Live Rust*, it was time to chart a course for the 1980s.

With and Without Geffen, 1980–1988

HAWKS & DOVES

Young kicked off the decade with *Hawks & Doves*, an unfocused album. Each of the tracks on side one was recorded at a different studio. The ensemble included Tim Drummond on bass and the Band's Levon Helm on drums. Young performed his own harmony vocals. The five tracks on side two were all recorded at the same studio. The side two ensemble included Ben Keith on steel guitar and Dobro and Rufus Thibodeaux on fiddle. The harmony vocals were by Ann Hillary O'Brien and Ben Keith. Most of the tracks have an acoustic foundation. "Little Wing" is about staying put and holding your own when faced with adversity. (At one point, Young thought of composing an album of songs with titles drawn from songs he admired from other composers. Thus, the title "Little Wing" was drawn from the Jimi Hendrix song. "Goin' Back," on Young's *Comes a Time* album, nodded to the Gerry Goffin–Carole King song popularized by the Byrds.)

"The Old Homestead" is a long story-song. Between some of the verse breaks, a theremin plays. There are incongruous images in the lyrics of a "prehistoric bird," a "naked rider," and a "phone booth" that form an opaque narrative. The narrator encounters a shadow who asks, "Why do you ride that crazy horse?" Doggett thinks the song is about Young's dealings with his superstar mates Crosby, Stills, and Nash.[1] "Lost in Space" is another acoustic performance that is more folk music in character than other tracks on the album. The narrative is as incomprehensible as the prior cut.

"Captain Kennedy" is about the military, war, and youth. Young may have chosen the name "Kennedy" because of its iconic status in the United States.

Among other things, the name represents a hope that was extinguished. The track is a story-song in the mid-1960s folk music tradition. It has a blues structure and an opening guitar line that brings to mind a Dylan tune circa 1963. The narrator is a "young mariner" who wishes to "kill good." His aim is to surpass his "father" (Captain Kennedy) who "lost" at war and struggled with the sea for the remainder of his days.

The lead-off track on side two, "Stayin' Power," has a bit more of a beat than the earlier tracks on side one. Its basis is in 1930s and 1940s Texas swing music. The piano plays steady, syncopated chords in a manner reminiscent of Sly and the Family Stone's "Hot Fun in the Summertime." The words present a simple affirmation of love by the narrator to his "baby." The song was written for Young's wife in response to her recovery from a serious health problem. Rick Nelson could have done an admirable job with "Coastline." The song has a late 1950s-early 1960s aesthetic both lyrically and musically. Young even sings, "Ooowee, baby" at the top of one verse.

"Union Man" is another of Young's spontaneous studio tension breakers. In this case, there may be a subtext related to issues that the American Federation of Musicians had with club disc jockeys. Young affects a southern accent parody in his talk-singing vocal delivery. The scene is a union meeting where Young is the moderator. Someone in the ranks yells out, "Live music is better." And the gathered members all "signify by sayin' 'Ay.'" Young's narrator again plays the part of the lower middle class southerner in "Comin' Apart at Every Nail." He talks about problems finding employment and the weakness of the military. After every line of verse, the background vocalists sing the song's title. When the narrator says the "fences are comin' apart at every nail," he refers in part to the weakening of borders to illegal aliens, but the phrase is also an allegory for the state of the union.

The title track, "Hawks & Doves," closes the album. Hawks and doves, in national affairs parlance, refer to the military establishment and antiwar peace proponents, respectively. The cut is one of the few on the album with an electric guitar in the instrumentation. The song may be patriotic or it may be ironic. It is not hard to imagine red, white, and blue country artist Toby Keith singing the chorus, "Ready to go, willin' to stay and pay, U.S.A., U.S.A." The chorus answers unquestioningly why we fight. The reason is "So my sweet love can dance another free day." It is a scary song if it is not tongue in cheek. Young sets a scene of people "on their knees...prayin'." This reflects the idea that the country will be victorious in battle because God is on its side. The narrator goes on to say that those who are opposed to war "just don't know." *Hawks & Doves* did not perform as well on the charts as Young's late 1970s albums. It reached Number 30 shortly after Ronald Reagan was elected President of the United States.

Where the Buffalo Roam Soundtrack

Young provided the music for the film *Where the Buffalo Roam,* which was released in 1980. He sang the traditional "Home on the Range" in an a cappella fashion over the opening credits. The performance closes with a brief harmonica coda. Much of the incidental music in the film is based on the musical theme of "Home on the Range," and much of it is performed on electric guitar, with various effects added. An instrumental version of "Home on the Range" performed by a large ensemble with a horn section is played over the closing credits. Young's collaborator David Briggs assisted with the film's soundtrack.

*Re*ac*tor*

Young returned to collaborating with Crazy Horse for his next album *Re*ac*tor.* "Southern Pacific," the charting single release from the long-player, chugs along like a good train song should. The song begins with the sound of a locomotive bell clanging and a whistle blowing. The musical atmosphere is reminiscent of Texas band ZZ Top in both the guitar line and the rhythm. The lyric is about the lack of concern for the tried and true, whether it be the worker who has labored his whole life or the railroad itself. The young and the unproven are valued over experience in a mixed-up world. Young often expresses a nostalgia for a past that cannot be brought back.

"Shots," the album closer, is about the potential for violence in all we undertake. The barrage of sound by the band makes the listener feel as though she or he is in the midst of a battle. The instruments are mixed as loud as the vocal, so it sounds as though Young is straining to compete with the music as he sings. Gun "shots" are described as a "venom in the sky." Young sings about military skirmishes where land troops "move the borders on the ground," but he also points out the strife that takes place in a household between two lovers. Disillusioned partners "learned to pretend" after they "met their dream's end." Disillusionment can lead to domestic violence. Although Young complained in "Southern Pacific" of how older people are so easily replaced, his hope for the future as expressed in "Shots" is in youth. Using a family beach scene as an allegory, his wish is that "children" will "join their fathers' castles together again."

*Re*ac*tor* kicks off with "Opera Star," a track that touches on the tension between high brow and low brow culture. Young sings a rough vocal over a fast tempo. In the chorus, the narrator proclaims, "You were born to rock, you'll never be an opera star." Sonically, "Surfer Joe and Moe the Sleaze" is similar to the album opener. At one point the phased guitar in the instrumental break after the second chorus borrows from George Harrison's "While My Guitar Gently Weeps." Young starts off the song with the words

"Here's a story," but he does not reveal too much about the two charac-ters in the title. They are beach people; one rides the waves and the other works the boardwalk. Fred Goodman suggested that the song is targeted at two Reprise record label executives, Mo Ostin and Joe Smith.[2] "T-Bone" is 9 minutes and 14 seconds of some of the hardest music to listen to. Young sings two lines, "Got mashed potatoes" and "Ain't got no T-Bone" over the same guitar riff and hand claps ad infinitum. Goodman notes the connection between this "maddeningly repetitive music" and the intensive therapy that Young and his wife were involved in with their disabled child.[3]

There is not much substance to the lyric of "Get Back on It." Forging ahead with a mellow, traveling vocal, Young's narrator expresses the myth of moving on, the myth of freedom to go where one pleases down the "high-way." In "Motor City," Young's narrator wonders what happened to the proudly manufactured products that were made in the United States in a dif-ferent era. The song has a polka beat. This is a nod to the eastern European enclaves in the United States such as the concentration of Polish people in the Detroit suburb of Hamtramck. Typically, the residents of these ethnic enclaves were blue collar workers who populated the industrial plants and mills of the United States when workers were proud of what came off the assembly line. Young addresses the balance of trade and its threat to the U.S. economy. His narrator, who affects a lower-middle class drawl in his vocal delivery, complains, "There's already too many Datsuns." The narrator sings the praises of his "army jeep." Not only is the sentiment patriotic (in its mili-tary reference), but the icon of the jeep hearkens back to the time when the phrase "Made in the USA" meant it was the best. The narrator is also against modernization (again showing Young's fondness for the past). Not only does his jeep have "no digital clock," it "Ain't got no clock." The drawl in the vocal delivery and the narrator's lack of grammatical prowess suggest that the lyric is a parody. Young is telling people who blame their problems on others to look in the mirror first.

"Rapid Transit" combines elements of 1950s rock and roll and 1960s rock music. The lyrics are obscure, although they do express something about conformity and following like sheep ("I'm standing in my line"). The track opens with an introduction similar to the Spencer Davis Group's "I'm a Man" from the mid-1960s. Young stutters his way through the lyrics like a 1950s rock and roll idol. The lyrics on the inner sleeve spell it out. He opens the song by singing, "Rrrrrapid Transit" and follows that with "Pppppppub-lic service." The chorus has nothing to do with these images of conformity, public utilities, and the government as expressed in the verses. The chorus lyrics are a tribute to surf music. He mashes together several phrases into one, singing in one line, "Hang ten pipeline let's go trippin'." "Hang ten" is a surfer's expression related to placement of feet on a surfboard. "Pipeline" was a Top 5 surf instrumental hit single by the Chantay's in 1963. "Let's Go Trippin" is also a surf music instrumental. Written and first recorded by

Dick Dale, it was popularized by the Beach Boys, featuring Carl Wilson on lead guitar on the California group's Number 1 *Concert* album from 1964. Other than continuing his fascination with the culture of southern California, Young's phrase does not cast any light on the song's meaning.

GEFFEN RECORDS

From 1969 through 1981, Young's solo albums were all released on the Reprise label. In 1982, Young decided to move on. Media mogul David Geffen started Geffen Records in 1980 with several signing coups including Elton John, Donna Summer, and, most impressively, John and Yoko Ono Lennon. Young signed a five-album contract with Geffen in 1982. Each album explored a different genre. From the beginning, his relationship with Geffen was tumultuous. He delivered an album titled *Island in the Sun* that the label rejected. His first release on the label delved into electronic music. He submitted a country-tinged album that the label again rejected. He followed that with a rockabilly album. From, there he turned back toward the country-and-western collection that had been rejected earlier, and, with help from Willie Nelson and Waylon Jennings, was successful in getting an official release. He was sued by Geffen for not making music typical of Neil Young. Once the suit was dropped, he jumped into the big drums and synthesizers of 1980s pop. For his last album in the Geffen deal, he returned to his hard rocking colleagues Crazy Horse.

TRANS

Of the eight tracks on *Trans,* released in 1982, five are steeped in machine-generated sounds. The other three tracks, the two that lead off each side of the vinyl release plus the closing track, are more in the tradition of earlier Young material, particularly his country rock and hard rock work. The players included Frank Sampedro, Ralph Molina, and Billy Talbot of Crazy Horse; Nils Lofgren, who played on both *After the Gold Rush* and *Tonight's the Night;* Ben Keith of the Stray Gators and various Young album appearances; Bruce Palmer, the Buffalo Springfield bassist; and Joe Lala, percussionist with the Stills-Young Band.

The album kicks off with "Little Thing Called Love." It does not really set the tone for the record because it is based more in country rock than Young's experiments with machine music. Over a popping country rock beat, he sings about the complicated emotion called love. The track was the only *Billboard* charting single off the album. It is easy to see why Geffen picked it and possibly why it was sequenced at the top of the disc. The production fit in with the music buyer's perception of what a Neil Young song should sound like in the early 1980s. Plus it was upbeat and the production gives the feeling that the musicians at the session were having fun.

The side two opener "Hold on to Your Love" has a 1960s pop feel to it. One can imagine Rick Nelson taking a turn at the lead vocal. You can also hear something of Beach Boy Carl Wilson in Young's delivery. A number of Young's vocals have the feel of Wilson's work from the early 1970s. The instrumentation features a crying pedal steel guitar after the readings of the title line, a Farfisa organ similar in sound to that of 1960s group the Sir Douglas Quintet and a reverbed surf guitar. These ingredients combine to give the production the feel of the earlier era. The message of the lyric is to stay with the one you love.

The album closer "Like an Inca" is a long track in the spirit of Young's earlier work with Crazy Horse. It is a wordy song, but it moves along in a good groove. The rhythm has a Latin, Santana-like character, and some of the backing vocals in the final verses are reminiscent of the Beach Boys. Lyrically, Young sets his sights on an earlier civilization that seemed to have a better understanding of life than the people of contemporary society. In the chorus, he sings of the "beautiful" structures designed and constructed by the Aztecs and the Incas.

The remaining five songs are sung in a disembodied, machine-altered vocal, sometimes at a high pitch. Young would later explain that the album's vocals were influenced by his experiences with his young disabled son's communication challenges.[4] The early 1980s saw the advent of the personal computer and Young was curious. The first of the machine music tracks in the album sequence is "Computer Age." The synthesizer is prominent in the mix and reminiscent of music coming over from England and Europe during the era. Although the vocal sounds robotic, ironically Young is proclaiming in the lyric that life must triumph over the machine. While "cars and trucks" and "bikes and vans" rush by, the narrator maintains his sense of humanity in the rat race. He is "more than just a number." Unlike the machine, he physically feels the "hot sun."

The theme of "We R in Control" is the threat of the ubiquitous computer taking over all of life. In a mesmerizing delivery he lists things that are controlled including the "flow of air" and "heat" and the "TV sky." The year 1984 has arrived. In a high-pitched vocal, Young sings of the "Transformer Man." It is left unclear who the "transformer man" is, but the narrator "feel(s) electrified" by him. Years later it would be revealed that Young's second son is the "transformer man." "Computer Cowboy (AKA Syscrusher)" tackles the invasion of the farm (the last bastion against modernity) by computer-age technology. The computer cowboy's livestock all "have numbers." Ironically combining the old and new, at the close of the track, Young sings, "yippee yi yippee yi ay" in his machine-transformed vocal style. Young also revisits his Buffalo Springfield song "Mr. Soul" from 15 years earlier and gives it the electronic music treatment with synthesizer and altered vocals. The track has less emotion than the original version.

"Sample and Hold" was a single release that did not crack the *Billboard* Top 100, but it was dance-floor friendly. Continuing with the machine-enhanced vocal effect, the foundation of the production is a Eurodisco beat. The lyrics are machine formal. In the first verse, one altered voice asks "Hair" and a deeper, disembodied voice fills in the answer "Blonde." This goes on for several lines of verse as the remainder of the form or questionnaire is completed. There is more guitar in the mix than the other computer-influenced songs on the album. The production opens with a barrage of single notes from an electric guitar. In the middle of the song, Young uses a fuzz tone effect on his guitar lead.

The narrator, in his robot voice, is arranging a purchase of a companion with whom to have sex, one he can "sample and hold." The deeper meaning of the lyric is that love and intimacy and openness and vulnerability between partners is replaced solely with sensual satisfaction of the self. The manufacturer assures the narrator "you'll be satisfied when you...see your unit come alive." Young's scenario, too, was a prophecy of the proliferation of cybersex and Internet romance that did not really become popular until more than a decade later.

EVERYBODY'S ROCKIN'

After diving into machine-enhanced vocals and synthesized instruments, Young took a hard turn and reinvented himself and his studio musicians as Neil and the Shocking Pinks for his album-length tribute to rockabilly, *Everybody's Rockin'* (1983). The Shocking Pinks include Ben "King" Keith on alto saxophone and lead guitar, Tim Drummond on upright bass, Karl Himmel on snare, Larry Byrom on piano and backing vocals, and Anthony Crawford and Rick Palombi on backing vocals. True to the spirit of rockabilly, three of the tracks clock in at less than two minutes and another two are only 12 and 16 seconds over the two-minute mark.

Young wrote six of the songs on the album. The record begins with two he did not write. He opens with Bobby Freeman's "Betty Lou's Got a New Pair of Shoes," a Top 40 hit from 1958.[5] Freeman is a rhythm-and-blues singer, but Young transforms the track into a fast-paced, Sun Records-style rock and roll burner. The tight band stops and starts the song in a number of spots as in an Elvis Presley rock-and-roll number. The production includes a saxophone in the break over a Jerry Lee Lewis-style piano line.

Young follows the Freeman track with his reading of Slim Harpo's "Rainin' in My Heart," a Top 40 single from 1961. It is a slow dance song in the style of Fats Domino's "Blueberry Hill." The vocal is heavily echoed like those of the rockabilly era recording artists. "Payola Blues" is a bald attack on corruption in the music industry. Young talks at the beginning and says the song is for Alan Freed. Freed, of course, was the Cleveland and New York disc jockey who became the whipping boy at the Congressional investigation of payola in the music industry in the late 1950s. Young suggests that the dishonesty he witnesses in the music industry in the 1980s would make Freed look like a "saint." As Young voices his complaint, his backing vocalists sing,

"Cash-a-wadda-wadda," acknowledging the rampant practice of exchanging cash and favors to get a record played on the air.

In "Kinda Fonda Wanda," Young acknowledges earlier artists of rock and roll. He lists a number of women who do not compare to "Wanda." Each of the names is from a 1950s or early 1960s single. He "went with Mary Lou," tipping his hat to Ronnie Hawkins's "Mary Lou." He follows by mentioning "Peggy Sue" (Buddy Holly), "Donna" (Ritchie Valens), "Barbara Ann" (the Regents), "Jenny" (Little Richard), "skinny Minnie" (Bill Haley), "Long tall Sally" (Little Richard), "short fat Fanny" (Larry Williams), "Miss Ann" (Little Richard), and "Mary Ann" and "Betty Lou" (Bobby Freeman). Unlike some of the veiled lyrics of the 1950s rock and rollers whose songs he mentions, the narrator sings he "screwed runaround Sue." It is interesting that he chooses Dion's woman who plays around to have sex with and then he insults her by saying she "wasn't as good as Wanda."

Continuing the sexual tone, Young uses the common euphemism of the "jellyroll" for the male member in "Jellyroll Man," the track that kicks off side two of the vinyl release. The track is powered by a rocking piano over a swinging ensemble. Young's narrator sings "I've got to have it right now," and "it" is not a jam-filled pastry. Neil and the Shocking Pinks follow with a cover of Jimmy Reed's "Bright Lights, Big City." The production has a bluesy, rolling rhythm, with Young's echoed vocal on top. Young counts off "1, 2, 3, 4" to start off his fast-paced rockabilly composition, "Cry, Cry, Cry." Ben Keith casts a nod to Scotty Moore, Elvis Presley's guitarist, in his lead guitar break.

The final cover is "Mystery Train," popularized by Presley in 1955. The band plays to a chugging rhythm and Young's vocal is mixed similar to Presley's vocal on his version. The album closes with the title track, written by Young. "Everybody's rockin'" including "Ronnie and Nancy...on the lawn." The reference is to Ronald and Nancy Reagan, the standing President and the First Lady at the time the album was recorded. On the first lines of the verses, Young's voice is only backed up by Karl Himmel's drums and particularly by the tom toms. The stand-up bass leads the band into the final bars of the session. After kicking up a cloud of sawdust over 24 minutes and 36 seconds, the Shocking Pinks vanish into thin air. And label executive David Geffen was not happy. He sued his artist for making recordings (*Trans* and *Everybody's Rockin'*) that were neither "commercial" nor "characteristic" of Young's body of work.[6]

OLD WAYS

Old Ways (1985) is an ambitious and affectionate look back at traditional country-and-western music. Geffen had rejected a prior version of the album that Young had offered to the label before the rockabilly issue. Young recruited a topnotch cast of country artists to aid in realizing his country music vision. Waylon Jennings, Willie Nelson, and Denise Draper share vocals with Young. Eight of the ten tracks were recorded at The Castle in Franklin, Tennessee. The sessions for the album date back to January 1983.[7] The album opens with the only cover version in the set. "The Wayward Wind" was a Number 1 bestseller for Gogi Grant in 1956. The composition was also recorded by Patsy Cline and Gene Vincent and His Bluecaps. Young performs a spirited version in a duet with Denise Draper. She takes the second verse by herself making the tale a conversation between the guy and the gal. The soaring strings add an old-country sheen to the track. Bela Fleck appears in a cameo role on banjo. Terry McMillan's harmonica adds a lonely mood to the presentation. Young affects a bit of a rural tone in his vocal delivery in this song about a "restless" and "wanderin'" character.

Waylon Jennings shares vocals with Young on the next track, a more upbeat production. Terry McMillan's turn on the Jew's harp adds a distinct character to "Get Back to the Country." The lyric begins autobiographically. Young sings about striking "gold" in his "younger" days "with a rock 'n' roll band." But now it is time to return to the roots, to simpler things and a simpler time. He notes that his lifestyle is not all that simple. He discusses the mechanics of touring ("Big buses and truck unload"), but he realizes that to stay grounded, he has to "Get back to the country."

Willie Nelson joins Young on "Are There Any More Real Cowboys?" The lyric differentiates people who work the land and who drive "dusty pickup(s)" and "pray for . . . rain," from the kind of "cowboy" that abuses drugs and wears "sequins" like Glen Campbell's "Rhinestone Cowboy." Although the subject of the song is not music, the lyric is also applicable to artists not authentically country in genre who jumped on the country music band wagon to stay in the spotlight, as Alan Jackson noted in "Gone Country" a decade later. Young also addresses the subject of family farmers struggling to stay ahead of their debts, as well as fighting the invasion of suburban sprawl. Nelson and Young, along with singer John Mellencamp, organized the first of the series of Farm Aid concerts the same year that *Old Ways* was released. The proceeds of the Farm Aid concerts assist family farmers who are at financial risk.

"Once an Angel" is a song of devotion from the narrator to his bride. The vocalist confesses his faults and appreciates the forgiveness he receives from his "angel." Young sings with a country-style delivery over Ralph Mooney's pedal steel guitar and Hargus "Pig" Robbins's honky-tonk style piano. The eight female background vocalists enhance the production with their wordless support and give a heavenly character to his affection for his wife. Their singing brings the track to a close.

"Misfits" is a long story-song with an opaque narrative. Musically, it fits with the rest of the set, but lyrically it does not. Joe Allen's stand-up bass starts off the production. Most of the scene is set in Texas. The words have to do with astronauts and their communication with Houston, a prostitute in a Texas hotel, and a lone alcoholic in Custer State Park in South Dakota.

The characters are not connected. "California Sunset" is a live performance recorded on stage during an *Austin City Limits* telecast. Rufus Thibodeaux, who contributes to half the songs on the album, is featured on fiddle. The stage band also features Young's musical stalwarts Tim Drummond on bass, Spooner Oldham on piano, and Ben Keith on pedal steel guitar. Drummond and Oldham appear on only two tracks on the disc. Keith appears on the same two tracks and adds Dobro to a third cut. The song is a rousing, spirited number with harmony vocals by Anthony Crawford. The lyric is a love letter to the natural beauty of the Golden State.

The title track opens with Ralph Mooney's steel guitar. Young and Jennings share the vocals. The rhythm moves along at a spry clip. "Old Ways" is about how it is difficult to break old habits. "My Boy" is a sweet song addressed to the narrator's son as he comes of age. The lyric expresses the universal wonder and amazement among parents when they realize their children have grown up in what seems like a brief period of time and are preparing to leave the roost. Young plays banjo on the track.

The story of "Bound for Glory" takes place along the Trans-Canada Highway. It is a tale of a lonely truck driver with a wife and two children at home and a young woman "hitchhiking with her dog." Young sings the first two verses, Jennings sings the middle two, and they sing the last two verses in unison. They sing the choruses together as well. Thibodeaux's fiddle divides the song into thirds. As fate would have it, the "trucker" and the "girl" were "bound" to find each other. When "the sun came climbing up the cab" (a strong and subtle lyrical impression by Young), the couple are still together. The assumption is they were intimate. Young observes, in a creative turn on words, that the two "were looking for love at second sight." The phrase could mean one of two things. They may have each found the love they were looking for after past failures. Or a relationship between them might continue beyond the initial impulse of emotion. Waylon Jennings again sings with Young on the closing track "Where Is the Highway Tonight?" The narrator reveals a nostalgia for his restlessness. Although he seems to be happy in his relationship, he becomes wistful for his freedom when he hears a certain "haunting melody" that triggers past yearnings to move on.

In the liner notes, Young offers "belated thanks" to Buffalo Springfield member Jim Messina and George Grantham of Poco for playing bass and drums, respectively, on Young's first solo album in 1969. Messina and Grantham were thanked on the *Decade* (1977) album, but Young did not specify for what at the time.

LANDING ON WATER

With *Landing on Water* (1986), Young wholeheartedly embraced the 1980s big drums and synthesizers pop music aesthetic. The musicians on the album are Young, Danny Kortchmar, and Steve Jordan. All three are credited on synthesizer and vocals. Young adds lead guitar, Kortchmar plays guitar, and Jordan plays drums. Several tracks feature the San Francisco Boys Chorus. The disc begins with the reggae-styled "Weight of the World" with big drums and synthesizer. The narrator talks about discovering freedom in the security of a romantic love. "Violent Side" has the same instrumental sound as the opening cut. In this track, the drums and synthesized bass are louder than the vocal in the mix, and there are points where Young is yelling his vocal line. In some measures, Young does a call and response with the Boys Chorus. The theme of the lyric is the fighting of personal demons. The narrator sings of a "stranger" who is "following me." The "stranger" is himself.

Young slows down the tempo with "Hippie Dream." Still, the guitar competes to be heard with the overpowering drums and synthesizers. As he has done before, Young looks back at the past, but his view here is jaundiced. He sings, "wooden ships were…a hippie dream." According to his narrator, nothing of substance came from the peace movement and the antiwar demonstrations of the late 1960s and early 1970s. The wooden vessels the lyric refers to are a pointed reference to the Crosby, Stills, and Nash song "Wooden Ships." The classic track is about the reconciliation of warriors no longer under the wing of leaders who march them to their demise. In "Wooden Ships," a dialogue takes place between two combatants. One asks for food from the other who then shares with him. But to Young's narrator in 1986, those lyrics from 1969 represented only a dream. Not only was the peace represented by "Wooden Ships" a dream, but the dream is "capsized in excess." The seduction of wealth and substance abuse led to complacency. People were too selfish to care about removing strife from the world or bringing harmony among its tribes. The narrator differentiates himself from those who are cushioned in contentment. He will continue to make music to proclaim the changes that need to be made to bring amity in the world community. It is not "over" for him.

"Bad News Beat" is reminiscent of a danceable Hall and Oates track from the early 1980s. The song is about the moment when you discover you have lost your love to another. "Touch the Night" sounds like a song by the group Journey with a choir thrown in the mix. The song begins to unfold a narrative about a fellow who "walked away" from an automobile accident. The next verse speaks of a woman who "walked away" from a guy. The guy may be the one who was involved in the car crash, and she may have been fatally injured in the crash, and "walked away" in a different way. No matter what happened, whether he is "between two…street lamps" or "between the shadows of his memory," he is without her.

"People on the Street" has a Doobie Brothers character. On several phrases, Steve Jordan and Danny Kortchmar provide a sweet soul delivery in their supporting vocals. The bass line pops over big drums and screaming synthesizers. The lyrics are full of urban impressions: "concrete canyon walls," "the avenue," "grates," "a muffled scream from the alley," and "the siren wails."

The scene is set, but the ingredients do not form a coherent narrative. Young sings several verses of "Hard Luck Stories" in a higher register than normal. The rhythm drives along at a good clip. The narrator addresses a fellow who was burned by love and then keeps burdening the narrator with his woes. The narrator tells the guy to keep his problems to himself.

"I Got a Problem" starts with a scream and goes into a rocking guitar that plays one pounding hook. Synthesizers are not present in the song. Young tips his hat to two musical icons in the track. In the second verse, he sings, "There must be some way outta here," echoing Bob Dylan's phrase from "All Along the Watchtower." In two instances, he sings about "break(ing) out in a cold sweat" and follows with a "Huh" as the late James Brown might have in his performances of his hit record "Cold Sweat." Lyrically, it is ironic that this song follows the previous song, as the narrator is telling people about his "problem." In the lyric of the prior song, the narrator chastised the fellow for sharing his burdens with others.

The pressure of living in a stressful world is manifested in the fast-paced rhythm of "Pressure." Young sings of the strain that comes from being bombarded by the media. The narrator "felt the pressure in a TV way." He mentions "video jocks" (MTV broadcasters) and "max head room," a reference to the computerized talk show host Max Headroom. As the production draws to a close, the drummer starts pounding away, and, from the tense musical interlude, the narrator screams right into the beginning of the final track on the disc, "Drifter." In a sentiment similar to his 1970s song, "Love Is a Rose" ("lose your love when you say the word 'mine'"), the narrator sings, "I'll stay until you try to tie me down." The theme is the desire to move on when you see fit, to be assured of your freedom. He sings, "I like to feel the wheel, put down the top and let it roll." The track and the album end with a big 1980s finish of drums pounding and synthesizers sounding like blaring trumpets.

LIFE

Since signing with Geffen, Young had not recorded a full album with Crazy Horse. The last album credited to Young and Crazy Horse was 1981s *Re*ac*tor,* his last release on Reprise before moving on. The three band members of Crazy Horse appeared on *Trans,* Young's first release on his new label, along with several other musicians. Except for one track on that album, "Like an Inca," *Trans* was nothing like a Crazy Horse album. Young regrouped with Crazy Horse for *Life* (1987), the release that would fulfill his obligation to Geffen. The album was recorded live at the Universal Amphitheater in Los Angeles. Studio overdubs were subsequently added to the tracks.

"Mideast Vacation" begins the disc with a slow dance beat. Although it is just Young and Crazy Horse in the production, there are influences of the 1980s pop music aesthetic. The drums and bass are up front in the mix. After a couple of verses, there is a synthesizer that sounds like someone is bending a sheet of aluminum back and forth. The track opens with the sound of a jetliner taking off; the sound effect is repeated later in the song as well. The tone of the lyric is patriotic. Whether it is ironic or not is difficult to decipher. The first verse opens with mention of the 1950s-era television series *Highway Patrol* that starred Broderick Crawford. Young reminisces about watching the crime drama and recalls that he did not realize then that "I'd be black and white for life." The phrase has a double meaning. The television broadcast was in black and white; however, the narrator is also saying that he sees everything as right or wrong; there are no shades of gray. He sets a scene in the Mideast where people shout "Death to America," which causes him to want to "fight." He describes himself as "Rambo in the disco." When the local people burn him "in effigy," he is satisfied.

Harmonica and piano open "Long Walk Home." Young continues the patriotic theme in a challenge to the United States. He asks, "America, where have we gone?" Using the corporate "we," the narrator suggests that he is culpable as well. While synthesized explosions occur throughout the piece, Young notes the losses of the United States "From Vietnam to…Beirut." In "Around the World," while life goes on, the military industrial complex works behind the scenes. Couples "fall in love" while governments topple and new ones emerge. "Surfers" share the ocean with "submarines." While farmers work in "planted fields," a Star Wars defense system is being constructed. The production opens with big drums and guitars, with a melody that echoes the Led Zeppelin song "Black Dog." The singer is angry in his echoed voice that recalls 1950s teen idol Eddie Cochran. He asks why there is war; "why…hate" and "why…incinerate." In the midst of this track about the overshadowing of the military, Young talk-sings one verse that is a short catalog of pickup lines. This seems out of place unless it refers to armed forces personnel on leave. The track closes with a drum roll and random guitar chords to feedback to a cymbal crash ending the coda mess.

A Spanish guitar begins "Inca Queen" as Young returns lyrically to the early empire. The ambiance of the recording is enhanced by the sounds of birds and native voices and hand drums. The song is full of impressions of the mountain civilization including mystical glimpses of "floating safety boats." When Young sings the chorus line "Inca Queen has come," he accents every beat in the measure. "Too Lonely" recalls the 1980s power pop of the Romantics. Young shout-sings the economical lyrics. The narrator has a "fast car." The woman he focuses on has "big lips" and a "tight dress." Both are "too lonely to fall in love." They are not looking for a commitment longer than the length of the night.

"Prisoners of Rock 'n' Roll" was Young's lyrical response to Geffen Records for threatening to sue him for making music that was not characteristic of Neil Young. The track has less of a 1980s feel to it, particularly in the rock drums. The vocalists sing purposely off-key. At several points, the lyrics pointedly criticize the record company executives. Young sings that they "never listen" to the company men who attempt to "change" the band. He also describes the executives as "clowns" who want to "water down" his music. The song has a strong rock beat with power chords from the guitars. In the spirit of rock and roll, the musicians just want to play. The track was a wave of goodbye to the Geffen label.

The band plays sparely and in the background in the slow-tempo "When Your Lonely Heart Breaks." The emphasis in this song about the heartache of love and loneliness is on the melancholy vocal. The narrator tells the protagonist not to park in the midst of his sorrows but to seek another "love." He sings in such a downhearted way, however, that you wonder if he takes his own advice. The song ends with a single, quiet electric guitar line. The last track, "We Never Danced," is co-produced by Jack Nitzsche. He collaborated with Young on several string-laden compositions including "Expecting to Fly," "A Man Needs a Maid," and "There's a World." There are no strings in this track, but Nitzsche's hand is evident in the mellow, atmospheric character of the production. The words offer mystical impressions of a "ballroom floor" located "between heaven and earth" and a place where "no lies" and "no pain" exist. Young repeats the title line a number of times. "We Never Danced" expresses his frustration over his relationship that never clicked with his record company from 1982 to 1987.

CROSBY, STILLS, NASH, AND YOUNG: *AMERICAN DREAM*

After the steps and missteps of the Geffen years, Young turned to his old musical colleagues Crosby, Stills, and Nash and recorded an album with them. After an 18-year gap, *Déjà vu* (1970) was finally followed up by Crosby, Stills, Nash, and Young's next studio album *American Dream* (1988). Young composed four tracks for the album and co-wrote another two with Stephen Stills. The title track, composed by Young, opens the album. He sings the lead vocal of this Caribbean music influenced critique of the "American dream." When the listener hears Crosby, Stills, and Nash join in, one simply marvels at how versatile Young is and how varied his musical career has been. In addition to those fellows, he has sung and recorded with Willie Nelson and Waylon Jennings, and Nicolette Larson and Linda Ronstadt, and the guys from Crazy Horse and Danny Whitten, and Emmylou Harris and Denise Draper, and Richie Furay and Ben Keith and the list continues.

"American Dream" has a peppy, upbeat rhythm that seems incongruous with the lyrics. The subject of the song is the defrocking of a televangelist who was "caught...with the girl next door." Young wryly observes the sensationalist media as they stalk the shamed spiritual leader. Several times the four sing, "Don't know when things went wrong." How did the United States become a place where television evangelists are worshipped? And where the media can saturate their broadcasts with spectacle? The high register notes on Stills's keyboard work, Bob Glaub's bass guitar, and the hand claps give the title track its signature sound.

The theme of "Name of Love" is that whatever you do, "do it in the name of love." After almost every line of verse sung by Young, the trio of Crosby, Stills, and Nash chime in with that phrase. The song is addressed primarily to the powers who have control over peace or war on the international stage. Young challenges them to think before the next "bomb explodes" or "missile flies" if they can do those actions "in the name of love." The song has a bit of the 1980s power ballad guitar style and big drums aesthetic to it, but the message is timeless.

"This Old House" is pretty, but in a bittersweet way. The four singers harmonize beautifully, sometimes in different groupings of voices. At times the background vocals sound like classic Beach Boys harmonies. Young depicts a scene that on the surface appears to be one of domestic bliss. The "kids" and the narrator's wife sleep. The "old clock" ticks. But the narrator is pacing the "floor." Something is wrong. The family is losing their home. Young illustrates the scene with the wife's "garden" and the children's "swing" set that deepens the pain of separating the family from their "dream."

Young's narrator misses his love while he is away from her in "Feel Your Love." Like "This Old House," the emphasis is on the blending of the four voices of Crosby, Stills, Nash, and Young in the production. He wants time to pass on so he can "feel" his "love." With *American Dream*, Young kept his promise to his long-time musical mates to again record with them when David Crosby cleaned himself up from serious drug abuse.

THIS NOTE'S FOR YOU

As Young jumped around and experimented with different genres at Geffen (electronic music, rockabilly, country and western, 1980s pop), similarly, he dove into something he had not tried before on his first album back at his old label Reprise. *This Note's for You* (1988) is rhythm and blues and swing music with a horn band. Akin to his earlier rockabilly album being credited to Neil and the Shocking Pinks, the 1988 album is credited to Neil Young and the Bluenotes. The design of the album cover hearkens back to the graphics of the Blue Note label releases of the 1950s and 1960s.

The band consists of Young on guitar and vocals, Chad Cromwell on drums, Rick Rosas on bass, Frank Sampedro on keyboards, Steve Lawrence on lead tenor saxophone, Ben Keith on alto saxophone, Larry Cragg on baritone saxophone, Claude Cailliet on trombone, and John Fumo and Tom Bray on trumpet. Both Keith and Sampedro played different instruments than they typically did on Neil Young sessions. Ben Keith played string instruments (pedal steel guitar, slide guitar, Dobro, steel guitar) on earlier sessions. Here he is given responsibility for the alto sax. Sampedro is the rhythm guitarist for

Crazy Horse. For the horn band album, he is the keyboardist. Cragg's day job was as Young's guitar technician.

"Ten Men Workin'" is an appropriate song to open the set. The "ten men" refers to Young and his ensemble. They are introducing themselves to the listener. The horn sound is similar to that of the horn section of Southside Johnny and the Asbury Jukes. Young plays a B. B. King style guitar line in one break. In another break, the guitar plays in a jazz groove. When the guys are not blowing their horns, they are singing "ooh"s and "aah"s behind the singer like the horn bands of earlier days.

"This Note's for You" opens with a James Brown-style vocal attack. The song is slower paced than the album opener; its theme is about artists selling out and cashing in on product endorsements. Young "ain't singin'" for any business enterprise. The title is a take-off on a television commercial for Budweiser beer that featured the rhythm-and-blues singer Lou Rawls crooning "This Bud's for you." The tempo and mood slow down with "Coupe de Ville." Young delivers the vocal in a quiet voice that is accompanied by slow strumming to a jazz beat on the guitar, a muted trumpet, and brushes on the drum skins. Even though the narrator has fame and anything money can be buy, all he wants is the one who used to live with him but now is gone.

Young snarls his echoed vocal in "Life in the City." He paints a portrait of urban despair. And he wonders in the chorus if anyone cares about the abject poverty in the city. He points out that these issues are not limited to the city. He sings, "the farm goes to seed." Downtown businesses are closed and there is no night life. He complains there is nowhere to take his "dressed up" woman. "Twilight" has a Blood, Sweat, and Tears touch to it. The drummer taps the beat out on the snare while a peaceful saxophone line and single notes on a blues guitar roll over it. The narrator is missing his love and his daughter as he makes his way home. When Young sings tenderly of "making love" to his partner "while time stands still," the sentiment is reminiscent of Vincent Gallo's character's remark about "spanning time" to his victim-lover in the independent film *Buffalo '66*.

Similar in lyrical theme to the Hall and Oates Top 10 hit "Family Man" from five years earlier, "Married Man" is a swing number. The narrator asks the tempter to "respect (his) happy home." "Sunny Inside" borrows its rhythm and melody from Wilson Pickett's "In the Midnight Hour." The track has a 1960s soul feel to it. The narrator is blissful and satisfied with his relationship. This feeling is musically reflected in the upbeat horn lines. The narrator does not need anything else since he has her. Lyrically, the song is the flip side of "Coupe de Ville," the song of loneliness from earlier in the set. In "Can't Believe Your Lyin'," jazz chords on the guitar and quiet cymbals set the mood for another song of lost love. His lover has gone off to "another man workin' in my place."

The band speeds things up on "Hey Hey," an energetic performance that is ignited by a screaming trumpet and is supported by muscular horns. Young tips his hat musically and lyrically to Big Joe Turner's "Shake, Rattle, and Roll" in the final verse. In the midst of this celebration of his good-looking woman, he addresses her and tells her, "Get off that couch, Turn off that MTV." The set ends with the melancholy song "One Thing." The narrator envisions trouble ahead in his romantic relationship. Underneath, the slow strumming guitar chords, the brushes on the drums, and the lonely saxophone line set the mood for the sad and foreboding lyric. Although *This Note's for You* did not crack the Top 60 on the *Billboard* album charts, the release had a sharp focus and is enjoyable listening. After spending most of the decade alienating record company executives and fans, Young seemed to be getting his groove back.

Freedom, 1989–1997

FREEDOM

After focusing on one genre per album for the most of the 1980s (electronic, rockabilly, country and western, rhythm and blues, 1980s pop, Crazy Horse jam), Young created an ambitious, wide-reaching album that touched on a variety of styles. *Freedom* (1989) is the album that began the period that cemented Young's place in the rock pantheon. Every track on the album is strong. The album structure is similar to that of *Rust Never Sleeps* a decade earlier in that the album begins and ends with acoustic and electric versions of the same song.

"Rockin' in the Free World" is one of the classic anthems in the history of rock music. It is ironic given the despair that emanates from its lyrical material. Following the format of *Rust Never Sleeps,* which opens with a live acoustic version of "My My, Hey Hey (Out of the Blue)," the acoustic version of "Rockin' in the Free World" that opens the disc is a live recording. The live remote was at the Jones Beach Amphitheater on Long Island in New York. Young performs alone with his guitar. The first verse addresses the oblivious patriotism of Americans. While we sleepwalk around the "red, white and blue," there are people in the world that perceive us as "Satan." This is a prescient statement written a dozen years before September 11, 2001.

The song's lyrics suggest that "Rockin' in the Free World" was written in response to the inaugural address of President George Bush on January 20, 1989. When Young observes the patriotic "colors on the streets" while the homeless are "sleepin' in their shoes," he could easily be describing the District of Columbia on that Friday afternoon.

In the second verse, Young narrows his focus from the international stage to a domestic issue. He unfolds the story of a young, drug-addicted mother who can no longer function or sufficiently care for her child. It is a disturbing scene. She does not give the child up for adoption, but tosses the "baby" into a "garbage can." This scene was inspired by a sentence from the President's address. George H. W. Bush said, "There are young women to be helped who are about to become mothers of children they can't care for and might not love."[1]

Despite these international and domestic concerns, what do Americans do? They just "Keep on rockin' in the free world." Young underlines the national complacency by repeating the phrase over and over again in the chorus. The audience response (whooping it up in the middle of the performance, singing the chorus a cappella as the track fades out) further underscores how out of tune most of society is with the problems that face the United States. The country's citizens are so self-absorbed that they do not see the vulnerabilities of the nation.

"Crime in the City (Sixty to Zero Part 1)" is a long narrative. The ensemble is the same crew that recorded as the Bluenotes for Young's *This Note's for You* a year earlier. The only difference is that Frank "Poncho" Sampedro plays guitar rather than keyboards on this track. Although the ensemble is the same, the song is not a rhythm and blues or swing number like the tracks on the prior release. The production opens with a Spanish guitar. The saxophone solo sounds like it is supporting the soundtrack of a film noir. The spare notes from the horn line throughout give an ominous character to the reading.

The narrative is like a draft treatment of a film noir. The first verse speaks of a bank robbery, the lack of solace from family, sensationalist media and a "bungalow...surrounded" by law enforcement. The scene shifts in the second verse where the listener eavesdrops on a conversation between a recording "artist" and a "producer" in a studio. The producer is satisfied with the instrumental "track," but he complains to the artist that he still needs a song, so he commands an assistant to call in a "songwriter." Again, Young shows a clear eye for detail. As the producer ends his conversation with the assistant, he requests "a cheeseburger and a new *Rolling Stone*." The narrative could be autobiographical. Young may even be referring to the creation of this song within the lyric.

The narrative leaves the recording studio for good and returns to the city streets. In the third verse, a police officer talks about the risks and vulnerabilities in his profession and of corruption. He admits to having a "wad of cash" given to him by a "ten-year-old" boy who "looks up to" him. The next verse is from the point of view of a child who wishes he could see his father more often. He owns up to being both "good" and "bad." The implication is that his lifestyle is a result of being a product of a "broken home." This may be the same child who pays off the policeman in the prior verse. The final verse has little to do with the earlier verses except that it is also an urban scene. A discredited fireman who is in "prison...without parole" looks back at the times he "sassed back" to a variety of authority figures including his mother, a "teacher" and a "preacher." Like the police officer and the young boy, the firefighter's place in life is an outcome of growing up in the urban environment.

The tempo slows down in "Don't Cry." The track is performed by a power trio featuring Young on guitar, Rick Rosas on bass, and Chad Cromwell on drums. Young uses a lot of distorted fuzz-tone guitar in the production. Several times the sound is like a sharp shock or an explosion. Rosas's bass guitar is also up front in the mix. The lyric is about a couple breaking up after living together. The narrator describes the "disappointed eyes" of his love. The vocal is full of quiet emotion that is counteracted by the bursts from Young's guitar. "Hangin' on a Limb" is one of three country rock style tracks on the album. Young plays acoustic guitar and Linda Ronstadt joins him on harmony and supporting vocals. The track has a pretty melody that is enhanced by the gentle vocals. The lyric is an allegory for a steadfast guy who waits for a roaming woman to join him in a romance.

There is no Part 2 to "Crime in the City (Sixty to Zero Part 1)." But "Eldorado" is a noir-style counterpart to the earlier cut that develops in a Mexican landscape. The instrumentation is intriguing in that it combines a Spanish guitar line with a fuzz-tone electric guitar, as well as castanets. In the first verse, there are victims with serious, if not mortal, wounds from gunshots. Whether this has actually happened in the narrative, or is only what the "gypsy" sees in her "crystal ball," is not clear. In another spot, there is gambling or the exchange of money for another purpose at the "Gold Hotel." In a disparate combination, ladies in "diamonds and sable" walk aside a "garbage heap." Meanwhile, a clandestine operation takes place at an airport. "Money changes hands" and a "briefcase snaps" closed in the cabin of an airplane. The final scene focuses on a matador in a bullring facing his traditional adversary. There is no clear connection between the various scenes. There is death. There are things done in secret. The song creates a wary mood.

"The Ways of Love" has a country sense to its production. As with "Hangin' on a Limb," Linda Ronstadt joins Young on vocals. Ben Keith adds pedal steel guitar to the track, which, along with Young's acoustic guitar and harmonica, contributes to the country color. Chad Cromwell plays a drop beat on the drum kit that adds a bounce to the shuffling rhythm. The song is about a couple whose relationship is going to break the heart of someone else. Such are the risks of love. The Bluenotes crew appears again on "Someday." On this cut, Sampedro plays keyboards as he did on *This Note's for You*. Musically the track is reminiscent of Bruce Springsteen and the E Street Band. Ben Keith's alto sax solo sounds like the solos of Clarence Clemons, and Sampedro's keyboard playing suggests the work of Roy Bittan. Again, Young's narrative is not connected, and it seems difficult even to find a unifying mood in the lyrics. Also, the lyrics seem to be at odds with the upbeat character of the instrumental track.

Young begins the song by singing about the World War II German general Erwin Rommel. The narrator suggests he had a conversation with the military leader. The second verse speaks of a televangelist. Musically, Young adds an interesting vocal line here, as the male background vocalists chant "Praise the Lord" in low notes behind his lead. The focus shifts to the construction workers who built the "Alaska pipeline." In the final verse, Young's narrator directs his attention to his love and asks that they enter a close embrace. Structurally, the verses are similar. The last line of each verse basically repeats the previous line. And there is an idea that things will happen or "might" happen "someday." The future is inevitable but it may be hopeful, too.

It is hard to imagine that Barry Mann, Cynthia Weil, Jerry Leiber, and Mike Stoller would have ever envisioned a version of "On Broadway" like the one Young presents when they composed the song. The trio of Young, Cromwell, and Rosas take the song to its power trio limit. It is a stepping shuffle with big drums behind Young's angry delivery. After he sings the line about playing "this here guitar," Young goes into a distorted, fuzz-drenched solo. As the song approaches its close, there is shouting as the rhythm of the guitar chords breaks down over the big drum beat.

Young's use of the term *wrecking ball* is novel in the song of the same name. Rather than referring to the object used in demolition, in "Wrecking Ball" the term refers to a formal dance or "ball." The song possesses a mesmerizing ambiance. The track begins with a quiet piano figure and Cromwell keeping time with a drumstick tapping the edge of the snare. The lyric begins with an autobiographical glimpse. Young sings that one can "read" his "life" on the "radio." And reflecting again on the down side of celebrity, he says there is "nowhere to hide." Although the verses do not form a linear narrative, the unifying theme is his interest in the one he desires to be with, the one with the "smoky eyes." In the last verse, he wants to call the person, but he does not want to because "you might say hello." The listener easily identifies with the situation. The complex emotions of love and infatuation are universal. Why is the dance a "wrecking ball"? When two people take the step and fall in love, anything can happen, and the relationship often ends in pieces on the ground. Emmylou Harris covered the song for the title track of her *Wrecking Ball* (1995) release. She and producer Daniel Lanois constructed an ethereal reading of Young's composition.

"No More" is a different kind of song and is not typical of Young's work. Part of the reason is his vocal delivery. He stretches out the notes in the verses. The song has a pop aesthetic. But the chorus transitions to a jazz riff accented by the drummer's hi-hat cymbal. Although the track uses standard instrumentation, albeit two basses are playing, Frank Sampedro's acoustic guitar and Ben Keith's keyboards contribute a unique sound to the introduction. The song is about substance abuse and creativity. He may be connecting the two, or only bringing up two subjects. The first verse talks about addiction and the difficulty one has kicking the habit. Young's narrator is "free" of it now. And so, he sings "no more." The next verse deals with searching for the muse to continue to create as you once did. He asks, "Where did the magic go?" In the final verse, he speaks to the recording artist's desire to do his best, but in the end, he is only trying to get enough material to fill the album. He is resigned to that affliction.

"Too Far Gone" is the last of the country-and-western-soaked tracks on the disc. Sampedro plays mandolin and Keith adds the pedal steel guitar to bring out the country flavor of the performance. The narrator asks if his lifestyle was too much for the love interest who has departed. His only tangible memory is the scent of "perfume" on the "empty pillow."

The band kicks in at full throttle for the electric reprise of "Rockin' in the Free World." Unlike the acoustic, album-opening version of the composition, the electric version was recorded in the studio. Lyrically, the song is the same except the electric closer adds one more verse. The first two verses, as noted earlier, speak to the public complacency in the United States to both international threats and domestic issues. The third verse suggests that the same sentiments reside in the upper levels of government. As noted in the discussion of the acoustic version of "Rockin' in the Free World," the lyrics are a response to President George H. W. Bush's inaugural address in 1989. In the third verse, Young borrows specifically from the speech. In Bush's address, he stated, "I have spoken of a thousand points of light, of all the community organizations that are spread like stars throughout the nation, doing good."[2] This led to the beginning of the Points of Light volunteer program. Young sings, "We got a thousand points of light for the homeless." In other words, the government has fooled itself into believing it has solved its domestic social problems through the recruitment of volunteers. Similarly, in his address, Bush said, "We as a people have such a purpose today. It is to make *kinder* the face of the nation and *gentler* the face of the world" (emphasis added). Young turns to the international theater and cynically addresses the American "kinder" and "gentler" military industrial complex. He speaks of the United States' "kinder, gentler machine gun hand." "Rockin' in the Free World" is a powerful statement that closes a strong album.

RAGGED GLORY

After two album releases without the full Crazy Horse band, Young returned to collaborate with the trio on *Ragged Glory* (1990). The opening cut, "Country Home," updates the country rock side (Crazy Horse style) of *Everybody Knows This Is Nowhere* for the 1990s with some exuberant guitar lines. The lyric is about getting back to your roots and to a simpler place. "White Line" is a traveling-down-the-highway kind of song. As in "Southern Pacific" almost a decade earlier, the listener feels like he or she is being transported down the ribbon of highway by the rolling tempo. On a couple of verse-ending words, the background vocals have a Byrds-like character. When the narrator sings about the "white line" being "a friend of mine," he could be referring to the solid line along the edge of the highway that keeps the trucker out of the drainage ditch as he barrels down the interstate through the night. Or he could be talking about drugs, and specifically, a line of cocaine. Just like drugs, the taste for the road can be addicting. Once the freedom of moving on is felt, it is hard to stay away from it. The lyric is also about a romantic relationship, although the status is vague. Being with his love made him feel like he "pulled a whole load behind." Despite the heavy baggage, she was a help and caused him to focus, but he let her go.

"F*!#in' Up" asks an eternal question. Just as the Apostle Paul wrote in his letter to the Romans, "for what I would, that do I not; but what I hate, that do I," Young asks, "Why do I keep fuckin' up?"[3] The song begins with Molina pounding on the tom-toms, and then the fuzz guitar kicks in with bent note power chords that carry through the track. The verses are full of images that seem not to coalesce. There are "dogs" and door "keys" and a "mindless drifter" and a "flowing gown." The "mindless drifter" prowls about and may hurt someone and then wonder why he acts the way he does.

"Over and Over" has a more upbeat melody, although the narrative carries the story of a romance to a sad conclusion. Young draws warm tones from his electric guitar as he lays down a sinuous guitar line in the introduction and in the instrumental breaks following an uptempo groove. The narrator remembers fondly the good times the couple had when they "danced beneath the silver rain." But love is a "broken circle." More often than not, the romantic relationship becomes damaged and breaks. "Love to Burn" is about the risk of opening up to a romance. The narrator is admonished by a "spirit" to be vulnerable, to "let your guard down," even though, as he points out in one example, "lovers" come together, have a child, and then ask, "Why'd you ruin my life?" The long song has several extended breaks featuring heavy rock guitar lines.

"Farmer John" is similar in lyrical theme to the Beach Boys' "Farmer's Daughter," but that is where the similarities end. Don "Sugarcane" Harris and Dewey Terry wrote the song in 1959 and released it as a single under the moniker of Don and Dewey. The track did not enter the *Billboard* Hot 100. The British group the Searchers recorded a two-minute rave up version of the song in 1963. The Premiers enjoyed a Top 20 hit with the track in 1964. Young and Crazy Horse slow down the tempo. The track has a goofy heavy-step beat that is accented with annoying "whooh-ooh-ooh" background vocals from Crazy Horse. The performance is as irritating as the Beach Boys' cover version of "Long Tall Texan." Young began performing "Farmer John" in the early 1960s with his youthful ensembles.[4]

The band returns to a good, rocking song on "Mansion on the Hill." The stories in this composition and the Bruce Springsteen song that shares the same title are different, but both songs deal with something that is tangible and close, yet unattainable. Young's narrator is on a search to get off the "road of tears." In the chorus, he describes the "mansion" as a place where "psychedelic music" is played and "peace and love" exist. He may be referring to a time in the past that just cannot be retrieved.

Young asks where are the people who cared, the people of compassion, in "Days That Used to Be." It is a nostalgic look back. He also addresses the seduction of possessions and how they used to be less important. The band adds a bit of Creedence Clearwater Revival's sound in the introductory chords. But the song really borrows melodically from Bob Dylan circa 1964, particularly from the songs "My Back Pages" and "Chimes of Freedom," which both appeared on *Another Side of Bob Dylan*. An early working title for the track was "Letter to Bob," clearly suggesting that Young knew whose music he was drawing from for the song.[5]

"Love and Only Love" is a long, mid-tempo rocker that features a powerful, fast-moving bass line from Billy Talbot. Talbot was inspired through these sessions. His playing adds a strong, driving character to the material on *Ragged Glory*. Talbot and Molina keep the rhythm moving, so the tracks do not have the meandering, sparse quality of earlier Crazy Horse productions. "Love and Only Love" is more than nine minutes long and has only two verses (one repeated) and three readings of the chorus, yet the listener never feels like the track loses direction. The message of the song is simple. Young begins each chorus singing, "Love and only love will endure." Amen.

"Mother Earth" promotes environmental awareness and care. Young speaks of how greed has damaged the environment. He asks, "how long can (the earth) give and not receive." Young looks to the future and warns that if we are not good stewards of the natural resources we have been blessed with, then we will "trade away our children's days." It is a sobering statement with which to lyrically end the album. The song was recorded live at an early Farm Aid benefit; you can hear the ambient sounds of the audience during the performance, as well as applause at the end of the track. Young and Crazy Horse sing in unison on the echo-enhanced vocals. The track is drenched with Young's heavily distorted fuzz-tone guitar effects. The melody is borrowed from the traditional song "The Water Is Wide."

WELD

Young released two live albums in the 1970s. One was a disc of all new material (*Time Fades Away*) and one was a retrospective (*Live Rust*). He did not release any live albums in the 1980s. (*Life* was recorded live but was heavily transformed in the studio.) *Weld* is the first of four live albums released by Young between 1991 and 2000.

Like *Live Rust*, *Weld* is a career-spanning live album. Although five of the tracks are from his most recent release at the time, *Ragged Glory*, and two are from *Freedom*, the prior release, the remaining nine tracks are drawn from albums released in 1979 or earlier. There are three songs from *Rust Never Sleeps*. The album closes with two cuts from *Tonight's the Night*. Young goes as far back as "Cinnamon Girl" from the first Crazy Horse album. He also performs a cover version of Bob Dylan's "Blowin' in the Wind." Nothing that Young released between 1980 and 1988 appears on the live set.

Young and Crazy Horse open with his *Rust Never Sleeps* classic "Hey Hey, My My (Into the Black)." The song is presented in all of its distortion and feedback-drenched ragged glory. "Crime in the City" is offered in a no-holds-barred rocking version that does not have the subtleties of the studio version. The presentation is more reminiscent of Young's electric versions of Bob Dylan's "All Along the Watchtower." Next up in the live set is Young's cover of Dylan's "Blowin' in the Wind." The tour from which the *Weld* performances were drawn took place during the Gulf War of early 1991. The world strife influenced Young's playing on the tour and is particularly evident in the opening of the Dylan classic. The performance begins with the sounds of air raid sirens, automatic weapons fire and the screeching sounds of missiles raining down. The arrangement of the ballad is reminiscent of "Mother Earth" from the *Ragged Glory* album, both in the choral singing of the band and the distorted guitar instrumental backing.

Young and the band follow with a powerful and committed version of "Welfare Mothers." Young adds several popping, distorted, fast-paced electric guitar solos. The song reaches its pinnacle at the close, as the band musically portrays the turbulence of a single woman with children living on the dole. As Young and bassist Billy Talbot shout couplets back and forth at each other, and someone else sings the title phrase, Ralph Molina adds crashing cymbals and snare rolls to the distorted guitars to create a cacophony.

"Love to Burn" is an extended, simmering performance of the song that does not stray far from the *Ragged Glory* studio version. The band presents an exuberant version of "Cinnamon Girl" that is an improvement over the original in that it does not end too quickly. Young repeats one of the verses and expands the coda. "Mansion on the Hill" is a straightforward reading of the song from the album. "F*!#in' Up" is performed with wilder guitar solos, unruly background vocals, and closes with 90 seconds of feedback and crashing drums.

Disc 2 of *Weld* begins with a nine-minute version of "Cortez the Killer." The pace is a little bit slower than the studio version. Ralph Molina offers crisp percussion and a muscular beat on "Powderfinger." Talbot's pumping bass leads the way in "Love and Only Love," as it did on the studio version, and even picks up the pace a notch. Young adds heavily distorted guitar in the jams. Crazy Horse's background vocals sound good for a live recording. Young, however, strains to reach notes on this performance. The band does not stop as it kicks into "Rockin' in the Free World," with Talbot again leading the way on electric bass. In this eight-minute-plus version, Young again uses a lot of distortion on his lead guitar lines. The band speeds up the tempo after the second verse about the young woman and her child. Then, they slow things down for the "points of light" verse, minimizing the sound to the bass and drums and the rhythm guitar. The band picks up for a distortion-filled jam before the group sings the chorus in a cappella fashion. Then the band goes through a number of false endings, heading toward a big finish, but then retreating, and then moving forward like a wave, and retreating again, and finally rising up to distorted notes and banging on the percussion to the end of the set. Young shouts, "Crazy Horse!" as the musicians exit the stage.

Young and Crazy Horse return for a four-song encore that opens with a 13-minute version of "Like a Hurricane." The long jams spotlight rhythm guitarist Frank "Poncho" Sampedro playing the Univox Stringman keyboard synthesizer under Young's distorted and high-pitched lead guitar lines. After an extended, feedback-filled ending that sounds like a thunderstorm drawing near, Young tells the audience that there is "time for one more." The band breaks into the clumsy beat of "Farmer John" as Young's distorted fuzz tone takes the lead. The song ends with a cappella "whooh-ooh-ooh" vocals, which the guys on stage exchange with the audience until only the audience is doing the wordless sounds to the finish.

The band leaves the stage and returns to applause for their *Tonight's the Night* segment. Drummer Ralph Molina sets the tempo and the mood for "Tonight's the Night" by beginning the song by only stepping on the foot petal of his hi-hat cymbals. Talbot joins in on bass, followed by Young's lead guitar. Molina expands his use of the drum kit, first to the tom-toms and then to the bass drum. With his snare shot, the band is off and running into the eight-minute performance led by Talbot's mesmerizing bass line. As noted earlier, the lyric talks about Bruce Berry, a casualty of a fatal drug overdose. Young knew Berry from his work as part of Crosby, Stills, Nash, and Young's road crew. In the live version, Young can be heard screaming, "Go, Bruce, play that guitar." After a feedback ending, Young indicates that the recorded concert is the last show of a long tour. He expresses his appreciation to the "families" and "road crew" that have been with the band over the "last 54 shows." He tells the audience that the band has "some more trash for you" and the concert closes with "Roll Another Number (For the Road)." Young sings a country-style vocal over a mid-tempo shuffle. It is a heavy, country-rock performance with melodic distorted fuzz guitar thrown in by Young. As the audience cheers in appreciation of the band's performance, the sound fades bringing the two-disc set to a close.

ARC

Arc is a 35-minute aural patchwork that primarily consists of guitar distortion and feedback, as well as drum rolls and crashing cymbals culled from endings of the songs recorded on the *Ragged Glory* tour. The piece is loosely connected by recurring loops from several songs including "Like a Hurricane" and "Love and Only Love." Originally, *Arc* and *Weld* were packaged together, which may be why the album did not even crack the Top 150 best-selling albums on the *Billboard* charts when it was released.

HARVEST MOON

With its pointed reference to his successful *Harvest* album of 20 years earlier, many listeners consider *Harvest Moon* to be the clear followup to the earlier album. In addition to its mellow arrangements, much of the cast was the same, including background vocalists Linda Ronstadt and James Taylor. *Harvest Moon* (1992) was Young's first full acoustic-based album since *Old Ways* seven years earlier. Peaking at Number 16, it was Young's highest charting studio album since *Rust Never Sleeps* recorded 13 years earlier. The Stray Gators provide the instrumental backup with Kenny Buttrey on drums, Tim Drummond on bass, Ben Keith on pedal steel guitar, and Spooner Oldham on keyboards. Linda Ronstadt and Nicolette Larson are prominent in the vocal support, although James Taylor, Astrid Young, Ben Keith, and Larry Cragg (Young's guitar technician) also provide supporting vocals. Young tinkered with some of the included tracks for a number of years. "You and Me" dates back to the early 1970s. "Unknown Legend" and "One of These Days" had also been around for a number of years.[6]

Linda Ronstadt sings in the choruses of the opening track "Unknown Legend." The lyric is about a restless woman who has settled down but still is wistful for the highway. The protagonist daydreams of her times on a "Harley-Davidson" motorcycle. The Stray Gators provide a warm feel in the instrumental track under Young's gentle lead vocal. The title of "From Hank to Hendrix" makes it sound as though the subject of the song is a musical hall of fame, but the phrase is used by Young to delineate a period of time. The track has a tender melody and vocal from Young. Just as they had done 20 years earlier on "Heart of Gold" and "Old Man," Linda Ronstadt and James Taylor contributes backing vocals in the choruses. At the outset of the song, the narrator appears to be offering a sweet tribute of devotion to his bride. They have been together from the time of Hank Williams (or possibly Hank B. Marvin, lead guitarist of the British instrumental group the Shadows) through Jimi Hendrix. He notes that he "believed" in her and he "loved (her) smile" through the period from Marilyn Monroe to Madonna. But then the hammer comes down transforming the mood from sweet to bitter. The narrator observes that the two are on the path to "divorce California-style." Again, Young shows how much he can say through an economical use of words. The phrase "divorce California-style" is pregnant with meaning and symbolism as a result of the celebrity culture that is spotlighted in the United States. Several phrases suggest that the marital problems stem from the narrator's life in the music business. In the first verse, he talks about being "with this old guitar doin' what I do." Later, he says, "The same thing that makes you live can kill you in the end." The rock-and-roll lifestyle can take its toll on a marriage.

Young duets with Nicolette Larson through most of "You and Me." He provides the only instrumental accompaniment on his acoustic guitar. The narrator assesses his life and love and urges the one he addresses to let love into a defensive heart. The title track has remained a cornerstone of the Neil Young catalog over the years. The production has a signature, lilting shuffle opening that immediately casts a warm glow. Linda Ronstadt adds the background vocalizing on "Harvest Moon." The lyric is a tender affirmation of love.

All six supporting vocalists add a poignant quality to the antiwar song "War of Man." The additional singers' presence is particularly felt in the choruses when they sing, "No one wins, It's a war of man." The lyrical images are of fear and the search for sanctuary in the face of imminent destruction. The instrumental track lends a foreboding sense to the setting as a result of the driving beat and the acoustic guitar runs before the vocalists sing the choruses. "One of These Days" is a song of reflection similar to "You and Me." The difference is that in this lyric, he considers his friendships and work associations rather than his romantic relationship. Elements of the lyrics are autobiographical. Young thinks of those he played music with and says he did not mean to "burn any bridges"; however, he admits, "I let some good things go." This could easily relate to his stints with Buffalo Springfield and Crosby, Stills, Nash, and Young. The chorus speaks of how the narrator will mend his broken relationships by composing a "long letter" to his "good friends." But he does not commit to when he will "sit down." The act of restoration will happen "one of these days." It is easy to put off things that matter.

As he had done a number of times for Young in the past, Jack Nitzsche arranged the strings for the track "Such a Woman." The production is backed by an 18-piece string orchestra along with Nicolette Larson and Astrid Young on vocals and the Stray Gators providing the instrumental foundation. Nitzsche's arrangement has much more vitality than his orchestral work on the *Harvest* album. Of Nitzsche's orchestra arrangements, the one for "Such a Woman" comes closest to reaching the heights of the soaring beauty of Young's "Expecting to Fly." Young delivers a quiet vocal in praise of his spouse. The lyric is a pledge of love. She slays him. He sings, "No one else can kill me like you do."

"Old King" is an ode to the bond between the narrator and his deceased "hound dog." The banjo sets the tone for the song that the listener can imagine hearing at a contra dance at the local VFW post. Apparently the hound was a fearless canine who would "jump off the truck in high gear." "Dreamin' Man" has an ethereal character formed primarily by Astrid Young and Nicolette Larson's background vocals. The narrator admits that his problem is that he is a "dreamin' man." What is difficult to decipher is whether his dream is to hurt or love the one he has "sweet dreams" of. While he sits dreaming in his Ford minivan, he carries a "loaded gun." In the second verse, he admires her beauty while she walks through the "mall." It is unclear whether he is appreciating the attractiveness of his partner ("I see your curves and I feel your vibrations") or if he is stalking her.

As on his previous studio album, *Harvest Moon* ends with a song that expresses Young's concern with the state of the natural environment. And like "Mother Earth" on *Ragged Glory*, "Natural Beauty" is recorded live in front of an audience. The ensemble consists of Young, Nicolette Larson on vocals, Spooner Oldham on keyboards, and Kenny Buttrey on percussion. The track has a different feel than the remainder of the album in part as a result of the concert performance at the Civic Auditorium in Portland, Oregon. But there is something else in the 10-minute track that sets it apart. It could be the vibraphone that percolates through the production or Larson's vocals. The lyric deals with the "Amazon" rain forest. The singer wonders what it would have been like to see the world "before it touched (man's) hand." Young's lyrics, however, also take a number of tacks that seem to have nothing to do with the earth and her splendor. He casts forth a variety of unrelated audiovisual impressions including the "cry" of a "newborn," the fading of a "perfect echo...into an anonymous wall of digital sound," "cowgirls" at a "rodeo," and the video playback of a failure "deep inside (his) soul." As the audience applauds at the close, Young splices in a snippet from the Rykodisc release *A Month in the Brazilian Rainforest*. This focuses the song on the verse about the Amazon river region and underscores the fragility of the "natural beauty" of the earth.

"PHILADELPHIA"

In 1993, Young was commissioned to write a song for the Jonathan Demme film *Philadelphia*. The movie focuses on the story of an attorney (played by Tom Hanks) who is dying of AIDS. Young's track plays over the final scene ("Remembering Larry") of the film and was nominated for an Academy Award. "Philadelphia" is an atmospheric piano ballad with a synthesized keyboard added for some accents. Young sings in a higher register than usual. The lyrics relate to the film's theme, but not in a direct way of simply borrowing from the script narrative. Rather, Young sings of not being "ashamed of love" and of "secrets" that become "unfurled." The narrator sings of acceptance. He asks the "city of brotherly love" not to "turn" its "back" on him.

UNPLUGGED

Young followed up *Harvest Moon* with a live set for the MTV channel's acoustic-based *Unplugged* series. He opens the concert by reaching back to his first solo album to perform "The Old Laughing Lady." Young provides the only instrumental accompaniment (acoustic guitar) and plays the song at a faster tempo than on the 1968 studio album. He then goes further back to the Buffalo Springfield days and plays a slow-paced version of his electrifying "Mr. Soul," a song he also covered in an electronica version on the *Trans* album 11 years earlier. This time, Young steps back and recasts "Mr. Soul" as a country blues shuffle. He plays a blues harmonica line at the outset, during the break, and at the close of the tune. There is an uneasiness or a portending of gloom in the significantly slowed-down rhythm.

"World on a String" brings no audience recognition at the outset; it seems the audience is not familiar with *Tonight's the Night*, the album the track is drawn from. The performance does not have the rock edge the studio version has, and Young adds a strained cast to his vocal.

The first official release of Young's composition "Stringman" is on the *Unplugged* set. A version was to have been included on the aborted *Homegrown* release from 1975. The theme of "Stringman" is loss—loss of principles and loss of a loved one. Young sings in a hushed voice over his own piano accompaniment. "Like a Hurricane" is performed at the same tempo as the original, with pump organ and harmonica accompaniment. The instrument gives the song an otherworldly, transcendent character.

Young then turns to "The Needle and the Damage Done," his tale of the grip of drug addiction. Considering the lyric, the reaction of the audience is confusing. They whoop it up and clap to the beat, as if the song has an uplifting, sunny message. When Young wrote the lyric "some of you don't understand," he must have had a premonition of audience reaction to the composition. The song is performed on acoustic guitar just as he had played it on his Spring 1971 tour.

The one composition Young chooses to play from his association with Crosby, Stills, and Nash is "Helpless." In the liner notes, he dedicates the performance of the song to his parents, his brother Bob, his sister Astrid and "the Irish side." Backed by his piano and harmonica and Nils Lofgren on accordion, along with Nicolette Larson and Astrid Young on backing vocals, Young offers a straight reading of the nostalgic song about growing up in Ontario.

"Harvest Moon" is the first of three tracks from Young's then-current album *Harvest Moon* performed during the *Unplugged* set. The presentation is close to the studio original right down to guitar technician Larry Cragg's percussion contribution with a broom against the stage floor. "Unknown Legend" and "From Hank to Hendrix" (which closes the concert) are also close to the studio takes from a year earlier. Larson and Astrid Young (who both contributed to the earlier *Harvest Moon* album) cover the vocal Linda Ronstadt provided on the studio version of "Unknown Legend." In the bittersweet "From Hank to Hendrix," the West Coast audience whoops it up in reaction to the lyric about "divorce California-style." No matter where a performer sings, the local audience will react in recognition of their home region.

The love of a father for his child comes out clearly in Young's acoustic reading of "Transformer Man," issued in its studio version on the *Trans* release. Just as "My Boy" was written for Young's oldest child, "Transformer Man" expresses Young's love for his second son. The acoustic guitar and the backing vocals give the song a gentle character that was masked by the electronic effects of the 1982 studio version. "Look Out for My Love," originally issued 15 years earlier on *Comes a Time,* is played in a brighter version for the *Unplugged* audience. The dual guitars of Young and Nils Lofgren add an interesting mini-acoustic jam to the performance. "Long May You Run" is presented in a fond version with the whole band. An electric guitar figure provides highlights over the predominantly acoustic ensemble. The background vocalists opt not to re-create a Beach Boys harmony sound over the "Caroline No" line as was done in the Stills-Young Band studio version.

Young had originally recorded a performance for *Unplugged* in New York, but did not like the end result.[7] So he went to a studio in Los Angeles and recorded a new performance there for the MTV series.

LUCKY THIRTEEN: EXCURSIONS INTO ALIEN TERRITORY

A compilation of tracks from Young's Geffen years, *Lucky Thirteen: Excursions into Alien Territory,* was also released in 1993. The collection includes four compositions that were not previously released. The liner notes state that these songs are part of the *Neil Young Archives.* During the past decade and a half, there have been a number of announcements that the *Archives* will be released. As of this writing, they are scheduled to appear in 2008.

"Depression Blues" is a country-and-western-flavored, mid-tempo song about the lack of control the individual has as the world changes around him. He counts his blessings. He has a "woman that loves (him)" and they have "got the kids." But his complaint is that things are "bein' bought" up and the "magic" has disappeared. Rufus Thibodeaux's fiddle work and Spooner Oldham's organ lines give the instrumentation its country character. The song was recorded in 1983 during the sessions for the original *Old Ways* album that was set aside and replaced by Young's rockabilly release *Everybody's Rockin'.*

"Get Gone" is one of several live-in-concert tracks in the collection. It was recorded in Dayton, Ohio while Young was touring with the Shocking Pinks, his rockabilly support band. The lyric is semiautobiographical. The narrator reminisces about tooling around in an old Buick with his bandmates and making music simply for the joy of it. The story unfolds with the narrator and his band becoming famous but then dying in a plane crash. The song's conclusion is a metaphor for the collapse of Young's first group, Buffalo Springfield. The song has a Bo Diddley/"Not Fade Away"-style rhythm.

"Don't Take Your Love Away from Me" is simply a plea from the narrator to his lover to stay with him. Recorded live at the same show in Dayton as "Get Gone," the instrumentation includes two saxophones and a trumpet. The song is a bluesy, mid-tempo rocker. "Ain't It the Truth" has a randy character. It is a popping blues with a melody that is reminiscent of the Standell's "Dirty Water," but at a faster speed. The track was recorded live in 1988 with Young's Bluenotes horn band at the Agora in Cleveland. The narrator celebrates the shape of his lover's body and asks his "babe" to "make love" to him. In another verse, Young mentions several food items that are metaphorically related to sexual foreplay. Young adds some blues harp to the track, and the horn section provides backing vocals. The shout of "Hey" just before the close of the song gives the performance a James Brown character. *Lucky Thirteen* also includes a live version of "This Note's for You," the title track of Young's 1988 album. Recorded in Hollywood, the performance is taken at a slower tempo than the studio recording.

SLEEPS WITH ANGELS

Kurt Cobain of the Seattle grunge band Nirvana committed suicide in spring 1994. In his suicide note he quoted from Young's *Rust Never Sleeps* album. This had a profound effect on Young and shaded *Sleeps with Angels* (1994). The title track centers on the life of Cobain and his wife, Courtney Love. Because of the timeliness of the lyric plus the widespread airplay of "Change Your Mind" on album-oriented rock radio stations, *Sleeps with Angels* broke into the Top 10 of the *Billboard* top-selling albums in fall 1994. On the opening track, "My Heart," Young plays tack piano, Frank Sampedro plays bass marimba, and Billy Talbot plays the vibes. The listener realizes immediately that this is not a typical Crazy Horse album. There are long jams and raucous moments that are signature Neil Young and Crazy Horse, but the mood is more sober and softened.

The tack piano contributes a childlike character to "My Heart." The production is reminiscent of the Beach Boys' late 1960s music, particularly the songs of *Friends* (1968) and *20/20* (1969). Young delivers a quiet vocal over the prominent tack piano and vibes that sound almost like a pedal steel guitar in this ballad. Again, Young tosses out lyrical images that create more of a mood or visual tone than tell a story. The scene in the first verse connects a "shepherd" and a "flock" and a "star" at night. It may be a reference to Christmas, or simply to a pastoral evening setting. In the second verse, he wonders if the power of "love" can conquer the loss of "dreams." The choruses have a similar lyrical structure, although he replaces words and phrases. The gist of the chorus is that the narrator has a vague feeling that he has to do something or be "somewhere," but he just cannot remember what or where.

The opening cut segues into a mid-tempo jazz groove led by the high notes of Young's flute playing. In the choruses, Young sings, "Are you feeling alright, Not feeling too bad myself." He delivers an extremely restrained version of Wilson Pickett's exuberantly delivered similar lines from his hit single, "Land of 1,000 Dances." Young uses several guitar effects that add interest to the performance of "Prime of Life." At one point, he plays a series of power chords, in another break he plays a series of single notes a la B. B. King, and in another place he adds feedback that sounds like a low-note siren. In the lyric, Young returns to the age of royalty. There is a "castle" and a "king and queen." He begins the song with a carefully-constructed visual image of "shadows climb(ing)" a "garden wall." There are glimpses of family life in a different era evidenced by running "footsteps" and "paper doll(s)." The bridge has nothing to do with the rest of the royal scene. Young's narrator sings sparely of love and lust. When he sees someone, it takes his "breath away."

"Driveby" transforms the set to a more somber mood. Young offers a strained vocal over the slow-tempo track that features Sampedro's piano playing. The lyric is about a drive-by shooting, about the fragility of life and senseless violence. The event is "random." The victim is a "delicate" young woman. The background singers quietly repeat the word "drive-by" over and over at the end of each verse, adding to the dusky tone of the production. At one point, they sing the word too quickly, throwing off the rhythm, thus highlighting the random and unexpected character of such a cold act as a drive-by killing.

Young's distorted fuzz-tone guitar leads off the out-of-kilter rhythm of the title track. The background vocals rush in at the end of lines, which additionally throws the rhythm off track. As mentioned earlier, the lyrics unfold a tale of Kurt Cobain and his wife Courtney Love. The story continues to the time Cobain killed himself. After several lines, the supporting vocals sing the phrases "too late" and "too soon." It was "too late" to help the suicide victim, but "too soon" to see him leave this world. At the close, the background vocalists sing the word "tonight" pointing back to Young's earlier song about death and rock and roll, "Tonight's the Night." The graphics on the compact disc also relate back to the *Tonight's the Night* album. On the 1975 vinyl album, the orange color of the Reprise label on the vinyl was replaced with white letters over a field of black, highlighting the somber subject matter of the title track. Young returned to the same white-letters-on-a-black background motif for the *Sleeps with Angels* compact disc label to reflect the sad atmosphere of the recording.

"Western Hero" is a quiet song carried along by Sampedro's playing at the grand piano. The track has a bit of a country tinge. The lyric begins with a look at the frontier hero of the Old West, the hero popularized in film and television. The scene dashes ahead to both the Pacific and European theaters of World War II. Young even quotes from "The Star Spangled Banner," emphasizing the patriotic air of the picture. The singer wonders where the heroes he mentions have gone. Young sings, "he's just a memory." The new heroes have a mercenary instinct; they are lauded for making the big bucks. The constitution of our heroes is "different now."

"Change Your Mind" is a 14-minute, mid-tempo, sparely played jam by Young and Crazy Horse. Young offers a subdued vocal in the simmering number. The guys from Crazy Horse strain and almost reach the high notes when they repeatedly sing the title phrase at the end of several verses and in the closing section of the production. Influenced by the method of recent short fiction, Young makes lists of action verbs in this song about romantic relationships. The verbs include "distract," "support," "embrace," "convince," "protect," "restore," "reveal," "soothe," "destroy," "confine," "distort," "control," "conceal," and "reveal." All these words come into play in the life cycle of a relationship. Structurally, the song has four narrative verses separated by four verses of lists. There are no choruses, although the narrative verses end with similar phrases with some word substitutions. Each narrative verse contains an action verb that is used to begin the list verse that follows that particular verse. So, for example, when Young sings, "Destroying you with this" in the narrative verse, he begins the next list verse with "Destroying you." The gist of the lyric is that entering the web of love can make a difference, for better or worse. In the closing repetitions of the title, Young adds a guitar line in the manner of Roger McGuinn's guitar work with the Byrds.

The only track on the album on which the songwriting credit is given to Young plus the three fellows in Crazy Horse is "Blue Eden." The cut is a slow-burning electric blues number. Young's vocal performance is reminiscent of the style of the late Bob "the Bear" Hite of the blues band Canned Heat. The track is purposely sequenced after "Change Your Mind," as the first verse lists six of the action verbs mentioned in the prior cut and adds "comfort" and "console." There are few lyrics in the six-minute-plus production. The performance opens with a two-minute instrumental of acoustic and fuzz-tone blues lines that set the mood. The lyrics do not present a comprehensible narrative. Each of the three verses borrows from another song on the album. The first verse points to the emotions and actions of a romance, as similarly presented in "Change Your Mind." The second verse talks about meeting a "friend" once "again," repeating lines from "Train of Love." And the final verse echoes words from the earlier cut "Driveby." Young sings of how the idea of deeming oneself as "invincible" is "part of life." He absolutely screams the word "life" before the instrumentalists proceed into the long coda, suggesting we are more fragile than invulnerable.

"Safeway Cart" has a slow, ominous rhythm accented by Talbot's bent notes on the bass. Drummer Molina keeps the beat with a tick-tock sound from a stick hitting the snare. He contributes a sense of time passing by in an inevitable manner that leaves the listener with a bad feeling. Young's harmonica gives the performance a touch of blues, but the song cannot really be classified as a blues. The narrative is murky. The only constant is that the scene is a "ghetto dawn." The unattended supermarket shopping cart emits an image of an unkempt area on the poor side of town. But after bringing up the picture of the cart, Young sings of "a sandal mark on the Savior's feet." It is an intriguing image, yet it is difficult to connect with the other brush strokes Young uses to paint the scene.

"Train of Love" has the same melody and rhythm as "Western Hero." Even the bridge is the same. It is as though Young had two sets of lyrics for the musical composition and did not want to part with either. The instrumentation is varied, although Sampedro sits at the grand piano on both tracks. The two tracks have the same emotional feel and similarly delivered lead vocals by Young. The lyric is primarily about love; the "train" is an allegory for connecting partners together in affection.

In "Trans Am," Young turns to a theme that he has dealt with before. Inevitably things change, and not necessarily for the better. He creates a narrative that sweeps across history, as he had accomplished with the lyric of "Western Hero." Young talk-sings the lyric in a quiet voice like an old story-teller. He opens the narrative on the frontier, with the stage set with "wag-ons" and a "plow" and two characters named "Seth" and "Merle." Soon, there is a "cowboy" and the "Santa Fe" railway. Young offers some word play in the second verse. He writes of the "gates of Eden Park" referring to both the Biblical gates of Eden and to Bob Dylan's 1965 song "Gates of Eden." Young presents an intriguing image of the gates: "One was swinging and one was hanging." You can hear the gates creaking in your mind. The picture he paints also ties the "gates" back to the gates of ranches in the West. As in Dylan's compositions of the mid-1960s, there are numerous obscure and/or nonsensical references in "Trans Am." The story of "Seth" and "Merle" came to the narrator from a Pontiac Trans Am automobile. The "cowboy" said he rode the railway "before the tracks were laid." In the third verse, Young shifts the setting to a business convention for "global manufacturing." In the final verse, the narrator and a buddy head out on Route 66 to help a gal with a disabled Trans Am, although the only problem with the car we hear of is that a "headlight" is out. The only constant in the four verses is the appearance of the Trans Am in each.

"Piece of Crap" is another of those songs by Young that sounds as though it was cooked up in the studio. The song is kick-started with some raucous power chords that move into distorted bent notes. The members of Crazy Horse sing intentionally rough background renditions of the title phrase that sound like "crap." The song is a relatively short (three-and-a-quarter-minutes), high-speed survey through products that face a dissatisfied consumer. Young tosses in a couple of references relating to buying products that will save the environment, but he still ends up with a "piece of crap." The song ends quickly with one of the Crazy Horse guys shouting out the title phrase.

"A Dream That Can Last" brings closure to the set as Young sits down again at the tack piano. The instrumentation connects the track back to the opening number. And like the opener, there is a Beach Boys' childlike quality to the performance. At times, Young's vocal sounds like he is channeling the late Beach Boy Carl Wilson, particularly in the last half of each of the two verses. He starts the introduction by hammering a high note on the piano (as a novice pianist may). The narrative is a vision of "heaven," a place where people do not "die" and "there is a better life." The lyric brings to closure the religious imagery that appears throughout the set. The first verse of the open-ing song "My Heart" alludes to Christmas. The title track suggests a suicide victim "sleeps with angels (tonight)." The cut that borrows its disconnected verses from three other songs in the collection is titled "Blue Eden," a refer-ence to the paradise that is also noted in "Trans Am." And in "Safeway Cart,"

Young makes mention of a "sandal mark on the Savior's feet." These references tie in with the album centerpiece, the subject of which was one who decided to leave this life for something more peaceful.

MIRROR BALL

Young has performed with a variety of music ensembles over the course of his career. He has played with Crazy Horse; the Stray Gators; and Crosby, Stills, Nash, and Young. And of course, he has recorded with a wide variety of musicians not in those groups, including Nils Lofgren, Chad Cromwell, and Rick Rosas. In the mid-1990s, in the midst of the grunge band era, Young collaborated on an album with the Seattle-based band Pearl Jam. Although the individual members of the group are credited in the liner notes, Pearl Jam is not mentioned in the packaging of *Mirror Ball* (1995). There are only references to the "Band," due to issues with Epic Records, Pearl Jam's label. The CD cover solely lists Young as the artist on the album. Be that as it may, the chemistry between Young and the band was successful. Young enjoyed his first Top 5 album since *Harvest* 22 years earlier.

The album has a different sound than any other Neil Young release. It was recorded in Seattle in January and February 1995. Pearl Jam producer Brendan O'Brien produced and mixed the disc. When Pearl Jam members Stone Gossard and Mike McCready are on electric guitar, Jeff Ament on bass, and Jack Irons on drums, obviously the result will be an album with instrumental tracks that sound like those of Pearl Jam. O'Brien created a muscular but somewhat murky tone for the set. He also mixes the instruments at the same level as Young's voice. Most of the album is fast-paced and there is little in the way of jamming. The songs are tight.

Two songs from the album received widespread airplay, "Downtown" and "Peace and Love." "Downtown" opens with a radio-friendly guitar riff that defines and extends through the track. The "Downtown" referred to in the lyric is a dance club. But it is not like any typical dance club. It is as if the narrator is viewing the locale through a looking glass or in a dream. There is "psychedelic" music (as in the *Ragged Glory* track "Mansion on the Hill"), but the clientele do not dance as they did in the psychedelic music era of the late 1960s. Rather, they dance the "Charleston" (of the 1920s) and the "limbo" (a dance craze of the early 1960s). In the second verse, the narrator warns the listener to be wary of the "gateman" upon entering the club with "your baby," because the guy at the door has "young blood in his eye." The sentiment is similar to Bruce Springsteen's "Tunnel of Love," in the scene where he pays the fellow at the gate and the guy's "eyes walk all over" his narrator's "angel." The third verse supplies the title of the album and continues this unreal mashing of disparate references. The "mirror ball twirlin'" is a reference to a key prop of discotheques and clubs of the disco era of the mid-1970s to early 1980s. But in the same verse, Young's narrator mentions the presence of Jimi Hendrix and Led Zeppelin at the "Downtown" cabaret. Hendrix, of course, died before disco emerged and Led Zeppelin played hard rock music. The odd mix of musical references bestows a hallucinatory character to the setting.

"What Happened Yesterday" is a very brief, slow-tempo track that sits in the album sequence between "Downtown" and "Peace and Love." It acts more as an introduction to the latter than as a coda to the former, although the lyrics relate to both. The song consists of one verse of 25 words. Young provides the only instrumental accompaniment on the pump organ. He sings quietly of how it is difficult to forget the past. And of course, all the musical references in "Downtown" are from the past. And the idea of "peace and love" seems forever attached to the antiwar protest movement of the late 1960s and 1970s. Young even mentions John Lennon in the lyric. The foundation of Lennon and his wife Yoko Ono's work was their campaign for peace. The quiet pump organ of the brief cut segues into the electric guitar chords of "Peace and Love" and the tempo picks up. The lyrics are economical. Most of the verse lines are only three words. They paint impressionistic glimpses. The sentiment of the first verse is that "peace and love" are necessary for future generations to survive. In the second verse, the narrator wonders if the feelings of "peace and love" were only a fad from an earlier era. In the third verse, Young speaks of "Lennon's goodbye." A voice of peace was lost and there are cracks in the crusade to continue to proclaim the value of "peace and love."[8] This is the only track to which Pearl Jam lead singer Eddie Vedder contributes any lead vocals. He sings the lyrics of the two bridges for which he also wrote the words. As in Young's main verses, Vedder wrote short phrases for the bridges. His narrator glimpsed "peace and love" and embraced the concepts, but they seem to have vanished from him.

The *Mirror Ball* set begins with a sea shanty titled "Song X." In the chorus, deep-voiced background vocalists sing "Hey ho away we go" as though they are pirates on the Main. The lyric is a conglomeration of diverse images including "Romeo and Juliet" and a "priest" and "cameras roll(ing)" on a movie set, as well as a physician and a "van." The accent is on the religious theme, as the band slows down at the end and Young repeats the second verse, singing slowly with emphasis on the "priest" and the penalty that resulted from breaking a precept of doctrine. As the track trudges along, the clearest lyrical point is that these characters (and the listeners, too, perhaps) are "on the road to never." From the plodding rhythm of this nightmarish sea shanty, Young and the band move into the faster-tempo rocker "Act of Love." Again the lyrics are opaque and several verses appear to have no connection. McDonough says the song deals with the various sides of the abortion issue.[9] In part of the song, the narrator addresses his "baby." He assures his partner that he will not do her any harm, but there are limits to what he can do to "help" her. One verse is about warriors mobilizing for a "holy war," which connects back to the mention of a "holy war" erupting in "Song X."

"I'm the Ocean" is a fast-paced rocker that includes Young's pump organ in the instrumental mix. The lyrics consist of nine verses (none repeated) and one reading of the chorus at the end. The chorus primarily consists of Young singing the title repeatedly. The verses are full of short phrases and compact images that do not connect to each other or the title of the track. A disjointed setting surrounds the narrator. The images include several automobiles, "voicemail," *Entertainment Tonight* and Native American "braves" situated on a "plain." Historically, the ideas and representations do not mesh, which is not unlike a number of Young's compositions; however, his non-narrative lyrics often create a mood. Although the music is pleasing, lyrically, "I'm the Ocean" leaves the listener perplexed. McDonough says the song is Young's look at his life in music.[10] The brief "Fallen Angel" that closes the *Mirror Ball* set reprises the musical theme of "I'm the Ocean." Young performs alone accompanying himself on the pump organ (which he also played in "I'm the Ocean"). It is one verse and only clocks in at a little over one minute, but like the earlier track, the lyrics are opaque.

After "I'm the Ocean," the band sets the tempo up a notch in "Big Green Country." The scene is the Old West. The spotlight is on a "rider" with a "leather bag." He is watched by "painted braves" who intend to "kill" him. At home, a woman waits, hoping he will return safely. The scene repeats several images from "I'm the Ocean." In the earlier track, in verse four, the "rider" is mentioned along with the "chieftain" and "braves." In verse eight, a woman "watch(es)" for him. "Truth Be Known" is a slow-tempo rock track performed by the full band. The three verses do not coalesce into a clear narrative.

"Throw Your Hatred Down" is the gem of the set. It is one in a line of antiwar songs written over the years by Young. The title phrase is founded in the words of the biblical prophecy that "they shall beat their swords into ploughshares."[11] Rather than throwing down their weapons for an instrument that produces life, Young goes to the core and commands the listener to surrender the emotion that leads to picking up a weapon. The production opens with driving and rocking guitars, bass, and drums that carry throughout the duration of the cut. The economical instrumental breaks are characteristic of the collaboration between Young and Pearl Jam. The lyrics suggest we live in a world shadowed by "sinful plans," a place where even at a young age we are forced to "choose" sides.

The third verse offers a creative and shrewd reference to the late folksinger Phil Ochs. Ochs wrote the antiwar anthem "I Ain't Marchin' Anymore," as well as the gentle folk tune "There but for Fortune," which was popularized by Joan Baez. Young sings "there but for circumstance" in "Throw Your Hatred Down" in a line that can easily be substituted with Ochs's phrase. Young follows with "dressed in gold lamé." Around 1970, Ochs began wearing a gold lamé suit on stage conjuring the image of Elvis Presley on his second greatest hits collection, *50,000,000 Elvis Fans Can't Be Wrong*. Ochs also wore the suit for the cover photo of his *Greatest Hits* (1970) release (which was a collection of new songs and not a retrospective.)

From the up-tempo "Throw Your Hatred Down," the band moves into the slow-burning rocker "Scenery." The track is a long (almost nine minutes) finale to the set (excluding the "Fallen Angel" coda) and, of the tracks on *Mirror Ball,* comes closest to echoing Young's extended jams with Crazy Horse. There is not a long instrumental jam, but the extended ending is reminiscent of the Crazy Horse work. Young quotes from "The Star Spangled Banner" in a number of compositions in his catalog including this track. Young's fascination with the American culture, given a keen sense because of his upbringing outside the country, has led him to notice the connections and contradictions between the words of the national anthem of the United States and the myths held by its citizens, as well as their activities. As the song simmers to its close, he repeats the phrase "home of the brave" half a dozen times. He also sings "land of the free" in the song's second verse.

The lyric is about the hegemonic use of those who believe they are fighting for a cause, yet, in the end, they are being used for the self-interests of a privileged few. The words suggest the tale of a fallen hero. The first line mentions a "grave," and Young also uses the words "worship" and "trust" and "danger" and "greed." The narrator sings, "the legend will outlive you." The song can be viewed as a requiem for those who give their lives for questionable causes.

BROKEN ARROW

The period from 1987 to 1997 was a time of concentrated collaboration between Young and Crazy Horse. During this time, they released four studio albums and two concert sets. The fourth of the studio albums is *Broken Arrow* (1996). Three dreamy soundscapes, "Big Time," "Slip Away," and "Scattered (Let's Think About Livin')" together give *Broken Arrow* its essence. All three tracks move at a slow tempo. The theme of "Big Time," as stated by the narrator, is that he still embraces the hopes and dreams of his youth. The first verse is in part autobiographical. Young's narrator speaks of driving "an old black car...to the land of suntan lotion." This parallels Young's experience of driving an old hearse from Canada to California in 1966. The narrator continues meditating while watching the "rippling" of the "bay" and reminiscing. The title may refer to the fact that even though Young has reached the "big time," he is still able to be the person he envisioned when he was in his youth.

"Slip Away" begins with a long instrumental passage that begins with the sound of Young's electric guitar opening up and spreading out like a starburst or a morning flower. The focus is on a woman, although we do not learn much about her. We know from the choruses that the sound of "music" carries her "away." She may be a celebrity, as she is transported in a "bulletproof stretch limousine"; and, furthermore, in an intriguing phrase, Young sings, "she lives in the TV sky." Or she may be a privileged recluse who lives vicariously through the electronic medium. The second verse adds little to the tale. The narrator paints a picture of an open landscape with a wind "turbine," a crying "baby," and pine trees. In "Scattered (Let's Think About Livin')," Young shows how adept he is at expressing universal emotions. Sometimes we feel as though we are sitting on top of the world. At other times, we do not know where we are in our emotional state. In a perceptive observation, Young notes in the first verse the fervent charge that can overcome us when we hear the "name" of a certain person, someone who we may have been involved with romantically or who may be a current infatuation. All in all, the lyrics are underscored by an optimistic feeling. As the subtitle of the song suggests, "let's think about living." In another admirable graphic lyrical image, he also tells the listener that it is possible to rise above gloominess as "a comet painted on the sky."

"Loose Change" has a rhythm in the style of signature Bo Diddley songs or "Not Fade Away." The introduction includes electric guitars and harmonica. Lyrically, the track opens and closes with lists. Five lines of the first verse begin with either "built a house" or "built a road." The construction takes the narrator through the emotions and practicalities of life. Every line of the last two verses begins with the phrase "some roads." He lists activities that have occurred on these highways of life. In the chorus, Young and his bandmates struggle to reach the high notes as they did on "Change Your Mind" a couple of years earlier. Before the last two verses, the tempo changes to a slower speed. The marching beat of the coda emphasizes the "shave-haircut-two-bits" rhythm of the track as it seems to continue ad infinitum to a close after nine minutes.

"Changing Highways" taps the same country vein that Young and Crazy Horse have mined since their first collaboration. The rhythm follows a two-step shuffle. It is an atypically short song for Young, clocking in at 2 minutes and 15 seconds. One can easily imagine the song being covered by the late Rick Nelson and his Stone Canyon Band. The production has that kind of early 1970s country-rock feel to it. The Crazy Horse background vocals are performed admirably, too, and have a Byrds-like character. The words are about the turns we face on the pathways of existence and the fate that brings people together.

"This Town" opens with a finger-picked figure on the electric guitar along with some snare taps. Then, the rhythm guitar moves in with an infectious "chucka-chucka" beat that dominates the instrumental track with its step rhythm pattern. The performance includes two brief soulful fuzz-tone guitar solos, which are precursors of similar solos used six years later on *Are You Passionate?* "This Town" has few words and they are more playful than sensible. The narrator does not sleep when he is "lyin' down," but rather when he is "walkin' around." It is not clear what the title of the track means, unless the narrator is suggesting that the citizens of the town do not approve of his lifestyle, but he does not care. For him, "it's okay."

Young sings very quietly on "Music Arcade" as though he does not want to wake up anyone. It is a solo performance with only his acoustic guitar (which is also played gently) for accompaniment. Lyrically, the four verses consist of glimpses of mostly mundane activities such as going to the "laundromat" or playing an "arcade" game or watching a "window washer." The track does not have a clearly coherent narrative. This is the third composition in which Young used the phrase "TV sky." He included it in "Slip Away," also from this collection, and in "We R in Control," from the 1982 *Trans* release. The "TV sky" can be intimidating, as it is a dome of broadcast signals that always covers the earth and its inhabitants. The only excitement in the musical presentation occurs at the end when Young strums the final chords loudly.

Broken Arrow closes with a cover of blues man Jimmy Reed's "Baby What You Want Me to Do." The production sounds like it is recorded at a roadhouse and, indeed, it is. According to McDonough, it was recorded during Young and Crazy Horse's extended stay in spring 1995 at a club called the Old Princeton Landing located near Young's Broken Arrow Ranch.[12] In the background throughout the performance, there is ongoing chatter and yelping and the sounds of glasses clinking. The quality of the recording is poorer than typical concert recordings. This gives the track the feel of an informal, audience taping. *Ragged Glory* (1990) and *Harvest Moon* (1992) are studio albums that also end with live recordings. In the case of the earlier releases, the live tracks both emphasized environmental concerns. The appending of a live recording to this album is not for the same purpose. Young's use of the live format for his reading of the Jimmy Reed song is a bow to the Elvis Presley *'68 Comeback Special*. In the tapings of the sit-down shows at NBC's Burbank studios, Presley performed "Baby What You Want Me to Do" at least five times.[13] Although the live ambiance of Young's track is grittier than that of a soundstage in Burbank, California or a big room at a casino (a favorite habitat of the performing Presley), Young connects to Presley through the live overlay. The rhythm section opens the track with a heavy bass-laden electric blues beat. Young channels the voice of Presley's contemporary Rick Nelson in his delivery of Reed's blues.

Aside from the three slow tracks at the heart of *Broken Arrow*, there is not a unifying theme to the collection. The album title and the compact disc graphics, which have a Native American theme, do not correspond with the lyrical themes of the disc. It is interesting that the album title is the same as Young's elaborate, landmark track that closed the second Buffalo Springfield album. There is nothing reminiscent of the song "Broken Arrow" on the disc.

YEAR OF THE HORSE

Year of the Horse (1997) is the third live collaboration between Young and Crazy Horse. The set is career-spanning. Young digs back to the Buffalo Springfield days and adds a rocker from *After the Gold Rush* (1970) and two tunes each from *Zuma* (1975), *Rust Never Sleeps* (1979), and *Life* (1987), the last of the Geffen albums. There is also a quiet song from *Comes a Time* (1978) and three songs from Young's latest studio album at the time, *Broken Arrow*. The dozen songs stretch across two compact discs, providing evidence of the extent of the jams between Young and the band. The album opens with Young addressing the audience and, perhaps, directing his remarks to someone who has badgered him with a song request. Young shouts out, "They all sound the same. It's all one song." So, what is his motive for introducing the set with this snippet of conversation? The songs were created in a period stretching from 1967 to 1996, so it is not like they all have the same rhythm or melody. He could be offering a philosophical statement about art. Maybe he is suggesting that all art is one. Or, possibly, he is criticizing the state of creativity in the music world and does not perceive anything new. Or, he could be referring to the production of the set. Most of the songs have a dreamy glow that unifies the sound of the collection.

The set opens strong with big power chords on "When You Dance," one of the two rockers included on *After the Gold Rush*. Young springs for the high notes in his lead break. The jam in the break offers a lot of high-volume distortion. Without missing a beat, the band moves into "Barstool Blues." The energy comes down a tad from "When You Dance," but Ralph Molina (active on his cymbal collection) and Billy Talbot on bass drive the performance home. Things slow down with a reading of "When Your Lonely Heart Breaks" that is led by deliberate low notes on the guitar. The echo on the voices adds a soft cast to the sober presentation. A keyboard playing only a few notes provides a quiet, steady background in the mix.

Fifteen years after the original issue of "Mr. Soul," Young reinvented the Buffalo Springfield rocker as a piece of electronica for the *Trans* collection. Eleven years later, on the *Unplugged* release, he slowed it down and played it as a country blues, accompanied only by his acoustic guitar and blues harp. For *Year of the Horse*, he plays it at a similar tempo, with the major difference being that Crazy Horse accompanies him on the ominous-sounding track.

The sequence shifts back to the electric side with the opening chords of "Big Time." The mid-tempo track is fueled by Frank Sampedro's big power chords on the rhythm guitar and Young's spare lead electric lines. All three live cuts from *Broken Arrow* that are included on the live set have softer edges than their studio counterparts, emphasizing even more so their dreamlike character. After "Big Time," "Pocahontas" continues the mid-tempo, dreamy mist character of the set. The track ends with Molina's tom-tom taps (acknowledging the Native American references in the lyrics) over Young's feedback. Returning to the acoustic guitar and harmonica, Young offers "Human Highway." It is a pretty reading, with Crazy Horse executing swell background vocals. The performance echoes the gentle ambiance of the *Comes a Time* set. Unlike *Live Rust* or *4 Way Street,* the acoustic set—or as Crosby, Stills, Nash, and Young used to say in concert—the "wooden music," is not placed at the beginning.

Rather, on this set, Young places one acoustic song in the middle of disc one and another at the end of the disc.

Disc two opens with two tracks from *Broken Arrow*, "Slip Away" and "Scattered." "Slip Away" begins with a long run of slow-tempo, distorted chords that sound as though one is listening to them through the haze of a dream. The long jam leads into a single-note melody from Young as Crazy Horse quiets down. At about the nine-minute mark, someone sings the title and grandiose chords lead to more high notes from Young. Stick rolls on the cymbals signal the finale of the track, which ends with guitar feedback. The opening riff of "Scattered" lifts the listener up a bit from the emotional burden of "Slip Away," but the production remains in the cloudy vapor of the dream. "Scattered" has a false ending in which the audience cheers, and then the chords rise up again and segue into the opening of "Dangerbird." The guitar opening has an industrial, wah-wah sound before moving into distorted power chords. Young sings in an ominous, serious tone. Molina keeps the band in a slow, considered tempo through the 13-minute jam-filled reading.

"Prisoners" is given a rowdy, energetic reading. If these tracks follow the sequence of the set list on the tour, this cut is where the band lets everything out, knowing that the end of the evening is in sight. Young closes the cut with a Jimi Hendrix-inspired guitar tour de force reading of "The Star Spangled Banner" with drum accompaniment from Molina. Young quoted the lyrics to the national anthem of the United States a number of times, but this is the only recording of him using the music to the anthem. The album closes with "Sedan Delivery" and its constantly changing time signature. Young says, "Smell the horse on this one," and opens with a series of random staccato guitar notes. Molina smashes his cymbals as though there is no tomorrow. Then the band stops on a dime, leaving Young alone with some random high-pitched notes to end the set.

The disc was a companion piece to the film by Jim Jarmusch of the same name that was also issued in 1997. The performances on the album release, however, are not identical to those in the film. The same year, Young provided the soundtrack music for Jarmusch's post-modern western *Dead Man*. Most of the music is spare, electric guitar chords with a lot of reverb. According to Simmons, the instrumentals were "improvised" while Young screened the film.[14] The film soundtrack includes a short, acoustic guitar piece and a brief pump organ addition. Approaching the end of the decade, Young looked to another old collaboration for his next musical adventure.

Looking Forward, 1999–2007

CROSBY, STILLS, NASH, AND YOUNG: *LOOKING FORWARD*

For the third time in 29 years, Crosby, Stills, Nash and Young gathered in the studio and released an album. *Looking Forward* (1999) completed the supergroup's twentieth-century hat trick. Young contributed four tracks including the title cut. Three tracks are slow-tempo, and the fourth is a peppy production. The three slow-tempo tracks were originally recorded for Young's next solo effort, but he offered them to Crosby, Stills, and Nash. Several of Young's studio musician regulars support the slow-tempo tracks. These include Ben Keith on pedal steel guitar and Dobro, Spooner Oldham on keyboards and pump organ, and Donald "Duck" Dunn on electric bass guitar. On Young's title composition, the four group members offer a tender harmony over Stephen Stills's and Young's acoustic guitars. The track has a warm, homey feel to it, as if the guys are hanging out singing and sharing music in a living room. (During the sessions, the vocalists shared one micro-phone to capture their harmonies.) The theme is optimistic. The narrator does not look back (which is rare in a Young lyric). He even underscores the idea of "looking forward" in a self-reflexive note. In the first verse, he sings of an "old wooden guitar." Several lines later, the narrator talks about composing the words to the tune and remarks that he is attempting not to use the word "old."

The rhythm and acoustic guitar strumming of "Slowpoke" is similar to Young's "Peace of Mind." The theme of the track is the pace of life and avoid-ing the temptation to rush. In the chorus, Young sings "when I was faster,

I was always behind." Reminiscent of the line from "On the Way Home," in which he sings, "though we rush ahead to save our lives," Young confirms the old adage of the faster we go, the further behind we get. Young's harmonica and Keith's pedal steel add pleasing accents to the tender track in which Young even sings, "the song is gentle." "Out of Control" is another delicate love song with sweet harmonies from the foursome. The narrator desires to protect his love, to "hold" and "cover." The key element of the production occurs when the time signature changes and Crosby, Stills, and Nash harmonize on Young's intriguing words "sky is fire, hell is blue."

"Queen of Them All" is unlike the other works Young contributed to the set. It is an upbeat mid-tempo rocker that is given a Caribbean feel by Young's celesta playing. The style and rhythm are more akin to the compositions of Young's bandmate Stephen Stills, in part because several of Stills' studio stalwarts support the track, including Joe Vitale on drums and Mike Finnigan on the Hammond B3 organ. The song has a happy beat for happy feet. Young's narrator even sings, "I really don't know why I feel so good." This is the same guy who told an audience decades earlier that the song "Don't Let It Bring You Down" was "guaranteed" to bring the listener to an emotional low. The narrator is excited that his lover is the "queen of them all." She is his steadying force.

SILVER & GOLD

Silver & Gold (2000) continues a line of acoustic-based, mellow albums that includes *Harvest, Comes a Time,* side one of *Rust Never Sleeps,* and *Harvest Moon.* Young employs the musicians that backed him on his contributions to the *Looking Forward* album a year earlier, including Ben Keith on pedal steel guitar, Jim Keltner on drums, Spooner Oldham on piano and organ, and "Duck" Dunn on bass guitar. Linda Ronstadt and Emmylou Harris add backing vocals on one song. The songs are compact and economical in their language. The album opens with "Good to See You," a song of greeting that is an appropriate introduction to the set. The theme is about returning to the hearth and to family companionship, but it is also about returning to one's roots to get one's bearings. The lyrics may be autobiographical, as Young alludes to the burden of life on the road (the "endless highway"). He also uses a clever, although ultimately bittersweet, image of "being the suitcase in your hallway."

The title cut is one of two older songs by Young that he resurrects for the set. "Silver & Gold" was composed in 1982, the year Young released the *Trans* album. The delicate, acoustic guitar performance is nothing like the electronica of *Trans.* An early version was recorded for the *Island in the Sun* album that Geffen rejected.[1] It is a song of devotion directed to the narrator's romantic partner. Young alludes to the fame and fortune that he let go. He sings that the burden of celebrity and riches "got so heavy that I had to rest." Wealth is temporal, "people" and "seasons" pass by, but the "love" between the narrator and his devotee goes on and on. In the second verse, Young hurries his words, stacking them on top of each other before the music moves on to the chorus. It is a technique that Joni Mitchell practiced but is atypical for Young in his vocal deliveries. Although not like "Sugar Mountain" in its melody, the track has an atmosphere reminiscent of Young's earlier composition. Young also attempted to record "Silver & Gold" during the *Old Ways* sessions.[2]

"Daddy Went Walkin' " follows a contra dance rhythm that is sent back in time by Young's "Home on the Range" harmonica style. The lyric is full of images of the rural, agricultural lifestyle. There is no story arc, but a mounding of images sets the scene. These include "tall weeds," "old plaid shirt," brown leather boots," and the "barnyard cat." The lyric is a paean to a simpler time and family values. The narrator speaks fondly of his "Daddy" who is the "sweetheart" of his "Mama." The tempo slows down for the chorus to a ballad style. The chorus seems out of place lyrically as well. Young sings about being careful for the "old man crossing the road." Perhaps he is suggesting that the manners of the country need to be applied to the city as well. Ben Keith's pedal steel guitar contribution in the bridge adds to the gentle character of the verse about "Mama" and "sweethearts." In a rare arrangement structure, Young sings the final verses almost a cappella, with just the slightest percussion accompaniment.

"Buffalo Springfield Again" is an affectionate, autobiographical look back at the musical companions with whom Young first found popularity. It is the first cut with a rock beat encountered on the set. The instrumental track is characterized by a couple of short acoustic guitar runs that Young plays after singing the title. Young does not put the blame on any band member for the group's breakup. Fame "ate" them "up." He paints an archetypal 1960s scene of an audience spread across a "big green lawn" listening to live music. In the last verse, Young suggests a reunion, as long as it is for "fun" rather than for money. The title of the track mimics the title of the second Buffalo Springfield album (*Again*), the collection that granted the band its legendary status. "The Great Divide" is a story of resignation sung over a mid-tempo shuffle. No matter how in "love" the couple is "on the carousel," they will get "caught...in the canyons of the great divide." The setting is a place full of "strangers walking...alone."

The theme of "Horseshoe Man" is the incomprehensibility of "love." The "Horseshoe Man" of the title is a cupid or blacksmith who repairs "heartbreak." Young emphasizes the theme of love. The last 11 lines of the lyric begin with the word "love." Seven lines end with the word "love." Young's electric guitar echoes the word at the end of several lines. The lyrics are profound in their simplicity. In the bridge, he sings, "love's the answer, love's the question." Young ends the song repeating the phrase, "I don't know about love." But who does?

The setting of "Red Sun" is a "railroad town" full of saloons with "happy sound(s)." Young again returns to the country. Emmylou Harris and Linda Ronstadt sing in unison with Young on the choruses. The chorus is unrelated to the verses. The threesome sing about "one" who is expected, as if they are referring to the return of a spiritual figure. Young offers another tender vocal delivery in "Distant Camera." Similar in theme to "Silver & Gold," the premise is a deep-rooted love that stands the test of time. Young draws clever visual images to underscore the track's title, including "life is a photograph fading in the mirror," "on the floor…daylight dances" and "love is a piece of dust shining in the sun." The acoustic guitar line that opens the track and appears near the end of the song is close in character to the melody of Young's hit single "Old Man."

The jewel of the set is "Razor Love," a song copyrighted 13 years earlier by Young. The first recording session for the song was in January, 1984. At one point, the track was considered for the *Old Ways* set.[3] Spooner Oldham's piano and percussionist Jim Keltner's hand shaker set the tone for the peaceful, melodic production. The words direct the narrator's affection to his sweetheart. His love is so sharp, so intense that it "cuts clean through" like a razor. In the first verse, he tells his lover that he will not abandon her as her father did. In the chorus, he revisits the idea of the burden of being separated from his romantic partner because of his lifestyle. He "make(s) a living like a Rolling Stone." Interestingly, he capitalizes Rolling Stone in the handwritten lyrics. So he is not applying a metaphor about shifting from place to place. Rather, he makes a living by touring and performing, the same way Charlie Watts, Keith Richards, and Mick Jagger do. Just before the "Rolling Stone" line, he sings the phrase "greedy hand" and repeats it directly afterward, as if the song skipped. By underscoring the notion of "greedy," the lyric reflects back to the title track. In "Silver & Gold," he spoke of letting go of a "treasure chest" that was bestowed on him when he first tasted fame. The "greedy hand, greedy hand" warning is intriguingly placed adjacent to the line about being a Rolling Stone, suggesting that the members of the English band did not release their hold on their treasure chest. Three of the 10 tracks on the album ("Good to See You," "Silver & Gold," and "Razor Love") bring up the thought of the narrator being separated from his love because of his lifestyle.

Young delivers the album closer, "Without Rings," in a somber voice and a lower register. Although it is an acoustic number, with Young providing sole accompaniment with his finger-picked guitar notes, the track does not fit in with the remainder of the album because of his vocal style and the lyrics. The images are more internal than external. He sings of "electrical energy" in his "brain." There is no sense of place as in the other tracks on *Silver & Gold*. There is a sense of time. He ends the song with a line about "flowers" growing through the cracked pavement where he rode with his targeted listener. And the track and set just simply end after the last delivered words. There is no big finish.

ROAD ROCK, VOL. 1: FRIENDS AND RELATIVES

Unlike *Silver & Gold,* which is unified by its predominantly acoustic arrangements and several intertwined lyrical themes, *Road Rock, Vol. 1: Friends and Relatives* (2000) is a patchwork of live tracks. Although recorded with the same cast on the same tour, the song selection and sequencing do not unify the set. Among the eight performances, there is an 18-minute jam session on "Cowgirl in the Sand," 10-plus minute readings of "Tonight's the Night," and "Words (Between the Lines of Age)," the debut of a previously unreleased Young composition, and a classic Bob Dylan song with a cameo appearance by Chrissie Hynde of the Pretenders. As the title suggests, the stage assemblage included friends (long-time Young musical collaborators Ben Keith, Spooner Oldham, and Donald "Duck" Dunn) and relatives (Young's half-sister Astrid Young and his wife Pegi Young). Percussionist Jim Keltner, who appeared on the immediately preceding studio release, joined the cast as well. The vocal support of the two women adds a distinctive character to old familiar songs that are remembered earlier with male background vocals.

Except for a couple of live tracks with Crosby, Stills, and Nash, the recorded, extended jam performances of Young were all with Crazy Horse up to this point. On *Road Rock,* Young jams with friends and relatives. Rather than building up to the long songs, the album begins with the longest, officially released version to date of "Cowgirl in the Sand." As noted earlier, the sequencing of the collection does not follow a typical flow. Astrid and Pegi Young contribute a fresh quality to the reading, with their voices echoing the verse lines and singing the chorus lines. Keltner's work on the drum kit, combined with short notes from Young's electric guitar, add a jazzy atmosphere to one of the extended instrumental breaks.

"Tonight's the Night" clocks in at exactly 10 minutes. Unlike the two studio versions on 1975s *Tonight's the Night* or the concert performances on *Live Rust* (1979) and *Weld* (1991), the *Road Rock* reading is not identified by the driving bass guitar line. Rather, Keltner's work on the hi-hat cymbals and the bass drum, the female vocals, Ben Keith's lap slide guitar, Young's screaming electric guitar licks, the occasional quiet segments with Young repeating the phrase "shaky, shaky voice," and the slowed-down tempo (in parts of the song) endow the performance with a singular atmosphere. The attributes combine to make the reading more eerie than past interpretations.

In 1972, Young released a long, behind-the-scenes studio version of "Words (Between the Lines of Age)" on the soundtrack recording *Journey through the Past.* He revisits the song on *Road Rock* with an 11-minute presentation. The song begins with its characteristic riff that goes on and on. Young leads the singing on the verses with minimal instrumentation, and then the group jams over the riff, with the singers repeating the phrase "lines of age" numerous times.

The bright and upbeat "Walk On" is an appropriate antidote to the dusky "Cowgirl in the Sand," which it follows in the concert sequence. The song's step rhythm gives it a danceable feature. Spooner Oldham adds a funky piano line to the performance. The one new song on the album, "Fool for Your Love," follows. The song has a rhythm-and-blues ambiance (accented by the women punctuating a number of lines with the word "fool"). The song's genesis was in the late 1980s *This Note's for You* sessions.[4] The melody borrows the hook from Bad Company's "Can't Get Enough." The lyric of the mid-tempo song is about the narrator's attempt to come to grips with the loss of his love to "another man." "Peace of Mind," one of two tracks performed in the set from 1978s *Comes a Time,* is next in the album sequence. The presentation is similar to the studio version. This is no surprise because, as they did 22 years earlier, Keith contributes pedal steel guitar and Oldham adds piano to the offering. Pegi Young sings the vocal that Nicolette Larson performed on the original.

Sandwiched between "Words (Between the Lines of Age)" and "Tonight's the Night" is the second helping from *Comes a Time,* the quirky "Motorcycle Mama." Astrid Young offers a powerful second vocal that, on the original, was contributed by Nicolette Larson. The stage band emphasizes the accented downbeat rhythm of the song in a slow funk reading. The album ends with an energetic and muscular, no-holds-barred cover of Bob Dylan's "All Along the Watchtower." The closer opens with big guitar chords and big drums. "Duck" Dunn adds a solid bass line that keeps the band moving at a good clip. His partner in the rhythm section, Keltner, contributes crashing cymbals. Chrissie Hynde, who performed Young's "The Needle and the Damage Done" five years earlier at the opening concert of the Rock and Roll Hall of Fame and Museum in Cleveland, sings the second verse of the Dylan tune alone. She and Young share vocal duties on the song's third verse. Young pulls out all the stops on his electric guitar in this finale. He plays with distortion effects and adds screaming high notes as the concert draws to its conclusion.

ARE YOU PASSIONATE?

From Chicago soul to Memphis soul and from Motown to sweet seventies soul, Young covers all the soul bases on *Are You Passionate?* (2002). In 1993, Neil Young toured with Booker T. and the MGs. Three of the band's members, keyboardist Booker T. Jones, bassist Donald "Duck" Dunn, and drummer Steve Potts comprise the instrumental core for the *Are You Passionate?* sessions. Along with Young on guitar (using a lot of soulful fuzz tone effects) and piano, they are supplemented by Crazy Horse member Frank "Poncho" Sampedro on guitar and Tom Bray on trumpet. Bray was part of the Bluenotes band on 1988s *This Note's for You*. Pegi Young and Astrid Young add their backing voices to the set.

Although the album was best known for the track Young wrote in response to the terrorist attacks of September 11, 2001, "Let's Roll," the song is not a key element musically in unifying the collection. Young channels his old musical partner Stephen Stills in both his vocal delivery and guitar style in "Let's Roll." The guitar line is atypical of Young's work. And it is easy to imagine Stills singing this song. The song is one of Young's journalistic responses, in the spirit of "Ohio" (1970) and "War Song" (1972). The title of the track, which is also the key phrase of the chorus, is taken from words spoken by Todd Beamer shortly before a group of passengers attempted to overcome the hijackers of United Airlines Flight 93 on that fateful Tuesday morning.[5]

The song begins ominously with the droning of a propeller plane engine followed by the ringing of a cell phone. Young's lyrical narration is from the point of view of one of the heroic passengers on board the flight. In the first verse, the narrator is speaking on a phone with his wife. He tells her he loves her before beginning the mission to take the plane back. In the second verse, the men pinpoint the locations of the hijackers and note they have to secure the cockpit. In the chorus, male background voices increase the tension by singing, "time is runnin' out." The third and fourth verses underline the fears of the would-be rescuers. The narrator remarks, "I hope someone can fly this thing." And, ironically, he seeks forgiveness for the actions they plan to take to regain control of the flight. Young sings the bridge in a higher register. He declares that "evil" must be confronted. After the third singing of the chorus, the lyric structure changes to a list of reasons for which to "roll." These include "freedom," "justice," and "truth." Interestingly, he adds "goin' after Satan." Twelve years earlier, in the lyrics of "Rockin' in the Free World," Young noted how the enemies of the United States perceived the nation as "Satan." Here, the tables are turned and the attackers of September 11 are now "Satan." The track is a patriotic broadside created in the wake of 9/11. Its lyrical sentiments echo in several of the album's cuts.

"Goin' Home" also does not fit with the soulful context of the album. The song is performed by Young and Crazy Horse. It sounds like a leftover work from 1996s *Broken Arrow*, but it was recorded around the time of the *Are You Passionate?* sessions. "Goin' Home" was created at a different studio and engineered by different personnel than the remaining tracks of the collection. The production is pushed along by Billy Talbot's energetic bass line and Ralph Molina's Native American-influenced drumbeats. The lyric again is vague. The locale of the first scene is the site of General George Armstrong Custer's defeat. The narrator proceeds from the historic site to the nearby town where he is "slicing through the cultures." The second verse is related to the music industry, one of Young's favorite subjects. He sings of a "fool who signed the paper to assorted slimes." The "fool" does this to keep the executives in the lifestyle to which they are accustomed. According to the narrator, when you sign on the dotted line, you "give your life away." The third scene relates back to the Little Bighorn location of the introductory scene. In this instance, there is more of a mystical slant. A woman drives her vehicle to the "battleground" where "a thousand warriors" are lined up. As the sounds of "battle drums" surround her, "her clothes...change into sky and stars." The chorus consists only of Young singing variations of "I'm goin' home." The return to the site of a Native American victory over the United States cavalry is a return to the narrator's roots, to his "home."

The album opens with "You're My Girl," a tender song of affection from Young to his daughter as she leaves home for college. The song is based on a slow tempo version of Otis Redding's "I Can't Turn You Loose" chord progression. Jones's keyboard work and Young's Steve Cropper-style guitar licks give the song a Memphis-Stax Studios soul character. The words express the universal feelings of parents witnessing the departure of children from the nest. Young sings, "please don't tell me that you're leaving just yet."

Young channels the talk-singing style of songs like the Chi-Lites' "Have You Seen Her?" in the spoken-sung "Mr. Disappointment." The song has a simmering rhythm. Young opens with a heavy fuzz-tone effect on his electric guitar. He offers the spoken lyrics in a gravelly voice. The narrator is saddened by the exit of his love from his life. "Differently" uses the call-and-response structure of soul music that finds its origins in church worship services. Young's vocal articulation is suggestive of Atlantic recording artist Darrell Banks's "Open the Door to Your Heart" and similar productions from the late 1960s. Most of the verse lines open with the male background vocalists singing the title word "differently," and Young answering with a variety of responses. The narrator attempts to convince his "babe" that he will change and live life "differently." In one verse that appears autobiographical, Young sings of how his wife told him to pay more attention to his "little girl" before she grew up and left. He regrets not heeding the advice more.

"Quit (Don't Say You Love Me)" is another slow love song heavy on the backbeat that is enhanced by the soulful background vocals of Pegi Young and Astrid Young. The narrator affirms his love for his "baby" in the midst of her accusations. The female voices are used in a dialogue as they play the part of the accuser telling the narrator, "don't say you love me." The title track is sequenced after "Let's Roll." "Are You Passionate?" is a slow-tempo, slow-dance number characterized by Young's repeating the same notes at the piano. The narration is cloudy. The words begin with eight questions related to emotional actions. But then in the bridge, the scene shifts to a battle zone. The narrator is a "soldier" responsible for launching "missiles...that kept you free." The patriotic sentiment relates back to the preceding track

"Let's Roll." In the next verse, the "soldier" has been captured and is a "prisoner...cleaned up for public display." Young returns to the question structure from the beginning of the song. The questions at the end of the song, however, are more related to the lyrics in the bridge. They deal with the challenges of facing hostile external forces rather than emotions. Young ask, "are you scared?" and "do you wish...it would stop?" The passion he refers to in the title is the civic support for activities that keep the United States "free."

"When I Hold You in My Arms" follows "Goin' Home" and returns the set to its soulful mood. The melody, stated by Jones's organ and Young's piano, brings to mind Motown soul, and specifically, Smokey Robinson and the Miracles' "You Really Got a Hold on Me." The lyric is about embracing a stable romantic relationship while everything changes around you. The singing by the female vocalists recalls the work of Claudette Rogers Robinson of the Miracles. "Be with You" uses the same chord progression as the album opener "You're My Girl," but with a faster tempo in a danceable workout. The production is influenced by the Isley Brothers (during their Motown years) and the Chambers Brothers reading of "I Can't Turn You Loose." Young leads with another Steve Cropper-style guitar line. Steve Potts's tambourine work adds an upbeat feel to the mix. The narrator expresses his devotion to his "baby."

"Two Old Friends" channels Curtis Mayfield and the Impressions' classic hit "People Get Ready." Young's fuzz-tone guitar solo recalls the Impressions' track directly. The spiritual images of the verses are supported by the gospel-soul instrumental track. The first verse speaks of a meeting between a "preacher" and "God" at the "Golden Gate," which refers both to the entrance to heaven and the bridge over the San Francisco Bay. A number of images in the song have double meanings. The "preacher" wishes for a time when "love and music is everywhere." "God" responds that the "world has changed" and the wish will not come true. Young suggests there was a time when "love and music" permeated the landscape "when The Band played *Rock of Ages*," a reference to the 1971 concert album by the group. "Rock of Ages" also relates to the eighteenth-century Christian hymn. In the final verse, the "two old friends," "God" and the "preacher," determine that faith still exists. The chorus is a prayer. The narrator desires to be removed from "evil." He confesses to being sinful. He acknowledges his "old black heart."

The album closes with a bit of Miami soul, similar in feel to the Timmy Thomas track "Why Can't We Live Together" of the early 1970s. "She's a Healer" has a Latin groove fueled by soulful, female background vocals, Booker T. Jones's organ playing, and Tom Bray's muted trumpet line. Several verses end with the phrase "when the good times roll" as Young borrows from Shirley and Lee's 1950s rhythm-and-blues hit "Let the Good Times

Roll." The lyrics, which follow a blues structure (A-A-B-C), are about the narrator's affection toward his woman.

GREENDALE

Greendale is a concept album, or rock opera, that is set in a rural area. In lieu of a libretto, in the booklet included in the compact disc package, Young writes about each of the songs, adding information not included in the lyrics. He also sheds light on his experiences writing the songs. One theme that Young expresses with wonder is that he does not know what is going to happen to the characters until he starts writing. He explains that he wrote one song a day on the way to the recording studio. The main characters in the tale include a couple named Edith and Earl Green, who run the Double E Ranch; their daughter Sun Green, a young woman with developing activist tendencies; their nephew, Cousin Jed Green; two grandparents, Grandma and Grandpa Green; and a California Highway Patrolman, Carmichael, whom Jed shoots during a routine traffic stop. The devil is a recurring, minor, albeit significant, character in the tale. Working in the studio with Crazy Horse for the first time since *Broken Arrow* seven years earlier, *Greendale* is akin to a long musical jam with lyrics. Three of the tracks are longer than 10 minutes.

Grandpa and Cousin Jed sit on a "porch" in "Falling from Above," the opening track. Grandpa tries to read the paper. Meanwhile, the narrator focuses on the "guy singin' this song." Young asks about himself, "Is there anything he knows that he ain't said?" He lists what he is singing the song for: "freedom," "love," and "depressed angels." There are a number of different things going on lyrically that do not relate to the story of the town of Greendale. In another section of the song, the narrator mentions a "hero" and an "artist" discussing their "goals and visions" for the future. Young brings up the "religious wars" that face the "human race." In describing a new day at the Double E ranch, Young borrows from Bob Dylan's lyrics to "New Morning." Young opens a verse, "Hear that rooster crowin'" and several lines later adds "It's a new morning." Dylan's song opens with the words, "Can't you hear that rooster crowin'?" A theme repeated several times is that "a little love and affection... will make the world a better place." So the track introduces characters and adds a general view of what is happening in the world around Greendale. The song has a mid-tempo rock music foundation.

The band picks up the tempo on the electric blues rock track "Double E." The narrator notes that Sun Green's parents are overprotective. But when they are absent, "she's hot enough to burn the house down." The listener also learns that Grandma lives in the past, in "the summer of love." "Devil's Sidewalk" takes place along the coast. A "captain" addresses a "helmsman" and a "mate." This is the only scene that takes place along the water, and it does not seem to have a lot to do with the overall story, except that the captain appears to be warning his laborers to stay away from Greendale. He calls it the "devil's sidewalk." As he talks about the town, ominous-sounding female background voices punctuate each line with the town's name. Young quotes from the Beatles' "Come Together" about having "to be free," and follows by adding, "John Lennon said that." The narrator then says he believes in "love" and "action," and the scene returns to the ship captain who remarks, "Who cares what you believe?" In his booklet comments related to the track, Young adds that Satan lives in the Greendale jail.

"Leave the Driving" is a quieter, electric guitar-based track. Although the title is derived from an old Greyhound bus lines advertisement, there is no connection between the action that takes place in the song and bus travel. The key dramatic moment of the album is contained in this track. Cousin Jed, carrying a significant amount of cocaine and marijuana, is stopped by the California Highway Patrol. He shoots and kills the officer. The image is highlighted by the narrator explaining that the killer's "life flashed before him like a black-and-white Super 8" film. And, adding the audio component, Young compares the "sound" of Jed's "future" to that of a "scratchy old 78" RPM record disc. Grandpa visits Jed in jail.

In another tangent from the main story arc, the narrator brings up terrorist networks on the "Internet" and relates how the government tells people that it can handle the threats ("leave the driving to us"). So the title appears in the song, but it is not related to the primary narrative. The song ends with wisdom from Grandpa who notes, "some people have taken pure bullshit and turned it into gold." In context, it is a knock against the media, a theme that is further crystallized as the story goes on. The more overarching meaning relates to the frustration of the artist who remains true to her vision yet suffers financially, while those who sell out are rewarded. In the booklet, Young writes that Cousin Jed in jail bears a "resemblance" to the devil, who, he noted earlier, likes to call the Greendale jail home. Young also explains that as he wrote the song, he was "surprised" that Cousin Jed shot the patrolman.

"Carmichael" is a slow-tempo rock song that opens with almost three minutes of instrumental jamming from Young and Crazy Horse. Young delivers the long lyric without emotion. The song focuses on the slain highway patrolman. At the outset, the listener learns that the law enforcement officer was having an affair with a woman named "Lenore." The next series of verses reconstructs a memorial service that his fellow officers held for "Carmichael." The final verses spotlight the widow's reaction to his passing. She did not show up at the memorial and she labels her late husband an "asshole" for getting himself "shot." But she also reminisces happily about a vacation to "Pebble Beach" where they met "Wayne Newton." The thought of the meeting with a celebrity gives a sense of the blue-collar status of Carmichael and his wife.

In the booklet discussion, Young states that even though Cousin Jed is in jail, "they're not gonna get him." He relates it to the "Cortez test," or what he said in the lyrics to "Cortez the Killer." In either case, there is no vindication for the victims.

In the song lyric, the widow adds that their relationship was strained when Carmichael went off to work that morning. In the booklet, Young writes that he learned from the song to "be nice to the one you love because you never know what's gonna happen."

"Bandit" opens with Young scratching his acoustic guitar strings. Unlike the remaining cuts on the album, "Bandit" is an acoustic track that Young talk-sings quietly over his acoustic guitar accompaniment. Melodically, Young borrows from the Beatles' "I'll Follow the Sun." As he did in "Falling from Above," Young quotes Bob Dylan. He recites Dylan's words from "Like a Rolling Stone" about being "invisible" and having "no secrets." And he follows with an acknowledgment to the composer, saying "Bob Dylan said that, something like that."

The lyrics do not mesh with the *Greendale* story. One section is about taking drugs. Another is a swipe at the music industry ("get past the negative thing the lawyers and business"). And then he talks about betting on a major league baseball game. In the written comments, Young states the song is about Earl Green, a painter by trade. He also says the story is unfolded in the instrumental portion of the production. Young writes, "you have to listen to the instrumentals to get this."[6] In the instrumental passage, Young explains, the devil bestows a new sense of creativity on Earl who then sells one of his new style paintings to Lenore, who owns the art gallery in town.

The focus of "Grandpa's Interview" is the invasive and sensationalist media. The song is a long (13 minutes) narrative over a mid-tempo rhythm. After the murder by Cousin Jed, Grandma and Grandpa Green seek sanctuary at the Double E ranch to avoid reporters and helicopters. Sun Green visits Jed in jail. We learn that Lenore, who was involved in an affair with Carmichael, also has a relationship with Jed. Young adds a sly comment about songwriting. Jed tells Sun that he has written a "new song" that is "longer than all the others combined" and the song has no meaning.

As the media close in on the Double E, Grandpa remarks that it is neither an "honor" nor a "duty" to "be on TV." After being accosted by a reporter, Grandpa collapses and dies. Young sings that he "died...for freedom of silence." In his written notes, Young shares that everyone in the studio was "depressed" that Grandpa died because he was a favorite character of the musicians. Again, Young was surprised that his story took this turn of events as he wrote *Greendale*. After Grandpa dies, there is a verse voiced by an unknown character who asks if someone can "shut up" the "guy who just keeps singin'." He wonders "where" the singer "comes up with this stuff." As in the opening track, Young turns the mirror toward himself.

After the passing of Grandpa, "Bringin' Down Dinner" has a slow, funereal character. The song's instrumentation includes only a church organ and a drum keeping the beat. Sun Green, who does not realize that Grandpa is dead, is carrying supper to him. Grandma makes a brief comment to the overprotected child that sets the tone for the remaining tracks. She encourages Sun to "go out now and see the world." In his written explanation, Young again expresses wonder that Grandpa died. He relates an autobiographical story about speaking with his father Scott Young, who was a sportswriter and novelist. The elder Young explained to his young child that he did not know what he was going to write when he sat down at his "Underwood typewriter."

Young has addressed environmental issues on several occasions in his songs ("Mother Earth" on *Ragged Glory*, "Natural Beauty" on *Harvest Moon*). He continues this tack on *Greendale*. The two closing tracks, "Sun Green" and "Be the Rain" deal with concern for the environment. The character Sun Green blossoms as an environmental activist in the 12-minute song titled after her. The loss of her grandfather sparked the 18-year-old to move out and realize her dreams. She demonstrates against a power company by chaining herself to a "statue" in the office "lobby." Young uses a megaphone effect on the microphone to voice Sun Green's words of protest. Her words address the California energy crisis of 2000 and 2001. She speaks of "rolling blackout(s)" and how "blame" is placed on the "governor." The media are all over Sun Green's activity, and, in this case, the character is glad to have the exposure, unlike her Grandpa earlier.

The song is broken up into several sections by a chorus in which the line "Hey Mr. Clean, you're dirty now too" is repeated with the megaphone effect. The music that accompanies the chorus and surrounds it borrows from the melody of Norman Greenbaum's "Spirit in the Sky." After the office lobby incident, the scene changes to a bar where Sun Green ends up dancing with Earth Brown. This adds an allegorical nature to Young's tale. Earth entices her to leave with him so that she can "be a goddess in the planet wars." In his written comments, Young puts his hope for the future in youth. Before they head for "Alaska," Sun went home to retrieve her cat. While she was away, however, the FBI searched her home, and an agent shot and killed the feline after it scratched him. Young adds the sound effects of the agents knocking on her door, the cat yelping, and the shot that killed the animal.

Director Jim Jarmusch, who filmed the *Year of the Horse* documentary about Young and Crazy Horse in 1997, applies the name of the "Sun Green" character to a woman with a similar disposition in the Bill Murray film *Broken Flowers*. In the film, "Sun Green" works at a florist and provides first aid to a nasty cut on the head of Bill Murray's character.

The story of *Greendale* ends with "Be the Rain," an upbeat, melodic rock tune. The background vocals by the "Mountainettes" (Pegi Young, Nancy Hall, Twink Brewer, and Sue Hall) add to the upbeat mood of the production. Sun Green and Earth Brown head off to Alaska to "save Mother Earth" despite adversity and their witness of the effects of pollution. Young lists the effects of the careless stewardship of earth's resources. Terrestrial and aquatic species disappear, timber supplies are low and farmland is laid waste by "corporate greed and chemicals." The waters of the planet, the "ocean," the "river," and the "rain" must remain pure for the earth to flourish.

In his notes, Young adds stage instructions for the tale's finale. A light shines on Sun Green. Grandpa sits in his "rocking chair." Cousin Jed and Officer Carmichael speak to each other at the jailhouse. And Sun's cat crosses the stage. Living or dead, the characters return to the stage. Young also sheds light in his writing about why, in the song's narrative, Earth leaves Sun while she is sleeping. The devil poisoned Earth's "bottle of water," which drove him to take in more and more water in an unending battle to remain cool and to cleanse himself. He could not be at peace around Sun. Young ends his written comments with Sun about to speak through "her megaphone." In 2007, it was announced that the tale of Greendale would be turned into a graphic novel.

PRAIRIE WIND

In 2004, Young was diagnosed with a brain aneurysm. Before his surgery he put down his thoughts about his family and his journey through the past in *Prairie Wind* (2005). The album is dedicated to Young's father Scott Young, who passed away shortly before the release of the recording. Some critics consider the album the completion of the *Harvest* trilogy, beginning with *Harvest* (1972) and followed by *Harvest Moon* (1992). They see the albums as part of a set because of their predominantly acoustic nature; however, identifying these three albums in this way excludes, for no apparent reason, other acoustic-based albums Young has recorded over the years including *Comes a Time* (1978) and *Silver & Gold* (2000).

The disc opens with the gentle track "The Painter." (As on *Greendale*, the tracks on *Prairie Wind* are sequenced in the order in which they were composed.) A message of the lyric is that everyone is given a painted backdrop to plow their way through as they go down life's path. The "painter" creates a landscape for life. The narrator meditates on finding his place in history. There are "long road(s)" both "behind" and "ahead." He warns of losing your way if you "follow every dream." The second verse focuses on a specific, older, hard-working woman the narrator admired, perhaps a mother or a grandmother. Young sings of his bond with his musical friends, some of whom have passed on. He notes, "we leave our tracks in the sound," in a clever image relating to making their marks on the musical landscape. We may not be able to "follow every dream," but we should follow the one that resonates with the creation that surrounds us.

"No Wonder" is the first of several songs that uses the term *prairie wind*. Young spent his formative years in western Canada, in Winnipeg, surrounded by prairie lands. The track has a more ominous quality than the opening number. The chorus (repeated three times in the song) emphasizes the passage of time, as he opens each reading with the phrase "tick tock." The "clock" reminds us that there is only so much time to "follow" a "dream" (as noted in "The Painter"). The choruses, all set in a church scene, paint key points in the cycle of life. In the first chorus, a couple prepares to be married, "seeking guidance from above." In the second, bells toll for "fallen soldiers." In the third, the marriage ceremony is complete and "happy people sing." The unity of the couple brings life, but we are also reminded of the strife that leads to death.

The first verses speak of a "bluebird" and the marching of time as indicated by the changing of the seasons (a "pasture" turns from "green" to "brown"). The "bluebird" is a reference to the minor hit single "Bluebird" by Buffalo Springfield. The bird symbolizes the music from "long ago" that will also "take (him) home." The "bluebird" is full of vigor like the music of youth.

The second set of verses relates to the televised *America: A Tribute to Heroes* benefit concert that took place on September 21, 2001, 10 days after 9/11. (Young participated in the concert. He sang John Lennon's signature composition "Imagine.") Young opens the verses with the phrase "amber waves of grain," borrowed from the second line of "America the Beautiful." He ties the image to both the "prairie wind" of his Canadian past and the United States. He continues with a line about hearing "Willie" (a reference to the country and western singer Willie Nelson) on the "radio," which reminds him of a "song from 9/11." The song is "America the Beautiful," which closed the tribute concert. Willie Nelson led the concert participants in a rendition of the patriotic hymn. Then, Young mentions comedian "Chris Rock," one of the announcers who took part in the tribute concert. He thinks about Rock telling the audience to stop sending "candles." The sound stages on which the concert took place were illuminated with many candles. Young notes that with the end of the concert, the "prairie wind" blows again. Life continues.

The third group of verses addresses Young's environmental concerns. The narrator remembers his family's wise use of natural resources. They only took what they needed to survive. The scene moves swiftly from the time "birds" were so plentiful that they "blocked out the sun" to a government office where an elected official takes a bribe from those responsible for killing off endangered species.

Young delivers "Falling off the Face of the Earth" in a quieter voice. The narrator wants to be sure he lets his "love" know how he feels in case he will no longer be around to say these tender words.

"Far from Home" is the first of three songs on the album that are enhanced by horns. The instruments add a soulful, country rhythm-and-blues character. Wayne Jackson of the Memphis Horns arranged the horn parts. Thomas McGinley and Jackson contribute the horn lines. Ben Keith's slide guitar and Young's harmonica add the country accents. The lyric opens with a bit of nostalgia as the narrator remembers how his "family" passed the enjoyment and love of music on to him. The "prairie" marks this lyric as well. Five times Young asks to be buried there. In the chorus, he sings of the "Canadian geese" that "filled the sky" in a sentiment similar to that of the birds that shadowed the sun in "No Wonder." Borrowing from the traditional "Home on the Range," he also speaks of how the "buffalo...roam(ed)" on the prairie. On the *Old Ways* album 20 years earlier, Young sang of the Trans-Canada Highway in "Bound for Glory." The narrator returns to the same roadway in this song as he attempts to hitchhike to "Nashville." As happened to Young in real life, the narrator dreams of getting a "big old car" and heading to the "promised land" where he will "really go far." Wherever he ends up in life, the narrator desires to come back to the "prairie" for his eternal rest where he will not be "far from home."

"It's a Dream" is a reminiscence of a "fading" lifestyle on the prairie. The song opens with just a piano. Later, strings enter and add an ethereal quality to the mix. Each verse presents a different scene. In the first verse the narrator notes that he avoids the bad news offered by the media as the new day presents itself. He assures the one that he has "been (with) through so many things" that he will protect her. The second verse focuses on a young carefree "boy" fishing below a bridge. The river mentioned in the lyric flows through Young's boyhood town. The sense is that the young fellow with the fishing pole continues a tradition that the narrator and his generation participated in as well. From a youngster, the song shifts to an elderly man in the final verse. Both of these folk inhabit a friendly town where the "old man" converses with a "policeman." Trains still stop at a "station" whose halcyon days have passed by. The narrator asserts that these scenes will become "just a memory."

"Prairie Wind" begins the second half of the album. The horns and the background vocalists singing about a "prairie wind blowing through (the) head" add an ominous feel to the title track. Before Young's father Scott Young died, he suffered from dementia. This adds a sad autobiographical note to the lyric. The song begins with the narrator attempting to recall what his father "said...before...time took away his head." The line is an intriguing combination of thoughts about memory. He struggles to recall the tales told by the elder who can no longer share them.

The narrator adds more thoughts about the prairie. He speaks of how he "tried" to convince those unfamiliar with it of the appeal of prairie life, but they do not understand. He adds a glimpse of that simple lifestyle that parallels the back cover photo of the album when he sings of a "farmer's wife hanging laundry." He notes the natural beauty of the northern lights and mentions the native religions that once held sway over the land he loves.

Young's parenthood experiences and his love and affection for his children have appeared in a number of tracks over the years. "My Boy," from *Old Ways,* was directed to Young's oldest son. The *Re*ac*tor* and *Trans* albums were influenced by the intensive therapy Young and his wife were immersed in with his second son. "You're My Girl," from *Are You Passionate?*, reflects on the time Young's daughter was about to go off to college. "Here for You" is also directed to Young's daughter as she reaches another milestone. In this case, she is about to graduate college and begin to make a life of her own. The upbeat, mid-tempo track relieves the tension of the ominous "Prairie Wind" that it follows in sequence. The music opens with Young's harmonica over his acoustic guitar, Keith's pedal steel guitar, the bass, and drums. Young assures his daughter that he will always "be" there for her but, on the other hand, he has no desire to "hold" her "down." He acknowledges, in a universal expression of the parent, that he will "miss" her. And, he offers a tender image of his "old heart beating for" her through all four seasons. He includes "summer," "winter," "spring," and "fall" to add a chronological structure to the lyrics. Naming the seasons also underlines the passage of time (like the "tick tock" of "No Wonder") and the passing of the mantle to the next generation. Young's wife, Pegi Young, joins in singing a portion of the lyric, affirming the love and devotion of both parents for their child.

Whether it is nonrenewable natural resources or a treasured musical instrument, we are only stewards of the gifts bestowed on us for a time. This is the message of "This Old Guitar." The song uses the acoustic guitar riff from "Harvest Moon," one of Young' best-known, acoustic-based tracks. Emmylou Harris shares the vocals with Young in several sections of the song. The lyrics speak of the power of music on the emotions and in speaking out on issues. The "old guitar" has been a "messenger in times of trouble…hope and fear." It also draws out "tear(s)" and "smile(s)."

"He Was the King" adds to Young's list of informal, off-the-wall studio blowouts that occasionally pop up on his albums. This song does not fit in the context of the set. The track is an offhand tribute to Elvis Presley. The recording begins with studio banter concerning the musical key in which the take should be played. All the verses begin with the phrase "the last time I saw Elvis" and all end with the title phrase. Each verse spotlights a different part of the Elvis mythos. The first verse recalls the incident of Presley shooting out a television screen. The second verse notes Elvis's penchant for gospel music. The third verse notes Presley's 1956 screen debut in *Love Me Tender*. The next verse presents the image of the Vegas Elvis performing for "blue-haired" women. The verses are not in chronological order. The fifth verse hearkens back to the days of the *Louisiana Hayride* radio broadcasts as Young paints a picture of the young Elvis "frontin' a three-piece band" while using the "back of a flatbed truck" for a stage. In the sixth verse, Presley rides in one of his famous Cadillacs. Young parodies Elvis by voicing Presley's famous phrase "thank you very much" before Young repeats the first verse as the tune draws to a close. The performance ends with more conversation between Young and his fellow musicians.

Prairie Wind closes with the sobering and hopeful "When God Made Me." Spooner Oldham's piano is the only instrumental accompaniment. And he plays it as though he is sitting in the sanctuary of a country church. A choir backs up Young; not a large choir as might be seen and heard at a televised mega-church service, but a small town choir one might hear at a village worship service. The lyric is a meditation on the Almighty. The narrator asks a series of questions related to the narrator's wonderment over what God was thinking when humankind was created. The narrator wonders if it is just humans or all "living thing(s)" that are created in God's image. He asks if God "envision(ed) the wars...fought in his name." These theological ruminations make a fitting close to an album unified by Young's consideration of his life and those who have touched it.

A concert film of Young performing most of the songs from *Prairie Wind* was released in 2006. Directed by Jonathan Demme, who also directed the Talking Heads' film *Stop Making Sense,* the *Neil Young: Heart of Gold* film focused on several nights of acoustic performances by Young and fellow musicians at the renowned Ryman Auditorium in Nashville. Oddly enough, while the film that celebrated Young's acoustic music side was opening to positive reviews around the country, Young released an album of new and controversial hard rock.

Living with War

Recorded in several weeks with drummer Chad Cromwell and bassist Rick Rosas, *Living with War* continues Young's work in musical journalism, which includes "Ohio" (1970), "War Song" (1972), and "Let's Roll" (2002). Unlike the earlier tracks, which were one-song reactions to events that were not meant to be the building blocks of a full, unified album, *Living with War* is an album-long protest against the Iraq conflict and George W. Bush and his administration. In interviews at the time of the album's issue, Young explained that he felt uncomfortable making the album, which to him was a sign that he was tapping into something that needed to be said.

A number of tracks include a full choir, which was Young's attempt to soften the blow of the message he presents. The album closes with the choir alone singing "America the Beautiful." In an edition of the album released later in 2006, *Living with War Raw,* the choir contribution is stripped from the album tracks. At the time of the release of the alternate version, Young remarked that the stripped-down version was the superior mix.

Although Young's focus is the U.S. involvement in Iraq, the album kicks off with another of his songs that expresses his environmental concern. The missive of "After the Garden" is that once the "garden" or creation has been destroyed and humankind can no longer survive, war and peace will be inconsequential. Young opens the song with a thinly veiled reference to Vice President Dick Cheney. He sings about a "shadow man runnin' the government." Young continues, "won't need no stinking war," a shrewd reference to the "stinking badges" line quoted by the adversary of Humphrey Bogart's character in *Treasure of the Sierra Madre*. The video for the song included excerpts from Al Gore's award-winning documentary about global warming, *An Inconvenient Truth*.

Young delivers his "Living with War" vocal with a broken heart, knowing that peace is a distant dream, and many families will suffer heartache before peace will come. The narrator "pray(s) for peace" and "vow(s) never to kill again." He inserts the phrase "how the west was won" in one verse. This is a reference to the popular film of the early 1960s, as well as a note on how the myths embraced by Americans, including the frontier myth, lead the nation into fruitless struggles. The background vocals by the full choir plus Tom Bray's trumpet add a sobering quality to the production. As he has done before, Young incorporates several lines from "The Star Spangled Banner" in the song. In the bridge he sings of "the rockets' red glare" and "bombs bursting in air" that "give proof...that our flag is still there." In this context, the words do not ring with the hope normally found in their reading.

In the late 1960s, John Lennon and Yoko Ono campaigned for peace. Lennon explained that they decided to use the same tools advertisers use to sell consumer products in the couple's advertising campaign for peace. In a tragic parallel, "The Restless Consumer" deals with the U.S. government's campaign to sell the Iraq war to the American citizens. The lyrics speak of the "Madison Avenue war." Young speaks of the crime of funneling resources into a war machine when people across the globe are "starving and dying." He also saves some of his vitriol for Madison Avenue itself. He does not need a "TV ad tellin' me how sick I am." The chorus repeats the phrase "don't need no more lies" over and over. Young's narrator is against "terror squad(s)" and a "Jihad," but he notes that unless there is communication between the warring adversaries, there will be no resolution.

On May 1, 2003, President Bush arrived on the deck of the USS Abraham Lincoln aircraft carrier in a Navy S-3B Viking jet and declared that "major combat" operations were complete in the Iraq conflict while a banner proclaiming "Mission Accomplished" flew behind him.[7] Beginning several months after Bush's declaration, these comments were criticized as premature, and the critique has only been further validated as coalition troops remain mired in Iraq in 2008. Young addresses the carrier incident in "Shock and Awe." He sings of "our chief...landing on the deck" and of a "golden photo-op." Young also mentions the "overconfidence" of the United States in its actions in Iraq. The title phrase comes from a military term describing a massive show of force to intimidate the enemy in the initial stages of a campaign. This strategy was used as the United States took offensive action against Iraq. Young looks at the effects of war. He notes the "bodies...brought home in boxes...(that) no one sees." He refers to the government's blocking of the media from seeing the return of fallen armed forces personnel to Dover Air Force Base in Delaware. (Young briefly refers to both this situation and the "mission accomplished" incident in the previous track, "The Restless

Consumer.") Young sings of the "children scarred for life" both physically from battlefield action and mentally from the loss of loved ones. The final sad observation in the closing verse is that none of this had to happen. Twice, he says, "we had a chance to change our mind."

"Families" is a sad, fast rocker with an infectious hook. The song is sung from the point of view of a soldier who wishes to be remembered honorably. It is not clear whether he survives the war, but the sense is that only his "spirit" is left at the end of the day. The emphasis is on the title term. The effects of war extend far beyond the battlefield casualties. Four verses end with the word "family" or a variant. The production provides evidence that Young can still create a great rock song that clocks in at less than two-and-a-half minutes.

The focus of "Flags of Freedom" is also the family. The narration is from the point of view of parents whose "son" marches "off to war." The scene is a small town ceremonial sendoff. "Flags...line old Main Street" and "church bells" ring. Interestingly, Young's lyric speaks of the "flags...blowin' in the wind." The flags, unfurled to express pride in the local warriors as they parade by, are ironically related to the famous song of Bob Dylan with antiwar sentiments. In "Blowin' in the Wind," Dylan asks "how many...cannonballs" have to be fired and "how many deaths will it take." Later, Young mentions "Dylan." The "sister" of the "son" who is heading out listens on her "headphones" to "Bob Dylan singin' in 1963." *The Freewheelin' Bob Dylan,* the album that included "Blowin' in the Wind," was issued in 1963. The sister's attention is momentarily diverted by the "president...on TV" and when she "turns" to look back at her "brother," he is gone. The image underscores the separation of families by war. In the final verse, Young wonders why Americans think they are any more patriotic than those they fight against. He suggests that those on the defensive "believe" in their "flags" as much as Americans do.

"Let's Impeach the President" is Young's unveiled attack on the sitting president of the United States. He accuses President Bush of "lying," "abusing...power," and "spying on citizens." Young also criticizes the president for misappropriating the religious beliefs of the electorate for his own purposes. In one section of the song, while the choir sings the words "flip, flop," Young splices in actual sound bites from the president. The Republican Party used the phrase "flip, flop" against the Democratic presidential nominee John Kerry in 2004 in reference to the party's accusations of Kerry's vacillation on issues.

Young turns the tables on Bush. For example, we hear Bush state, "war is my last choice." This is followed by Bush's words, "we're gonna smoke them out" and "bring them on." After announcing that "Hussein has weapons of mass destruction," followed by the president's remarks that no such weapons were uncovered, the section concludes with Bush declaring, "no one can now doubt the word of America." Young goes on to indict the president on domestic issues, including the tragic lack of response to the aftermath of Hurricane Katrina. Young said he used a poor melody on purpose for the song. Because of the message he wanted to get across, he used a melody that "pisses people off...and...aggravates" them.[8]

"Lookin' for a Leader" is about the search for someone who will right the country. Musically and lyrically, the song is the weakest element in the set. Young specifically mentions Barack "Obama" and "Colin Powell" as possible presidential candidates who can offer better leadership than George W. Bush. He notes the "desolation," "corruption," and "broken world" that are the results of the current administration in the White House. "Roger and Out" is the only slow tempo number on the disc. The instrumentation is electric, but the ambiance is quiet and respectful. Young's thoughts turn to an old friend, someone who he traveled with on the "Hippie Highway." The "good buddy" made the ultimate sacrifice for his "country." Young fondly reminisces about their times when they were "a couple of kids." The song may also be interpreted as Young's farewell to the late Bruce Palmer, bass guitarist, fellow Canadian, and founding member of Buffalo Springfield. Palmer died in 2004.

The insertion of "America the Beautiful" underscores Young's love, concern, and hope for the country he has called home for the past 40 years. The song is performed a cappella by the choir in an uplifting performance. The sequencing of the patriotic performance at the end of the album also relates back to the *America: A Tribute for Heroes* benefit concert for 9/11 victims, which also ended with a large ensemble singing "America the Beautiful."

CHROME DREAMS II

In the last quarter of 2007, Young released his 32nd solo studio album (including albums with backing by Crazy Horse or the Stray Gators, or any ensemble other than Buffalo Springfield or Crosby, Stills, Nash, and Young).[9] *Chrome Dreams II* is a collection of 10 songs, all but one of which were recently recorded. The title suggests the album is a sequel, but there was never an authorized Neil Young album with the Chrome Dreams title before this issue. Young recorded a collection of songs in the late 1970s that he decided not to release. Some of the songs, for example, "Like a Hurricane," "Homegrown," and "Pocahontas," appeared on other albums. The 2007 release does not resurrect any of the tracks that were shelved back in the 1970s. One track, however, that was recorded in 1988, is included on *Chrome Dreams II*. Two other songs were composed and recorded in different versions in the 1980s. The three older compositions begin the album sequence.

The album opens with a slow, shuffling beat. A harmonica, a strumming acoustic guitar, a lap pedal steel guitar, and brushes on the snare drum create a country flavor in "Beautiful Bluebird." Young begins the song by singing about going for a ride in his "old pickup truck." It almost sounds like someone is doing a parody of the mellow Neil Young. A version of the track was recorded during the *Old Ways* sessions. The Wyatt Earps (Ben Keith, Ralph Molina, and Young) provide the harmonies on the track. The background vocals are reminiscent of Crosby, Stills, and Nash, and it would have been easy to imagine the trio contributing their voices to the composition. Ben Keith's Dobro work adds a satisfying touch to the instrumentation. The lyric is about people who come into your life and then are gone. The person could be a lover, a family member, someone you made music with, or just someone that has touched your life in some way. But when she or he is gone, that is the end. There is no return to the way things were. In the chorus, Young sings of how he could reunite with the person if there was an open window to "heaven."

"Boxcar" is an allegory about life that uses railroad imagery. The narrator takes a path through life and is carried where fate or the "Great Spirit" takes him. He is resigned to face what comes before him. A lyrical thread through the album is faith and a higher power. In the opening track, the possibility of a reunion in heaven was noted. "Boxcar" does not have as bright a disposition as the opening cut. The rhythm of Young's banjo gives the country-flavored track an ominous cast. Young recorded a more rock-oriented, unreleased version in the late 1980s.

The one track taken from a session date almost two decades earlier is the 18-minute "Ordinary People." It is a wordy song, like "Last Trip to Tulsa," but unlike that early acoustic track, it has the slogging, electric jam-style rhythm of Young's work with Crazy Horse (although only Frank "Poncho" Sampedro of Crazy Horse appears on the track). The song was recorded with the Bluenotes band (including the horn section) that Young used on the *This Note's for You* sessions. Listening to the song, it is easy to realize why it would not have fit on the 1988 release. It sounds like Crazy Horse with horns, with a long lyrical narrative. If Bob Dylan had recorded *Blonde on Blonde* with Crazy Horse plus keyboard players Danny Federici and Roy Bittan of the E Street Band plus the horn section of the Asbury Jukes, it may have sounded something like this.

The lyric has a populist bent. Young sings of the "patch-of-ground" people. It is a story of the oppressed and those who take advantage of them, yet the narrator seems to understand both sides in this class tension. Young's tale is an updated, rock music complement to James Agee and Walker Evans's *Let Us Now Praise Famous Men*, their eyewitness account of Depression-era tenant farmers in Alabama.[10] Tom Bray adds a jazzy, muted trumpet solo in one of the breaks. Several saxophone solos play against Young's guitar lines. Each verse is a vignette of life. Some have to pay the price to make others happy. Some have to pay for what they have done wrong. Others go about their daily business. The narrator sings, "Ordinary people bring the good things back." He finds strong moral fiber in the "regular guy." The composition is an impressionistic look at the lives of everyday people.

"Shining Light" has a gospel cast. The heavenly background vocals sound like they could be coming from the Jordanaires on an Elvis Presley track. The slow tempo track has the clearest spiritual imagery of the numerous songs with a faith element in the collection. It is, for all intents and purposes, a hymn. The narrator addresses the song to the "Shining Light." He petitions the "light" to show its "love" and "compassion" to him. The narrator asks a series of questions, wondering what he may offer to the "shining light" so that he may "stand in its glow." The singer's heartfelt plea is to experience the "light" and "love" of the higher power. "The Believer" is an unabashed, affirmation of love by the narrator to his "baby," in whom he has "faith." The instrumentation is powered ahead by Molina's strong downbeat on the snare.

"Spirit Road" is a rolling-down-the-highway electric rocker that could have easily fit in with the *Ragged Glory*-era Crazy Horse sessions. The lyrics suggest that there are many stumbling blocks along the "Spirit Road" that can keep a person from finding "peace." The narrator encourages the "love lost friend" to keep moving on to "where you belong." "Dirty Old Man" is a grungy, old rocker that brings to mind tracks like "Piece of Crap" and other one-offs that Young has recorded through his career. Even here, though, Young continues to coax interesting tones from his guitar, bringing to the fore lines reminiscent of his work in 1995 with Pearl Jam on *Mirror Ball*. In the narration, the singer wrestles with the lure of alcohol and often loses the battle. Young's lyric adds an amusing detail of a "bag of frozen peas" on his "knees" to ease the pain from kneeling as he tries to "please" someone, by asking for forgiveness or through physical pleasure.

"Ever After" is a country gospel waltz with a strong downbeat courtesy of Crazy Horse's Ralph Molina on the drum kit. Again, the lyrics are drawn with religious allusions. Being in nature leads the narrator to pray among "the trees." He is convinced that there is "laughter" and "music" in the "ever after." The narrator is not dogmatic, however. He observes that there are "right" and "wrong" answers. He sings, "the one that I believe in is a wish in a song."

A mid-1970s funk guitar riff (in the style of the Ohio Players) undergirds the long (14 minutes) slow jam "No Hidden Path." In between the verses, Young continues to show his creativity in coming up with his spare electric guitar solos that he continues to conjure up almost 40 years since his first album with Crazy Horse in 1969. Again the lyrics contain spiritual allusions. Surrounded by nature, he "feel(s) the chosen one." As in "Shining Light," the lyrics of the chorus present a petition to a higher power. Young sings, "Show me the way and I'll follow." He acknowledges a force that keeps his "path" from being obscured.

The most interesting and unusual track (since it is unlike anything Young has done before) is the closing number, "The Way." Young is backed by a children's choir (the Young People's Chorus of New York City). The recording sounds as though Young is channeling public television's Mr. Rogers, "Sing"-era Carpenters, and the childlike melodies and productions of the late 1967 to 1969 Beach Boys albums, for example, *Wild Honey, Friends,* and *20/20.* Like other lyrics on the album, the song has a spiritual overtone. The narrator sings that if you are "lost" and "can't be found," there is a "way" to "get you back home" to "peace." Musically, *Chrome Dreams II* is Young's most varied album since *Freedom* in 1989.

REPRISE

The Neil Young *Archives* may finally be released in 2008 as announced. Of course, there have been rumors of its release since the early 1990s.[11] What is different this time, however, is that two live concerts from 1970 and 1971 were released in 2006 and 2007, respectively. So the *Archives* may soon appear. But with Neil Young, one never knows until his authorized work is actually available to the listener. He follows his own muse and does not care what the expectations are of anyone following his artistic career. In early 2008, Young announced that the *Archives* will be available in fall 2008. He created a stir by noting that the collection will not be available on compact disc, but only in the Blu-Ray and DVD formats.

Throughout his career, Young has lived in the moment. One day he will announce that he will never again work with Crazy Horse. A while later he will record a classic album with the band. Young follows what he hears in his head. If it's time for acoustic tracks, then that is what he will record. But if it's time for something else, he will move on to whatever musicians work best for the new music. When the *Heart of Gold* film was released, conventional wisdom would have put the artist on a tour promoting the *Prairie Wind* songs that made up the bulk of the filmed concert with the band from the film. Instead, Young quickly recorded a controversial, electric-rocking anti-war album (*Living with War*). And he followed it up with a tour with Crosby, Stills, and Nash, with whom he had not recorded since 1999.

At the dawn of 2008, Young continues to be active. In January, 2008, he debuted a film that he directed, *CSNY Déjà vu,* at the Sundance Film Festival. The documentary follows Crosby, Stills, Nash, and Young's Freedom of Speech Tour of 2006 and the reaction of its audiences. In the spring of 2008, a Dallas theater company was scheduled to debut a play based on Young's *Greendale* album. And Young was set to tour England and Scotland at the same time. Neil Young continues on his journey through the past to the future.

Discography

THE STUDIO AND CONCERT ALBUMS OF NEIL YOUNG

Neil Young. Neil Young, vocals, acoustic and electric guitar, harmonica, piano; various assisting instrumentalists and vocalists. "The Emperor of Wyoming" (Young); "The Loner" (Young); "If I Could Have Her Tonight" (Young); "I've Been Waiting for You" (Young); "The Old Laughing Lady" (Young); "String Quartet from Whiskey Boot Hill" (Jack Nitzsche); "Here We Are in the Years" (Young); "What Did You Do to My Life?" (Young); "I've Loved Her So Long" (Young); "The Last Trip to Tulsa" (Young). 33-1/3 rpm phonodisc. Reprise RS-6317, 1969. Reissued on compact disc as Reprise 2–6317.

Everybody Knows This Is Nowhere. Neil Young with Crazy Horse. Neil Young, vocals, acoustic and electric guitar, harmonica, piano; Crazy Horse (Danny Whitten, guitar, vocals; Billy Talbot, bass guitar; Ralph Molina, drums, vocals); various assisting instrumentalists and vocalists. "Cinnamon Girl" (Young); "Everybody Knows This Is Nowhere" (Young); "Round & Round (It Won't Be Long)" (Young); "Down by the River" (Young); "Losing End (When You're On)" (Young); "Running Dry (Requiem for the Rockets)" (Young); "Cowgirl in the Sand" (Young). 33-1/3 rpm phonodisc. Reprise RS-6349, 1969. Reissued in 1987 on compact disc as Reprise 2–2282.

After the Gold Rush. Neil Young, vocals, acoustic and electric guitar, harmonica, piano, vibraphone; various assisting instrumentalists and vocalists. "Tell Me Why" (Young); "After the Gold Rush" (Young); "Only Love Can Break Your Heart" (Young); "Southern Man" (Young); "Till the Morning Comes" (Young); "Oh, Lonesome Me" (Don Gibson); "Don't Let It Bring You Down" (Young); "Birds" (Young); "When You Dance I Can Really Love" (Young); "I Believe in You" (Young); "Cripple Creek Ferry" (Young). 33-1/3 rpm phonodisc. Reprise RS-6383, 1970. Reissued in 1987 on compact disc as Reprise 2–2283.

Harvest. Neil Young, vocals, acoustic and electric guitar, harmonica, piano; various assisting instrumentalists and vocalists. "Out on the Weekend" (Young); "Harvest" (Young); "A Man Needs a Maid" (Young); "Heart of Gold" (Young); "Are You Ready for the Country?" (Young); "Old Man" (Young); "There's a World" (Young); "Alabama" (Young); "The Needle and the Damage Done" (Young); "Words (Between the Lines of Age)" (Young). 33-1/3 rpm phonodisc. Reprise MS-2032, 1972. Reissued in 1987 on compact disc as Reprise 2277–2.

Time Fades Away. Neil Young, vocals, acoustic and electric guitar, harmonica; various assisting instrumentalists and vocalists. "Time Fades Away" (Young); "Journey thru the Past" (Young); "Yonder Stands the Sinner" (Young); "L.A." (Young); "Love in Mind" (Young); "Don't Be Denied" (Young); "The Bridge" (Young); "Last Dance" (Young). 33-1/3 rpm phonodisc. Reprise MS-2151, 1973.

On the Beach. Neil Young, vocals, acoustic and electric guitar, harmonica, banjo, Wurlitzer; various assisting instrumentalists and vocalists. "Walk On" (Young); "See the Sky about to Rain" (Young); "Revolution Blues" (Young); "For the Turnstiles" (Young); "Vampire Blues" (Young); "On the Beach" (Young); "Motion Pictures" (Young); "Ambulance Blues" (Young). 33-1/3 rpm phonodisc. Reprise R-2180, 1974. Reissued in 2004 on compact disc as Warner Bros. 48526.

Tonight's the Night. Neil Young, vocals, acoustic and electric guitar, harmonica, piano, vibraphone; various assisting instrumentalists and vocalists. "Tonight's the Night" (Young); "Speakin' Out" (Young); "World on a String" (Young); "Borrowed Tune" (Young); "Come on Baby Let's Go Downtown" (Danny Whitten); "Mellow My Mind" (Young); "Roll Another Number (For the Road)" (Young); "Albuquerque" (Young); "New Mama" (Young); "Lookout Joe" (Young); "Tired Eyes" (Young); "Tonight's the Night, Pt. II" (Young). 33-1/3 rpm phonodisc. Reprise MS-2221, 1975. Reissued in 1987 on compact disc as Reprise 2–2221.

Zuma. Neil Young, Crazy Horse. Neil Young, vocals, acoustic and electric guitar, harmonica, keyboards; Crazy Horse (Frank Sampedro, Billy Talbot, Ralph Molina); various assisting instrumentalists and vocalists. "Don't Cry No Tears" (Young); "Danger Bird" (Young); "Pardon My Heart" (Young); "Lookin' for a Love" (Young); "Barstool Blues" (Young); "Stupid Girl" (Young); "Drive Back" (Young); "Cortez the Killer" (Young); "Through My Sails" (Young). 33-1/3 rpm phonodisc. Reprise MS-2242, 1975. Reissued in 1989 on compact disc as Reprise 2–2242.

Long May You Run. The Stills-Young Band. Stephen Stills, vocals, guitar, piano; Neil Young, vocals, acoustic and electric guitar, harmonica, piano, synthesizer strings; various assisting instrumentalists and vocalists. "Long May You Run" (Young); "Make Love to You" (Stephen Stills); "Midnight on the Bay" (Young); "Black Coral" (Stephen Stills); "Ocean Girl" (Young); "Let It Shine" (Young); "12/8 Blues (All the Same)" (Stephen Stills); "Fontainebleau" (Young); "Guardian Angel" (Stephen Stills). 33-1/3 rpm phonodisc. Reprise MS-2253, 1976. Reissued in 1988 on compact disc as Reprise 2–2253.

American Stars 'n' Bars. Neil Young, vocals, acoustic and electric guitar, harmonica; various assisting instrumentalists and vocalists. "The Old Country Waltz" (Young); "Saddle up the Palomino" (Young, Tim Drummond, Bobby Charles); "Hey Babe" (Young); "Hold Back the Tears" (Young); "Bite the Bullet" (Young); "Star of Bethlehem" (Young); "Will To Love" (Young); "Like a Hurricane"

(Young); "Homegrown" (Young). 33-1/3 rpm phonodisc. Reprise MSK-2261, 1977. Reissued in 2003 on compact disc as Reprise 48525.

Comes a Time. Neil Young, vocals, acoustic and electric guitar, harmonica; various assisting instrumentalists and vocalists. "Goin' Back" (Young); "Comes a Time" (Young); "Look Out for My Love" (Young); "Lotta Love" (Young); "Peace of Mind" (Young); "Human Highway" (Young); "Already One" (Young); "Field of Opportunity" (Young); "Motorcycle Mama" (Young); "Four Strong Winds" (Ian Tyson). 33-1/3 rpm phonodisc. Reprise MSK-2266, 1978. Reissued in 1988 on compact disc as Reprise 2–2266.

Rust Never Sleeps. Neil Young, Crazy Horse. Neil Young, vocals, acoustic and electric guitar, harmonica; Crazy Horse (Frank Sampedro, Billy Talbot, Ralph Molina); various assisting instrumentalists and vocalists. "My My, Hey Hey (Out of the Blue)" (Young, Jeff Blackburn); "Thrasher" (Young); "Ride My Llama" (Young); "Pocahontas" (Young); "Sail Away" (Young); "Powderfinger" (Young); "Welfare Mothers" (Young); "Sedan Delivery" (Young); "Hey Hey, My My (Into the Black)" (Young). 33-1/3 rpm phonodisc. Reprise HS-2295, 1979. Reissued in 1987 on compact disc as Reprise 2–2295.

Live Rust. Neil Young, Crazy Horse. Neil Young, vocals, acoustic and electric guitar, harmonica, keyboards; Crazy Horse (Frank Sampedro, Billy Talbot, Ralph Molina). "Sugar Mountain" (Young); "I Am a Child" (Young); "Comes a Time" (Young); "After the Gold Rush" (Young); "My My, Hey Hey (Out of the Blue)" (Young, Jeff Blackburn); "When You Dance I Can Really Love" (Young); "The Loner" (Young); "The Needle and the Damage Done" (Young); "Lotta Love" (Young); "Sedan Delivery" (Young); "Powderfinger" (Young); "Cortez the Killer" (Young); "Cinnamon Girl" (Young); "Like a Hurricane" (Young); "Hey Hey, My My (Into the Black)" (Young); "Tonight's the Night" (Young). 33-1/3 rpm phonodisc. Reprise 2RX-2296, 1979. Reissued in 1988 on compact disc as Reprise 2–2296.

Where the Buffalo Roam. Neil Young, vocals, acoustic and electric guitar, harmonica, piano. Includes recordings by other artists as noted. "Buffalo Stomp" (Young, David Blumberg); Ode to Wild Bill #1 (Young); "All Along the Watchtower (Bob Dylan) (Performed by Jimi Hendrix); "Lucy in the Sky with Diamonds" (John Lennon, Paul McCartney) (Performed by Bill Murray); "Ode to Wild Bill #2" (Young); "Papa Was a Rolling Stone" (Norman Whitfield, Barrett Strong) (Performed by the Temptations); "Home, Home on the Range" (Traditional); "Straight Answers" (Dialogue by Bill Murray); "Highway 61 Revisited' (Bob Dylan) (Performed by Bob Dylan); "I Can't Help Myself" (Brian Holland, Lamont Dozier, Eddie Holland, Jr.) (Performed by the Four Tops); "Ode to Wild Bill #3" (Young); "Keep on Chooglin'" (John Fogerty) (Performed by Creedence Clearwater Revival); "Ode to Wild Bill #4" (Young); "Purple Haze" (Jimi Hendrix) (Performed by Jimi Hendrix); "Buffalo Stomp Refrain" (Young, David Blumberg). 33-1/3 rpm phonodisc. Backstreet MCA 5126, 1980.

Hawks & Doves. Neil Young, vocals, acoustic and electric guitar, harmonica, piano; various assisting instrumentalists and vocalists. "Little Wing" (Young); "The Old Homestead" (Young); "Lost in Space" (Young); "Captain Kennedy" (Young); "Stayin' Power" (Young); "Coastline" (Young); "Union Man" (Young); "Comin' Apart at Every Nail" (Young); "Hawks & Doves" (Young). 33-1/3 rpm phonodisc. Reprise HS-2297, 1980. Reissued in 2003 on compact disc as Warner Bros. 48499.

Re*ac*tor. Neil Young, Crazy Horse. Neil Young, vocals, acoustic and electric guitar, harmonica; Crazy Horse (Frank Sampedro, Billy Talbot, Ralph Molina). "Opera Star" (Young); "Surfer Joe and Moe the Sleaze" (Young); "T-Bone" (Young); "Get Back on It" (Young); "Southern Pacific" (Young); "Motor City" (Young); "Rapid Transit" (Young); "Shots" (Young). 33-1/3 rpm phonodisc. Reprise HS-2304, 1981. Reissued in 2003 on compact disc as Warner Bros. 48498.

Trans. Neil Young, vocals, acoustic and electric guitar, harmonica; various assisting instrumentalists and vocalists. "Little Thing Called Love" (Young); "Computer Age" (Young); "We R in Control" (Young); "Transformer Man" (Young); "Computer Cowboy (AKA Syscrusher)" (Young); "Hold on To Your Love" (Young); "Sample and Hold" (Young); "Mr. Soul" (Young); "Like an Inca" (Young). 33-1/3 rpm phonodisc. Geffen 2018, 1982. Reissued in 2002 on compact disc as Geffen 02018.

Everybody's Rockin'. Neil Young, vocals, acoustic and electric guitar, harmonica, piano; various assisting instrumentalists and vocalists. "Betty Lou's Got a New Pair of Shoes" (Bobby Freeman); "Rainin' in My Heart" (James Isaac Moore, Jerry West); "Payola Blues" (Ben Keith, Young); "Wonderin'" (Young); "Kinda Fonda Wanda" (Tim Drummond, Young); "Jellyroll Man" (Young); "Bright Lights, Big City" (Jimmy Reed); "Cry, Cry, Cry" (Young); "Mystery Train" (Junior Parker, Sam Phillips); "Everybody's Rockin'" (Young). 33-1/3 rpm phonodisc. Geffen 4013, 1983. Reissued in 2000 on compact disc as Geffen 490706.

Old Ways. Neil Young, vocals, acoustic and electric guitar, harmonica; various assisting instrumentalists and vocalists. "The Wayward Wind" (Stan Lebowsky, Herbert Newman); "Get Back to the Country" (Young); "Are There Any More Real Cowboys?" (Young); "Once an Angel" (Young); "Misfits" (Young); "California Sunset" (Young); "Old Ways" (Young); "My Boy" (Young); "Bound for Glory" (Young); "Where Is the Highway Tonight?" (Young). 33-1/3 rpm phonodisc. Geffen GHS-24086, 1985. Reissued in 2000 on compact disc as Geffen 069 490 705-2.

Landing on Water. Neil Young, vocals, acoustic and electric guitar, harmonica, synthesizer; various assisting instrumentalists and vocalists. "Weight of the World" (Young); "Violent Side" (Young); "Hippie Dream" (Young); "Bad News Beat" (Young); "Touch the Night" (Young); "People on the Street" (Young); "Hard Luck Stories" (Young); "I Got a Problem" (Young); "Pressure" (Young); "Drifter" (Young). 33-1/3 rpm phonodisc. Geffen GHS-24109, 1986. Reissued in 2000 on compact disc as Geffen 490799.

Life. Neil Young and Crazy Horse. Neil Young, vocals, acoustic and electric guitar, harmonica, keyboards; Crazy Horse (Frank Sampedro, Billy Talbot, Ralph Molina). "Mideast Vacation" (Young); "Long Walk Home" (Young); "Around the World" (Young); "Inca Queen" (Young); "Too Lonely" (Young); "Prisoners of Rock 'n' Roll" (Young); "Cryin' Eyes" (Young); "When Your Lonely Heart Breaks" (Young); "We Never Danced" (Young). 33-1/3 rpm phonodisc. Geffen 2–24154, 1987. Reissued in 2000 on compact disc as Geffen 490798.

This Note's for You. Neil Young, vocals, acoustic and electric guitar; various assisting instrumentalists and vocalists. "Ten Men Workin'" (Young); "This Note's for

You" (Young); "Coupe de Ville" (Young); "Life in the City" (Young); "Twilight" (Young); "Married Man" (Young); "Sunny Inside" (Young); "Can't Believe Your Lyin'" (Young); "Hey Hey" (Young); "One Thing" (Young). Compact disc. Reprise 9 25719–2, 1988.

Freedom. Neil Young, vocals, guitar; various assisting instrumentalists and vocalists. "Rockin' in the Free World" (Young); "Crime in the City (Sixty to Zero Part I)" (Young); "Don't Cry" (Young); "Hangin' on a Limb" (Young); "Eldorado" (Young); "The Ways of Love" (Young); "Someday" (Young); "On Broadway" (Barry Mann, Cynthia Weil, Jerry Leiber, Mike Stoller); "Wrecking Ball" (Young); "No More" (Young); "Too Far Gone" (Young); "Rockin' in the Free World" (Young). Compact disc. Reprise 9 25899–2, 1989.

Ragged Glory. Neil Young and Crazy Horse. Neil Young, vocals, guitar; Crazy Horse (Frank "Poncho" Sampedro, Billy Talbot, Ralph Molina). "Country Home" (Young); "White Line" (Young); "F*!#in' Up" (Young); "Over and Over" (Young); "Love to Burn" (Young); "Farmer John" (Don Harris, Dewey Terry); "Mansion on the Hill" (Young); "Days That Used to Be" (Young); "Love and Only Love" (Young); "Mother Earth (Natural Anthem)" (Young). Compact disc. Reprise 9 26315–2, 1990.

Arc. Neil Young and Crazy Horse. Neil Young, vocals, guitar; Crazy Horse (Frank "Poncho" Sampedro, Billy Talbot, Ralph Molina). "Arc" (Young). Compact disc. Reprise 9 26769–2, 1991.

Weld. Neil Young and Crazy Horse. Neil Young, vocals, guitar; Crazy Horse (Frank "Poncho" Sampedro, Billy Talbot, Ralph Molina). "Hey Hey, My My (Into the Black)" (Young); "Crime in the City" (Young); "Blowin' in the Wind" (Bob Dylan); "Welfare Mothers" (Young); "Love to Burn" (Young); "Cinnamon Girl" (Young); "Mansion on the Hill" (Young); F*!#in' Up" (Young); "Cortez the Killer" (Young); "Powderfinger" (Young); "Love and Only Love" (Young); "Rockin' in the Free World" (Harris, Terry); "Like a Hurricane" (Young); "Farmer John" (Harris, Terry); "Tonight's the Night" (Young); "Roll Another Number (For the Road)" (Young). Two compact discs. Reprise 9 26671–2, 1991.

Harvest Moon. Neil Young, vocals, guitar, harmonica, piano; various assisting instrumentalists and vocalists. "Unknown Legend" (Young); "From Hank to Hendrix" (Young); "You and Me" (Young); "Harvest Moon" (Young); "War of Man" (Young); "One of These Days" (Young); "Such a Woman" (Young); "Old King" (Young); "Dreamin' Man" (Young); "Natural Beauty" (Young). Compact disc. Reprise 9 45057–2, 1992.

Unplugged. Neil Young, vocals, guitar, harmonica, piano; various assisting instrumentalists and vocalists. "The Old Laughing Lady" (Young); "Mr. Soul" (Young); "World on a String" (Young); "Pocahontas" (Young); "Stringman" (Young); "Like a Hurricane" (Young); "The Needle and the Damage Done" (Young); "Helpless" (Young); "Harvest Moon" (Young); "Transformer Man" (Young); "Unknown Legend" (Young); "Look Out for My Love" (Young); "Long May You Run" (Young); "From Hank to Hendrix" (Young). Compact disc. Reprise 9 45310, 1993.

Sleeps with Angels. Neil Young and Crazy Horse. Neil Young, vocals, guitar, tack piano; flute, accordion, harmonica; Crazy Horse (Frank "Poncho" Sampedro, Billy Talbot, Ralph Molina). "My Heart" (Young); "Prime of Life" (Young); "Driveby" (Young); "Sleeps with Angels" (Young); "Western Hero" (Young);

"Change Your Mind" (Young); "Blue Eden" (Young, Frank "Poncho" Sampe-dro, Billy Talbot, Ralph Molina); "Safeway Cart" (Young); "Train of Love" (Young); "Trans Am" (Young); "Piece of Crap" (Young); "A Dream that Can Last" (Young). Compact disc. Reprise 9 45749–2, 1994.

Mirror Ball. Neil Young, vocals, electric and acoustic guitars, pump organ; Jeff Ament, bass guitar; Stone Gossard, electric guitar; Mike McCready, electric guitar; Jack Irons, drums; Brendan O' Brien, background vocals, electric guitar, piano; Eddie Vedder, background vocals. "Song X" (Young); "Act of Love" (Young); "I'm the Ocean" (Young); "Big Green Country" (Young); "Truth Be Known" (Young); "Downtown" (Young); "What Happened Yesterday" (Young); "Peace and Love" (Young, Eddie Vedder); "Throw Your Hatred Down" (Young); "Scenery" (Young); "Fallen Angel" (Young). Compact disc. Reprise 9 45934–2, 1995.

Broken Arrow. Neil Young, Crazy Horse. Neil Young, vocals, guitar, harmonica; Crazy Horse (Frank "Poncho" Sampedro, Billy Talbot, Ralph Molina). "Big Time" (Young); "Loose Change" (Young); "Slip Away" (Young); "Changing Highways" (Young); "Scattered (Let's Think About Livin')" (Young); "This Town" (Young); "Music Arcade" (Young); "Baby What You Want Me to Do" (Jimmy Reed). Compact disc. Reprise 9 46291–2, 1996.

Dead Man: Music from and Inspired by the Motion Picture Dead Man. Neil Young, acoustic and electric guitar, pump organ. "Guitar Solo, No. 1" (Young); "The Round Stones Beneath the Earth…" (Dialogue); "Guitar Solo, No. 2" (Young); "Why Does Thou Hide Thyself, Clouds…" (Dialogue); "Organ Solo" (Young); "Do You Know How to Use This Weapon?" (Dialogue); "Guitar Solo, No. 3" (Young); "Nobody's Story" (Dialogue); "Guitar Solo, No. 4" (Young); "Stu-pid White Men" (Dialogue); "Guitar Solo, No. 5" (Young); "Time for You to Leave, William Blake…" (Dialogue); "Guitar Solo, No. 6" (Young). Compact disc. Vapor 46171, 1996.

Year of the Horse. Neil Young, Crazy Horse. Neil Young, vocals, acoustic and elec-tric guitar, harmonica; Crazy Horse (Frank "Poncho" Sampedro, Billy Talbot, Ralph Molina). "When You Dance" (Young); "Barstool Blues" (Young); "When Your Lonely Heart Breaks" (Young); "Mr. Soul" (Young); "Big Time" (Young); "Pocahontas" (Young); "Human Highway" (Young); "Slip Away" (Young); "Scattered" (Young); "Dangerbird" (Young); "Prisoners" (Young); "Sedan Delivery" (Young). Two compact discs. Reprise 9 46652–2, 1997.

Silver & Gold. Neil Young, vocals, guitar, harmonica, piano; various assisting instru-mentalists and vocalists. "Good to See You" (Young); "Silver & Gold" (Young); "Daddy Went Walkin'" (Young); "Buffalo Springfield Again" (Young); "The Great Divide" (Young); "Horseshoe Man" (Young); "Red Sun" (Young); "Dis-tant Camera" (Young); "Razor Love" (Young); "Without Rings" (Young). Compact disc. Reprise 9 47305–2, 2000.

Road Rock, Vol. 1: Friends and Relatives. Neil Young, vocals, guitar, harmonica, piano; various assisting instrumentalists and vocalists. "Cowgirl in the Sand" (Young); "Walk On" (Young); "Fool for Your Love" (Young); "Peace of Mind" (Young); "Words (Between the Lines of Age)" (Young); "Motorcycle Mama" (Young); "Tonight's the Night" (Young); "All Along the Watchtower" (Bob Dylan). Com-pact disc. Reprise 9 48036–2, 2000.

Are You Passionate? Neil Young, vocals, guitar, piano; various assisting instrumental-ists and vocalists. "You're My Girl" (Young); "Mr. Disappointment" (Young);

"Differently" (Young); "Quit (Don't Say You Love Me)" (Young); "Let's Roll" (Young); "Are You Passionate?" (Young); "Goin' Home" (Young); "When I Hold You in My Arms" (Young); "Be with You" (Young); "Two Old Friends" (Young); "She's a Healer" (Young). Compact disc. Reprise 9 48111-2, 2002.

Greendale. Neil Young, Crazy Horse. Neil Young, vocals, acoustic and electric guitar, harmonica; Crazy Horse (Billy Talbot, Ralph Molina). "Falling from Above" (Young); "Double E" (Young); "Devil's Sidewalk" (Young); "Leave the Driving" (Young); "Carmichael" (Young); "Bandit" (Young); "Grandpa's Interview" (Young); "Bringin' Down Dinner" (Young); "Sun Green" (Young); "Be the Rain" (Young). Compact disc. Reprise 48533-2, 2003. Includes a DVD of Young performing the album solo on stage at Vicar St., Dublin, Ireland.

Prairie Wind. Neil Young, vocals, acoustic and electric guitar, harmonica; various assisting instrumentalists and vocalists. "The Painter" (Young); "No Wonder" (Young); "Falling off the Face of the Earth" (Young); "Far From Home" (Young); "It's a Dream" (Young); "Prairie Wind" (Young); "Here for You" (Young); "This Old Guitar" (Young); "He Was the King" (Young); "When God Made Me" (Young). Compact disc. Reprise 49593-2, 2005.

Living with War. Neil Young, vocals, acoustic and electric guitar, harmonica; various assisting instrumentalists and vocalists. "After the Garden" (Young); "Living with War" (Young); "The Restless Consumer" (Young); "Shock and Awe" (Young); "Families" (Young); "Flags of Freedom" (Young); "Let's Impeach the President" (Young); "Lookin' for a Leader" (Young); "Roger and Out" (Young); "America the Beautiful" (arranged by Young). Compact disc. Reprise 44335-2, 2006.

Live at the Fillmore East. Neil Young with Crazy Horse. Neil Young, vocals, acoustic and electric guitar, harmonica, piano; Crazy Horse (Danny Whitten, guitar, vocals; Billy Talbot, bass guitar; Ralph Molina, drums, vocals). "Everybody Knows This Is Nowhere" (Young); "Winterlong" (Young); "Down by the River" (Young); "Wonderin'" (Young); "Come on Baby, Let's Go Downtown" (Danny Whitten); "Cowgirl in the Sand" (Young). Compact disc. Reprise 44429-2, 2006. Recorded March 6 and 7, 1970 at the Fillmore East, New York, New York.

Live at Massey Hall 1971. Neil Young, vocals, acoustic guitar, piano, harmonica. "On the Way Home" (Young); "Tell Me Why" (Young); "Old Man" (Young); "Journey through the Past" (Young); "Helpless" (Young); "Love in Mind" (Young); "A Man Needs a Maid/Heart of Gold Suite" (Young); "Cowgirl in the Sand" (Young); "Don't Let It Bring You Down" (Young); "There's a World" (Young); "Bad Fog of Loneliness" (Young); "The Needle and the Damage Done" (Young); "Ohio" (Young); "See the Sky about to Rain" (Young); "Down by the River" (Young); "Dance Dance Dance" (Young); "I Am a Child" (Young). Compact disc. Reprise 43328-2, 2007. Recorded January 19, 1971 during the second show at Massey Hall, Toronto, Ontario, Canada.

Chrome Dreams II. Neil Young, vocals, acoustic and electric guitar, banjo, harmonica, grand piano, pump organ, Hammond B-3 organ, vibes, percussion; various assisting instrumentalist and vocalists. "Beautiful Bluebird" (Young); "Boxcar" (Young); "Ordinary People" (Young); "Shining Light" (Young); "The Believer" (Young); "Spirit Road" (Young); "Dirty Old Man" (Young); "Ever

After" (Young); "No Hidden Path" (Young); "The Way" (Young). Compact disc. Reprise 311932–2, 2007.

THE COMPILATION ALBUMS OF NEIL YOUNG

Journey through the Past (Soundtrack). Crosby, Stills, Nash & Young, Buffalo Spring-field, Neil Young, Stray Gators, Tony and Susan Alamo Christian Foundation Orchestra & Chorus. Neil Young, vocals, acoustic and electric guitar, harmonica, piano; various assisting instrumentalists and vocalists. "For What It's Worth"/ "Mr. Soul" (Stephen Stills, Young); "Rock & Roll Woman" (Stephen Stills); "Find the Cost of Freedom" (Stephen Stills); "Ohio" (Young); "Southern Man" (Young); "Are You Ready for the Country" (Young); "Let Me Call You Sweet-heart" (Leo Friedman, Slater Whitson); "Alabama" (Young); "Words" (Young); "Relativity Invitation"; "Handel's Messiah" (Handel); "The 'King of Kings' Theme" (Miklos Rozsa); "Soldier" (Young); "Let's Go Away for Awhile" (Brian Wilson). Two 33-1/3 rpm phonodiscs. Reprise 2XS 6480, 1972.

Decade. Neil Young, vocals, acoustic and electric guitar, harmonica, piano; Buf-falo Springfield; Crazy Horse; Crosby, Stills, Nash and Young; Stray Gators; various assisting instrumentalists and vocalists. "Down to the Wire" (Young); "Burned" (Young); "Mr. Soul" (Young); "Broken Arrow" (Young); "Expect-ing to Fly" (Young); "Sugar Mountain" (Young); "I Am a Child" (Young); "The Loner" (Young); "The Old Laughing Lady" (Young); "Cinnamon Girl" (Young); "Down by the River" (Young); "Cowgirl in the Sand" (Young); "I Believe in You" (Young); "After the Gold Rush" (Young); "Southern Man" (Young); "Helpless" (Young); "Ohio" (Young); "Soldier" (Young); "Old Man" (Young); "A Man Needs a Maid" (Young); "Harvest" (Young); "Heart of Gold" (Young); "Star of Bethlehem" (Young); "The Needle and the Dam-age Done" (Young); "Tonight's the Night" (Part 1) (Young); "Tired Eyes" (Young); "Walk On" (Young); "For the Turnstiles" (Young); "Winterlong" (Young); "Deep Forbidden Lake" (Young); "Like a Hurricane" (Young); "Love Is a Rose" (Young); "Cortez the Killer" (Young); "Campaigner" (Young); "Long May You Run" (Young). Three 33-1/3 rpm phonodiscs. Reprise 3RS 2257, 1976.

Lucky Thirteen: Excursions into Alien Territory. Neil Young, vocals, acoustic and elec-tric guitar, harmonica, piano; various assisting instrumentalists and vocal-ists. "Sample and Hold" (Young); "Transformer Man" (Young); "Depression Blues" (Young); "Get Gone" (Young); "Don't Take Your Love Away from Me" (Young); "Once an Angel" (Young); "Where Is the Highway Tonight?" (Young); "Hippie Dream" (Young); "Pressure" (Young); "Around the World" (Young); "Mideast Vacation" (Young); "Ain't It the Truth" (Young); "This Note's for You" (Young). Compact disc. Geffen 24452, 1993.

Mystery Train. Neil Young, vocals, acoustic and electric guitar, harmonica, piano, various assisting instrumentalists and vocalists. "Everybody's Rockin'" (Young); "Little Thing Called Love" (Young); "Mystery Train" (Junior Parker, Sam Phil-lips); "Around the World" (Young); "California Sunset" (Young); "Like an Inca" (Young); "My Boy" (Young); "Old Ways" (Young); "Once an Angel" (Young); "Rainin' in My Heart" (James Isaac Moore, Jerry West); "Transformer Man" (Young); "Bright Lights, Big City" (Jimmy Reed); "Bound for Glory"

(Young); "Betty Lou's Got a New Pair of Shoes" (Bobby Freeman). Compact disc. Universal International 493014, 2001.

Greatest Hits. Neil Young, vocals, acoustic and electric guitar, harmonica, piano; various assisting instrumentalists and vocalists. "Down by the River" (Young); "Cowgirl in the Sand" (Young); "Cinnamon Girl" (Young); "Helpless" (Young); "After the Gold Rush" (Young); "Only Love Can Break Your Heart" (Young); "Southern Man" (Young); "Ohio" (Young); "The Needle and the Damage Done" (Young); "Old Man" (Young); "Heart of Gold" (Young); "Like a Hurricane" (Young); "Comes a Time" (Young); "Hey Hey, My My (Into the Black)" (Young, Jeff Blackburn); "Rockin' in the Free World" (Young); "Harvest Moon" (Young). Compact disc. Reprise 48935–2, 2004.

ALBUMS WITH BUFFALO SPRINGFIELD AND CROSBY, STILLS, NASH, AND YOUNG

Buffalo Springfield. Buffalo Springfield. Neil Young (vocals, guitar, piano), Stephen Stills (vocals, guitar), Richie Furay (vocals, guitar), Bruce Palmer (bass guitar), Dewey Martin (drums). "For What It's Worth" (Stephen Stills); "Go and Say Goodbye" (Stephen Stills); "Sit Down I Think I Love You" (Stephen Stills); "Nowadays Clancy Can't Even Sing" (Young); "Hot Dusty Roads" (Stephen Stills); "Everybody's Wrong" (Stephen Stills); "Flying on the Ground Is Wrong" (Young); "Burned" (Young); "Do I Have to Come Right Out and Say It" (Young); "Leave" (Stephen Stills); "Out of My Mind" (Young); "Pay the Price" (Stephen Stills). 33-1/3 rpm phonodisc. ATCO 33–200-A, 1966. Originally issued as ATCO 33–200 which included "Baby Don't Scold Me" (Stephen Stills). The track was replaced by "For What It's Worth" on ATCO 33–200-A. Reissued in 1997 on compact disc as Elektra 62080–2. The reissue includes both the mono and stereo mixes of the album and both "Baby Don't Scold Me" and "For What It's Worth."

Again. Buffalo Springfield. Neil Young (vocals, guitar), Stephen Stills (vocals, guitar, keyboards), Richie Furay (vocals, guitar), Bruce Palmer (bass guitar), Dewey Martin (vocals, drums); various assisting instrumentalists. "Mr. Soul" (Young); "A Child's Claim to Fame" (Richie Furay); "Everydays" (Stephen Stills); "Expecting to Fly" (Young); "Bluebird" (Stephen Stills); "Hung Upside Down" (Stephen Stills); "Sad Memory" (Richie Furay); "Good Time Boy" (Richie Furay); "Rock & Roll Woman" (Stephen Stills); "Broken Arrow" (Young). 33-1/3 rpm phonodisc. ATCO SD 33–226, 1967.

Last Time Around. Buffalo Springfield. Neil Young (vocals, guitar, harmonica), Stephen Stills (vocals, guitar, keyboards), Richie Furay (vocals, guitar, keyboards), Jim Messina (bass guitar), Dewey Martin (vocals, drums); various assisting instrumentalists. "On the Way Home" (Young); "It's So Hard to Wait" (Richie Furay, Young); "Pretty Girl Why" (Stephen Stills); "Four Days Gone" (Stephen Stills); "Carefree Country Day" (Jim Messina); "Special Care" (Stephen Stills); "In the Hour of Not Quite Rain" (Richie Furay, Mickeala Callen); "Questions" (Stephen Stills); "I Am a Child" (Young); "Merry-Go-Round" (Richie Furay); "Uno Mundo" (Stephen Stills); "Kind Woman" (Richie Furay). 33-1/3 rpm phonodisc. ATCO SD 33–256, 1968.

Retrospective. Buffalo Springfield. Neil Young (vocals, guitar, harmonica), Stephen Stills (vocals, guitar, keyboards), Richie Furay (vocals, guitar, keyboards), Bruce Palmer (bass guitar); Jim Messina (bass guitar), Dewey Martin (vocals, drums); various assisting instrumentalists. "For What It's Worth" (Stephen Stills); "Mr. Soul" (Young); "Sit Down I Think I Love You" (Stephen Stills); "Kind Woman" (Richie Furay); "Bluebird" (Stephen Stills); "On the Way Home" (Young); "Nowadays Clancy Can't Even Sing" (Young); "Broken Arrow" (Young); "Rock & Roll Woman" (Stephen Stills); "I Am a Child" (Young); "Go and Say Goodbye" (Stephen Stills); "Expecting to Fly" (Young). 33-1/3 rpm phonodisc. ATCO 33–283, 1969. Consists of previously released material.

Déjà vu. Crosby, Stills, Nash & Young; various assisting instrumentalists. "Carry On" (Stephen Stills); "Teach Your Children" (Graham Nash); "Almost Cut My Hair" (David Crosby); "Helpless" (Young); "Woodstock" (Joni Mitchell); "Déjà vu" (David Crosby); "Our House" (Graham Nash); "4 + 20" (Stephen Stills); "Country Girl (1. Whiskey Boot Hill; 2. Down, Down, Down; 3. Country Girl [I Think You're Pretty])" (Young); "Everybody I Love You" (Stephen Stills, Young). 33-1/3 rpm phonodisc. Atlantic SD 7200, 1970.

4 Way Street. Crosby, Stills, Nash & Young; various assisting instrumentalists. "Suite: Judy Blue Eyes" (Stephen Stills); "On the Way Home" (Young); "Teach Your Children" (Graham Nash); "Triad" (David Crosby); "The Lee Shore" (David Crosby); "Chicago" (Graham Nash); "Right Between the Eyes" (Graham Nash); "Cowgirl in the Sand" (Young); "Don't Let It Bring You Down" (Young); "49 Bye Byes"/"America's Children" (Stephen Stills); "Love the One You're With" (Stephen Stills); "Pre-Road Downs" (Graham Nash); "Long Time Gone" (David Crosby); "Southern Man" (Young); "Ohio" (Young); "Carry On" (Stephen Stills); "Find the Cost of Freedom" (Stephen Stills). Two 33-1/3 rpm phonodiscs. Atlantic SD 2–902, 1971. Reissued in 1992 on compact disc as Atlantic 82408. The reissue adds: "King Midas in Reverse" (Allan Clarke, Tony Hicks, Graham Nash); "Laughing" (David Crosby); "Black Queen" (Stephen Stills); and "Medley: 'The Loner'/'Cinnamon Girl'/'Down by the River'" (Young).

Buffalo Springfield: Neil Young, Stephen Stills, Richie Furay, Jim Messina, Bruce Palmer, Dewey Martin. Buffalo Springfield. Neil Young (vocals, guitar, piano), Stephen Stills (vocals, guitar, keyboards), Richie Furay (vocals, guitar, keyboards), Bruce Palmer (bass guitar), Jim Messina (bass guitar), Dewey Martin (drums). "For What It's Worth" (Stephen Stills); "Sit Down I Think I Love You" (Stephen Stills); "Nowadays Clancy Can't Even Sing" (Young); "Go and Say Goodbye" (Stephen Stills); "Pay the Price" (Stephen Stills) "Burned" (Young); "Out of My Mind" (Young); "Mr. Soul" (Young); "Bluebird" (Stephen Stills); "Broken Arrow" (Young); "Rock & Roll Woman" (Stephen Stills); "Expecting to Fly" (Young); "Hung Upside Down" (Stephen Stills); "A Child's Claim to Fame (Richie Furay); "Kind Woman" (Richie Furay); "On the Way Home" (Young); "I Am a Child" (Young); "Pretty Girl Why" (Stephen Stills); "Special Care" (Stephen Stills); "Uno Mundo" (Stephen Stills); "In the Hour of Not Quite Rain" (Richie Furay, Mickeala Callen); "Four Days Gone" (Stephen Stills); "Questions" (Stephen Stills). Two 33-1/3 rpm phonodiscs. ATCO SD 2–806, 1973. All tracks are previously released except for the 9-minute version of "Bluebird."

So Far. Crosby, Stills, Nash & Young; various assisting instrumentalists. "Déjà vu" (David Crosby); "Helplessly Hoping" (Stephen Stills); "Wooden Ships" (Stephen

Stills, David Crosby); "Teach Your Children" (Graham Nash); "Ohio" (Young); "Find the Cost of Freedom (Stephen Stills); "Woodstock" (Joni Mitchell); "Our House" (Graham Nash); "Helpless" (Young); "Guinnevere" (David Crosby); "Suite: Judy Blue Eyes" (Stephen Stills). 33-1/3 rpm phonodisc. Atlantic SD 19119, 1974. Consists of previously released material.

American Dream. Crosby, Stills, Nash & Young; various assisting instrumentalists and vocalists. "American Dream" (Young); "Got It Made" (Stephen Stills); "Name of Love" (Young); "Don't Say Goodbye" (Graham Nash, Joe Vitale); "This Old House" (Young); "Nighttime for Generals" (David Crosby, Craig Doerge); "Shadowland" (Rick Ryan, Graham Nash, Joe Vitale); "Drivin' Thunder" (Stephen Stills, Young); "Clear Blue Skies" (Graham Nash); "That Girl" (Stephen Stills, Joe Vitale, Bob Glaub); "Compass" (David Crosby); "Soldiers of Peace" (Graham Nash, Craig Doerge, Joe Vitale); "Feel Your Love" (Young); "Night Song" (Stephen Stills, Young). 33-1/3 rpm phonodisc. Atlantic 7–81888–1, 1988.

CSN (Box Set). Crosby, Stills & Nash, various assisting instrumentalists and vocalists. "Suite: Judy Blue Eyes" (Stephen Stills); "Helplessly Hoping" (Stephen Stills); "You Don't Have to Cry" (Stephen Stills); "Wooden Ships" (David Crosby, Paul Kantner, Stephen Stills); "Guinnevere" (David Crosby); "Marrakesh Express" (Graham Nash); "Long Time Gone" (David Crosby); "Blackbird" (John Lennon, Paul McCartney); "Lady of the Island" (Graham Nash); "Song with No Words (Tree with No Leaves)" (David Crosby); "Almost Cut My Hair" (David Crosby); "Teach Your Children" (Graham Nash); "Horses through a Rainstorm" (Graham Nash, Terry Reid); "Déjà vu" (David Crosby); "Helpless" (Young); "4 + 20" (Stephen Stills); "Laughing" (David Crosby); "Carry On"/"Questions" (Stephen Stills); "Woodstock" (Joni Mitchell); "Ohio" (Young); "Love the One You're With" (Stephen Stills); "Our House" (Graham Nash); "Old Times Good Times" (Stephen Stills); "The Lee Shore" (David Crosby); "Music Is Love" (David Crosby, Graham Nash, Young); "I'd Swear There Was Somebody Here" (David Crosby); "Man in the Mirror" (Graham Nash); "Black Queen" (Stephen Stills); "Military Madness" (Graham Nash); "Urge for Going" (Joni Mitchell); "I Used to Be a King" (Graham Nash); "Simple Man" (Graham Nash); "Southbound Train" (Graham Nash); "Change Partners" (Stephen Stills); "My Love Is a Gentle Thing" (Stephen Stills); "Word Game" (Stephen Stills); "Johnny's Garden" (Stephen Stills); "So Begins the Task" (Stephen Stills); "Turn Back the Pages" (Donnie Dacus, Stephen Stills); "See the Changes" (Stephen Stills); "It Doesn't Matter" (Chris Hillman, Stephen Stills); "Immigration Man" (Graham Nash); "Chicago"/"We Can Change the World" (Graham Nash); "Homeward through the Haze" (David Crosby); "Where Will I Be?" (David Crosby); "Page 43" (David Crosby); "Carry Me" (David Crosby); "Cowboy of Dreams" (Graham Nash); "Bittersweet" (Graham Nash); "To the Last Whale … (A. Critical Mass B. Wind on the Water)" (David Crosby, Graham Nash); "Critical Mass" (David Crosby); "Wind on the Water" (Graham Nash); "Prison Song" (Graham Nash); "Another Sleep Song" (Graham Nash); "Taken at All" (David Crosby, Graham Nash); "In My Dreams" (David Crosby); "Just a Song Before I Go" (Graham Nash); "Shadow Captain" (David Crosby, Craig Doerge); "Dark Star" (Stephen Stills); "Cathedral" (Graham Nash); "Wasted on the Way" (Graham Nash); "Barrel of Pain (Half-Life)" (Graham Nash); "Southern Cross" (Rick Curtis, Michael Curtis, Stephen Stills); "Daylight Again" (Stephen Stills); "Thoroughfare

Gap" (Stephen Stills); "Wild Tales" (live) (Graham Nash); "Dear Mr. Fantasy" (Jim Capaldi, Steve Winwood, Chris Wood); "Cold Rain" (Graham Nash); "Got It Made" (Stephen Stills, Young); "Tracks in the Dust" (David Crosby); "As I Come of Age" (Stephen Stills); "50/50" (Joe Lala, Stephen Stills); "Drive My Car" (David Crosby); "Delta" (David Crosby); "Soldiers of Peace" (Craig Doerge, Graham Nash, Joe Vitale); "Yours and Mine" (David Crosby, Craig Doerge, Graham Nash); "Haven't We Lost Enough?" (Kevin Cronin, Stephen Stills); "After the Dolphin" (Craig Doerge, Graham Nash); "Find the Cost of Freedom" (Stephen Stills). Four compact discs. Atlantic 82319-2, 1991. Includes previously released material plus unissued recordings and alternate takes. Though Young does not receive an author credit for the collection, he is represented as composer and performer on a significant number of tracks.

Buffalo Springfield Box Set. Buffalo Springfield. Neil Young (vocals, guitar, piano), Stephen Stills (vocals, guitar, keyboards), Richie Furay (vocals, guitar, keyboards), Bruce Palmer (bass guitar), Jim Messina (bass guitar), Dewey Martin (drums). "There Goes My Babe" (demo) (Young); "Come On" (demo) (Stephen Stills); "Hello, I've Returned" (demo) (Stephen Stills, Van Dyke Parks); "Out of My Mind" (demo) (Young); "Flying on the Ground Is Wrong" (demo) (Young); "I'm Your Kind of Guy" (demo) (Young); "Baby Don't Scold Me" (demo) (Stephen Stills); "Neighbor Don't You Worry" (demo) (Stephen Stills); "We'll See" (demo) (Stephen Stills); "Sad Memory" (demo) (Richie Furay); "Can't Keep Me Down" (demo) (Richie Furay); "Nowadays Clancy Can't Even Sing" (Young); "Go and Say Goodbye" (Stephen Stills); "Sit Down I Think I Love You" (Stephen Stills); "Leave" (Stephen Stills); "Hot Dusty Roads" (Stephen Stills); "Everybody's Wrong" (Stephen Stills); "Burned" (Young); "Do I Have To Come Right Out and Say It" (Young); "Out of My Mind" (Young); "Pay the Price" (Stephen Stills) "Down Down Down" (demo) (Young); "Flying on the Ground Is Wrong" (Young); "Neighbor Don't You Worry" (remix) (Stephen Stills); "Down Down Down" (remix) (Young); "Kahuna Sunset" (Stephen Stills, Young); "Buffalo Stomp (Raga) (Richie Furay, Bruce Kunkel, Dewey Martin, Stephen Stills, Young); "Baby Don't Scold Me" (Stephen Stills); "For What It's Worth" (Stephen Stills); "Mr. Soul" (Young); "We'll See" (Stephen Stills); "My Kind of Love" (Richie Furay); "Pretty Girl Why" (previously unreleased mix) (Stephen Stills); "Words I Must Say" (demo) (Richie Furay); "Nobody's Fool" (demo) (Richie Furay); "So You've Got a Lover" (demo) (Stephen Stills); "My Angel" (demo) (Stephen Stills); "No Sun Today" (Eric Eisner); "Everydays" (Stephen Stills); "Down to the Wire" (Young); "Bluebird" (Stephen Stills); "Expecting to Fly" (Young); "Hung Upside Down" (demo) (Stephen Stills); "A Child's Claim to Fame (Richie Furay); "Rock & Roll Woman" (Stephen Stills); "Hung Upside Down" (Stephen Stills); "Good Time Boy" (Richie Furay); "One More Sign" (demo) (Young); "The Rent Is Always Due" (demo) (Young); "Round and Round and Round" (demo) (Young); "Old Laughing Lady" (demo) (Young); "Broken Arrow" (Young); "Sad Memory" (Richie Furay); "On the Way Home" (previously unreleased mix) (Young); "Whatever Happened to Saturday Night?" (Young); "Special Care" (Stephen Stills); "Falcon Lake (Ash on the Floor)" (remix) (Young); "What a Day" (Richie Furay); "I Am a Child" (Young); "Questions" (Stephen Stills); "Merry-Go-Round" (Richie Furay); "Uno Mundo" (Stephen Stills); "Kind Woman" (Richie Furay) "It's So Hard to Wait" (Richie Furay, Young); "Four Days Gone" (demo) (Stephen Stills);

"For What It's Worth" (Stephen Stills); "Go and Say Goodbye" (Stephen Stills); "Sit Down I Think I Love You" (Stephen Stills); "Nowadays Clancy Can't Even Sing" (Young); "Hot Dusty Roads" (Stephen Stills); "Everybody's Wrong" (Stephen Stills); "Flying on the Ground Is Wrong" (Young); "Burned" (Young); "Do I Have to Come Right Out and Say It" (Young); "Leave" (Stephen Stills); "Out of My Mind" (Young); "Pay the Price" (Stephen Stills) "Baby Don't Scold Me" (Stephen Stills); "Mr. Soul" (Young); "A Child's Claim to Fame" (Richie Furay); "Everydays" (Stephen Stills); "Expecting to Fly" (Young); "Bluebird" (Stephen Stills); "Hung Upside Down" (Stephen Stills); "Sad Memory" (Richie Furay); "Good Time Boy" (Richie Furay); "Rock & Roll Woman" (Stephen Stills); "Broken Arrow" (Young). Four compact discs. Rhino 74234, 2001. Includes unreleased and previously-issued tracks. Disc 4 consists of the debut *Buffalo Springfield* album in mono and the *Again* album in stereo. Both are in the original sequence except that both "For What It's Worth" and "Baby Don't Scold Me" are included on the debut album.

Looking Forward. Crosby, Stills, Nash & Young, various assisting instrumentalists and vocalists. "Faith in Me" (Stephen Stills, Joe Vitale); "Looking Forward" (Young); "Stand and Be Counted" (David Crosby, James Raymond); "Heartland" (Graham Nash); "Seen Enough" (Stephen Stills); "Slowpoke" (Young); "Dream for Him" (David Crosby); "No Tears Left" (Stephen Stills); "Out of Control" (Young); "Someday Soon" (Graham Nash); "Queen of Them All" (Young); "Sanibel" (Denny Sarokin). Compact disc. Reprise 47436, 1999.

THE SINGLES OF NEIL YOUNG, BUFFALO SPRINGFIELD, CROSBY, STILLS, NASH, AND YOUNG, AND THE STILLS-YOUNG BAND

Buffalo Springfield

"Nowadays Clancy Can't Even Sing" (Young); "Go and Say Goodbye" (Stephen Stills). 45 rpm phonodisc. Atco 6428, 1966.

"Burned" (Young); "Everybody's Wrong" (Stephen Stills). 45 rpm phonodisc. Atco 6452, 1966.

"For What It's Worth" (Stephen Stills); "Do I Have to Come Right Out and Say It" (Young). 45 rpm phonodisc. Atco 6459, 1967.

"Bluebird" (Stephen Stills); "Mr. Soul" (Young). 45 rpm phonodisc. Atco 6499, 1967.

"Expecting to Fly" (Young); "Everydays" (Stephen Stills). 45 rpm phonodisc. Atco 6545, 1967.

"On the Way Home" (Young); "Four Days Gone" (Stephen Stills). 45 rpm phonodisc. Atco 6615, 1968.

Crosby, Stills, Nash, and Young

"Woodstock" (Joni Mitchell); "Helpless" (Young). 45 rpm phonodisc. Atlantic 45–2723, 1970.

"Teach Your Children" (Graham Nash); "Country Girl" (Young). 45 rpm phonodisc. Atlantic 2735, 1970.

"Ohio" (Young); "Find the Cost of Freedom" (Stephen Stills). 45 rpm phonodisc. Atlantic 45–2740, 1970.

"American Dream" (Young); "Compass" (David Crosby). 45 rpm phonodisc. Atlantic 89003, 1988.

"Got It Made" (Stephen Stills); "This Old House" (Young). 45 rpm phonodisc. Atlantic 88966, 1989.

The Stills-Young Band

"Long May You Run" (Young); "12/8 Blues (All the Same)" (Stephen Stills). 45 rpm phonodisc. Reprise 1365, 1976.

"Midnight on the Bay" (Young); "Black Coral" (Stephen Stills). 45 rpm phonodisc. Reprise 1378, 1976.

Neil Young

"The Loner" (Young); "Sugar Mountain" (Live) (Young). 45 rpm phonodisc. Reprise 0785, 1968.

"Everybody Knows This Is Nowhere" (Young); "Emperor of Wyoming" (Young). 45 rpm phonodisc. Reprise 0819, 1969. Some pressings have a solo acoustic version of "Everybody Knows This Is Nowhere" on the A side.

"Down by the River" (Young); "The Losing End" (Young). 45 rpm phonodisc. Reprise 0836, 1969.

"Oh, Lonesome Me" (Don Gibson); "Sugar Mountain" (Live) (Young). 45 rpm phonodisc. Reprise 0861, 1970. "Oh, Lonesome Me" was recorded with Crazy Horse.

"Oh, Lonesome Me" (Don Gibson); "I've Been Waiting for You" (Young). 45 rpm phonodisc. Reprise 0898, 1970.

"Cinnamon Girl" (Young); "Sugar Mountain" (Live) (Young). 45 rpm phonodisc. Reprise 0911, 1970. Crazy Horse accompanies Young on "Cinnamon Girl."

"Only Love Can Break Your Heart" (Young); "Birds" (Young). 45 rpm phonodisc. Reprise 0958, 1970.

"When You Dance, I Can Really Love" (Young); "Sugar Mountain" (Live) (Young). 45 rpm phonodisc. Reprise 0992, 1971.

"Heart of Gold" (Young); "Sugar Mountain" (Live) (Young). 45 rpm phonodisc. Reprise 1065, 1972.

"Old Man" (Young); "The Needle and the Damage Done" (Young). 45 rpm phonodisc. Reprise 1084, 1972.

"Time Fades Away" (Young); "Last Trip to Tulsa" (Live) (Young). 45 rpm phonodisc. Reprise 1184, 1973.

"Walk On" (Young); "For the Turnstiles" (Young). 45 rpm phonodisc. Reprise 1209, 1974.

"Lookin' for a Love" (Young); "Sugar Mountain" (Live) (Young). 45 rpm phonodisc. Reprise 1344, 1975.

"Drive Back" (Young); "Stupid Girl" (Young). 45 rpm phonodisc. Reprise 1350, 1976.

"Hey Babe" (Young); "Homegrown" (Young). 45 rpm phonodisc. Reprise 1390, 1977.

"Like a Hurricane" (Young); "Hold Back the Tears" (Young). 45 rpm phonodisc. Reprise 1391, 1977.

"Sugar Mountain" (Live) (Young); "The Needle and the Damage Done" (Young). 45 rpm phonodisc. Reprise 1393, 1977.

"Comes a Time" (Young); "Motorcycle Mama" (Young). 45 rpm phonodisc. Reprise 1395, 1978.

"Four Strong Winds" (Ian Tyson); "Human Highway" (Young). 45 rpm phonodisc. Reprise 1396, 1978.

"Hey Hey, My My (Into the Black)" (Young); "My My, Hey Hey (Out of the Blue)" (Young, Jeff Blackburn). 45 rpm phonodisc. Reprise 49031, 1979.

"The Loner" (live) (Young); "Cinnamon Girl" (live) (Young). 45 rpm phonodisc. Reprise 49189, 1979.

"Buffalo Stomp-Ode to Wild Bill" (Young); "Soundtrack Dialogue" (Bill Murray). 45 rpm phonodisc. Backstreet/MCA 1878, 1980.

"Hawks and Doves" (Young); "Union Man" (Young). 45 rpm phonodisc. Reprise 49555, 1980.

"Stayin' Power" (Young); "Captain Kennedy" (Young). 45 rpm phonodisc. Reprise 49641, 1981.

"Southern Pacific" (Young); "Motor City" (Young). 45 rpm phonodisc. Reprise 49870, 1981.

"Opera Star" (Young); "Surfer Joe and Moe the Sleaze" (Young). 45 rpm phonodisc. Reprise 50014, 1982.

"Little Thing Called Love" (Young); "We R in Control" (Young). 45 rpm phonodisc. Geffen 7–29887, 1982.

"Sample and Hold" (Young) (extended); "Mr. Soul" (extended) (Young); "Sample and Hold" (Young). 12-inch single. Geffen 20105, 1983.

"Mr. Soul, Part 1" (Young); "Mr. Soul, Part 2" (Young). 45 rpm phonodisc. Geffen 7–29707, 1983.

"Wonderin'" (Young); "Payola Blues" (Young). 45 rpm phonodisc. Geffen 7–29474, 1983.

"Cry, Cry, Cry" (Young); "Payola Blues" (Young). 45 rpm phonodisc. Geffen 7–29433, 1983.

"Get Back To the Country" (Young); "Misfits" (Young). 45 rpm phonodisc. Geffen 7–28883, 1985.

"Old Ways" (Young); "Once an Angel" (Young). 45 rpm phonodisc. Geffen 7–28753, 1985.

"Weight of the World" (Young); "Pressure" (Young). 45 rpm phonodisc. Geffen 7–28623, 1986.

"Mideast Vacation" (Young); "Long Walk Home" (Young). 45 rpm phonodisc. Geffen 7–28196, 1987.

"Long Walk Home" (Young); "Cryin' Eyes" (Young). 45 rpm phonodisc. Geffen GEF 25, 1987

"Ten Men Workin'" (Young); "I'm Goin'" (Young). 45 rpm phonodisc. Reprise 7–27908, 1988.

"This Note's for You" (Live) (Young); "This Note's for You" (Young). 45 rpm phonodisc. Reprise 7–27848, 1988.

"Rockin' in the Free World" (Young); "Rockin' in the Free World" (Live) (Young).
45 rpm phonodisc. Reprise 7–22776, 1989.

"Eldorado" (Young); "Cocaine Eyes" (Young); "Don't Cry" (Young); "Heavy Love"
(Young); "On Broadway" (Young). Compact Disc Maxi Single. Reprise 2 OP2–
2651, 1989. Import. "Cocaine Eyes" and "Heavy Love" have not been issued
in the United States to date. "Don't Cry" is a different version than the track
on the *Freedom* album.

"Mansion on the Hill" (single edit) (Young); "Mansion on the Hill" (album edit)
(Young); "Don't Spook the Horse" (Young). Compact Disc Maxi Single.
Reprise 7599–21759–2, 1990.

"Over and Over" (Young); "Don't Spook the Horse" (Young). Audio Cassette. Warner Bros. 7599–19483–4, 1991.

"Harvest Moon" (Young); "Old King" (Young). Compact Disc Maxi Single. Reprise
18685–2, 1992.

"Long May You Run" (*Unplugged* version) (Young); "Sugar Mountain" (*Live Rust*
version) (Young); "Cortez the Killer" (*Rust Never Sleeps* soundtrack version)
(Young); "Cinnamon Girl" (*Rust Never Sleeps* soundtrack version) (Young).
Compact Disc Maxi Single. Reprise 41117–2, 1993. Import.

"Philadelphia" (motion picture soundtrack version) (Young); "Such a Woman"
(Young); "Stringman" (Young); (Young). Compact Disc Maxi Single. Reprise
41518–2, 1994. Import.

"My Heart" (Young); "Tired Eyes" (Young); "Roll Another Number" (Young).
Compact Disc Maxi Single. Reprise WO 266, 1994. Import.

"Piece of Crap" (Young); "Tonight's the Night Part 1" (Young); "Tonight's the Night
Part 2" (Young). Compact Disc Maxi Single. Reprise WO 261, 1994. Import.

"Downtown" (single edit) (Young); "Downtown" (album edit) (Young); "Big Green
Country" (Young). Compact Disc Maxi Single. Reprise 43588, 1995.

"Peace and Love" (single edit) (Young, Eddie Vedder); "Peace and Love" (Young,
Eddie Vedder); "Safeway Cart" (Young). Compact Disc Maxi Single. Reprise
9362–43608–2, 1995.

"Big Time" (album edit) (Young); "Big Time" (single edit) (Young); "Interstate"
(Young). Compact Disc Maxi Single. Reprise 43731–2, 1996. Import.

"Rockin' in the Free World" (Edit Mix) (Young); "Rockin' in the Free World" (Live
Freedom version) (Young); "Rockin' in the Free World" (*Weld* version) (Young).
Compact Disc Maxi Single. Warner Bros. 16197, 2004. The song appears on the
soundtrack of Michael Moore's documentary *Fahrenheit 9/11*. The maxi-single
was released in conjunction with the film.

OTHER RECORDED PERFORMANCES BY NEIL YOUNG

"The Sultan" (Young); "Aurora" (Young). The Squires. Young, guitar. 45 rpm phonodisc. V Records V 109, 1963. Young was part of the teenage Winnipeg group.
The two instrumental sides are his first recordings. The disc was only issued
regionally.

"It's My Time" (Ricky James Matthews, Young); "Go on and Cry." The Mynah Birds.
Young, guitar. In *The Complete Motown Singles Volume 6: 1966*. Five compact

discs. Hip-O Select, 2006. Young was the lead guitar player for the mostly Canadian group. They recorded a number of sides at Motown's Hitsville USA studios in Detroit. None were released at the time as lead singer Ricky James Matthews (aka Rick James) was arrested for being AWOL. "It's My Time" is a bouncy, folk-rock song reminiscent of the Los Angeles-based combo Love.

"Sea of Madness" (Young). Crosby, Stills, Nash and Young. Young, lead vocal, organ. In *Woodstock*. Three 33-1/3 rpm phonodiscs. Cotillion SD3–500, 1970. Recorded on August 18, 1969, Young is accompanied by David Crosby (vocals, guitar), Stephen Stills (vocals, guitar), Graham Nash (vocals), Dallas Taylor (drums) and Greg Reeves (bass guitar). Young provides organ accompaniment on Crosby, Stills and Nash's "Wooden Ships" (David Crosby, Stephen Stills).

"War Song" (Young). Neil Young with Graham Nash. Neil Young, vocals, electric guitar; various assisting instrumentalists and vocalists. In *Hard Goods*. Two 33-1/3 rpm phonodiscs. Warner Bros. PRO-583, 1974. Recorded and initially released as a 45 rpm single (Reprise 1099) in 1972 with "The Needle and the Damage Done" on the flip side.

"Helpless" (Young). Neil Young, vocals, guitar, harmonica; various assisting instrumentalists and vocalists. In *The Last Waltz*. Three compact discs. Rhino R2 78278, 2002. Originally issued as Warner Bros. 3WS-346, 1978. Young considered it to be "one of the pleasures of (his) life" to be on stage with the Band and their friends for the group's farewell performance on Thanksgiving 1976. Young's compatriot Joni Mitchell added background vocals while she was seated backstage.

"Four Strong Winds" (Ian Tyson). Neil Young, vocals, guitar, harmonica; various assisting instrumentalists and vocalists. In *The Last Waltz*. Three compact discs. Rhino R2 78278, 2002. Originally issued as Warner Bros. 3WS-346, 1978. Backed by the four-fifths Canadian group the Band, Young sang fellow countryman Ian Tyson's classic folk music composition.

"Home, Home on the Range" (Traditional). Neil Young, vocals, guitar, harmonica. In *Where the Buffalo Roam*. 33-1/3 rpm phonodisc. Backstreet/MCA 5126, 1980. The soundtrack album also includes four instrumentals written by Young including "Ode to Wild Bill #1," "Ode to Wild Bill #2," "Ode to Wild Bill #3 with Dialogue" and "Ode to Wild Bill #4," plus two instrumentals written by Young and David Blumberg including "Buffalo Stomp" and "Buffalo Stomp Refrain."

"The Needle and the Damage Done" (Young). Neil Young, vocals, guitar. In *Live Aid: The Day the Music Changed the World*. Digital Video Disc. Woodcharm/WEA International R2 970383, 2004. Young performed a solo, acoustic version of his song in front of 90,000 people who were jumping up and down, smiling and waving their arms in stifling heat, seemingly oblivious to the message of the song. Young sang, "I know that some of you don't understand," and based on the footage, it appeared most did not.

"Nothing Is Perfect (in God's Perfect Plan)" (Young). Neil Young, vocals, guitar, various assisting instrumentalists and vocalists. In *Live Aid: The Day the Music Changed the World*. Digital Video Disc. Woodcharm/WEA International R2 970383, 2004. Following the release of *Old Ways,* Young toured with the International Harvesters who appeared with him on the Live Aid stage on July 13, 1985.

"I Am a Child" (Young). Neil Young, vocals, guitar, harmonica. In *The Bridge School Concerts Vol. One*. Compact disc. Reprise 9 46824–2, 1997. Performed in 1986.

Young also contributes harmonica and vocal accompaniment to Nils Lofgren's "Believe" (Nils Lofgren) performed in 1991 and vocal accompaniment to Elvis Costello's "Alison" (Elvis Costello) performed in 1990.

"No More" (Young). Neil Young, vocals, guitar, harmonica; various assisting instrumentalists and vocalists. In *SNL 25: Saturday Night Live, The Musical Performances, Volume 2*. Compact disc. Dream Works 50206, 1999. Young performed the song on September 30, 1989 accompanied by Crazy Horse guitarist Frank Sampedro plus Charlie Drayton (bass) and Steve Jordan (drums). Young also performed "The Needle and the Damage Done" and "Rockin' in the Free World" on the same show.

"Just Like Tom Thumb's Blues" (Bob Dylan). Neil Young, vocals, guitar, harmonica; various assisting instrumentalists and vocalists. In *Bob Dylan: A Thirtieth Anniversary Celebration*. Two compact discs. Columbia C2K-53230, 1993. In the 1992 tribute concert commemorating the release of Dylan's debut in 1962, Young performed a folk-rock version of the song.

"All Along the Watchtower" (Bob Dylan). Neil Young, vocals, guitar, harmonica; various assisting instrumentalists and vocalists. In *Bob Dylan: A Thirtieth Anniversary Celebration*. Two compact discs. Columbia C2K-53230, 1993. In the tribute concert nicknamed "Bob Fest" by Young, he performed a blistering rock version of the song full of his trademark guitar pyrotechnics. Young also took lead vocal duties for the third verse of "My Back Pages," one of the closing performances at the concert.

"Philadelphia" (Young). Neil Young, vocals, piano, keyboards. In *Philadelphia*. Compact disc. Epic Soundtrax EK-57624, 1994. Young contributed the ballad to the soundtrack of the film.

"(Sittin' On) The Dock of the Bay" (Otis Redding, Steve Cropper). Neil Young, vocals, guitar, harmonica; various assisting instrumentalists and vocalists. In Booker T. & the MGs *Time Is Tight*. Three compact discs. Stax 4424, 1998. A live performance from 1993 when Booker T. & the MGs backed Young on tour is included on the Stax instrumental group's box set.

"Greensleeves" (Traditional). Neil Young, vocals, guitar, harmonica. In *Seven Gates: A Christmas Album by Ben Keith and Friends*. Compact disc. Reprise 9 45773, 1994. Young also sings a verse on "The Little Drummer Boy" with lead vocal by Johnny Cash.

"Homegrown" (Young). Neil Young, vocals, guitar, harmonica; various assisting instrumentalists and vocalists. In *Farm Aid, Volume One, Live*. Compact disc. Turn Up the Music, 2003. In this 1994 performance, Young was accompanied by Crazy Horse.

"Mother Earth (Natural Anthem)" (Young). Neil Young, vocals, guitar, harmonica; various assisting instrumentalists and vocalists. In *Farm Aid, Volume One, Live*. Compact disc. Turn Up the Music, 2003. Young played the pump organ in this 1995 performance.

"When Your Lonely Heart Breaks" (Young). Neil Young, vocal, electric guitar; Crazy Horse (Frank Sampedro, guitar; Billy Talbot, bass; Ralph Molina, drums). In *The Horde Festival 1997*. Compact disc. Hollywood, 1997.

"Last of His Kind (The Farm Aid Song)" (Young). Neil Young, vocals, guitar, harmonica; various assisting instrumentalists and vocalists. In *Farm Aid, Family Farmers Keep America Growing, Vol. 1, Live*. Compact disc. Turn Up the Music, 2003. Recorded in 1999.

"Imagine" (John Lennon). Neil Young, vocals, piano; various assisting instrumentalists. In *America: A Tribute to Heroes*. Two compact discs. Interscope 93188,
2001. Ten days after the September 11, 2001 terrorist attacks, Young performed
a straight reading of the Lennon masterwork in a somber, cracking voice at
the televised live fundraiser. Young also added pump organ accompaniment
to "Long Road," a song performed by Pearl Jam members Eddie Vedder and
Michael McCready at the same event. Additionally, Young played guitar on
"America the Beautiful," the finale led by Willie Nelson.

"Four Strong Winds" (Ian Tyson). Neil Young, vocals, guitar, harmonica, Pegi Young,
vocals. In *Live 8: One Day One Concert One World: July 2nd, 2005*. Digital Video
Disc. Woodcharm/EMI/Capitol C9–0946–3-41982–9-5, 2005. Twenty years
after his appearance at Live Aid in Philadelphia, Young and his wife Pegi took the
stage at the Live 8 concert in Toronto.

APPEARANCES BY NEIL YOUNG ON OTHER ARTISTS' RECORDED PERFORMANCES

"As We Go Along" (Carole King, Toni Stern). The Monkees. In *Head*. 33-1/3 rpm
phonodisc. Colgems 5008, 1968. Young adds guitar.

"You and I" (David Jones, Bill Chadwick). The Monkees. In *Instant Replay*. 33-1/3
rpm phonodisc. Colgems 113, 1969. Young adds guitar.

"Music Is Love" (David Crosby, Graham Nash, Young). David Crosby. In *If I Could
Only Remember My Name*. 33-1/3 rpm phonodisc. Atlantic SD-7203, 1971.
Also available on the *CSN* box set.

"Better Days" (Graham Nash). Graham Nash. In *Songs for Beginners*. 33-1/3 rpm
phonodisc. Atlantic SD-7204, 1971. Young contributed piano under the pseud-
onym Joe Yankee.

"Man in the Mirror" (Graham Nash). Graham Nash. In *Songs for Beginners*. 33-1/3
rpm phonodisc. Atlantic SD-7204, 1971. Under the moniker Joe Yankee, Young
added piano to the track.

"Furry Sings the Blues" (Joni Mitchell). Joni Mitchell. In *Hejira*. 33-1/3 rpm phonodisc. Asylum 7E-1087, 1976. On her "Coyote" album, Young adds a harmonica line throughout this slow tempo jazz–influenced track. In the same year,
Young also accompanied Mitchell on a live version of the song included in *The
Last Waltz* album set.

"Light of the Stable" (Steven Rhymer, Elizabeth Rhymer). Emmylou Harris. In *Light
of the Stable—The Christmas Album*. 33-1/3 rpm phonodisc. Warner Bros. BSK
3484, 1980. On the title track, Young, along with Dolly Parton and Linda Ronstadt, added "Hallelujah"s (literally) and other harmony vocals to the track.

"Tears Are Not Enough" (Bryan Adams, Jim Vallance, David Foster, Rachel Paiement,
Paul Hyde, Bob Rock). Northern Lights (Canadian All Stars). In USA for Africa.
We Are the World. 33-1/3 rpm phonodisc. Columbia USA 40043, 1985. In
this Canadian response to "We Are the World," Young was one of a number of
prominent Canadian musicians who contributed their voices to the benefit song.
He was the sixth soloist and sang five words, "somehow our innocence is lost."

"All That You Have Is Your Soul" (Tracy Chapman). Tracy Chapman. In *Crossroads*.
Compact disc. Elektra 60888–2, 1989. Young contributed acoustic guitar and
an understated, tinkling piano figure to the production.

"I Got ID" (Eddie Vedder). Pearl Jam. In *Merkin Ball*. Compact Disc Single. Epic 662 716, 1995. Young contributed electric guitar.

"Long Road" (Eddie Vedder). Pearl Jam. In *Merkin Ball*. Compact Disc Single. Epic 662 716, 1995. Young contributed pump organ.

"For a Dancer" (Jackson Browne). Linda Ronstadt & Emmylou Harris. In *Western Wall—The Tucson Sessions*. Compact disc. Asylum 62408–2, 1999. Behind Ronstadt's lead vocal, Young joins Harris in singing backing harmony. He also contributes harmonica.

"Across the Border" (Bruce Springsteen). Linda Ronstadt & Emmylou Harris. In *Western Wall—The Tucson Sessions*. Compact disc. Asylum 62408–2, 1999. Young adds a relaxed harmonica line to the instrumentation in addition to contributing harmony along with Harris in support of Ronstadt's lead vocal.

"You Don't Have to Go" (Jimmy Reed). Jerry Lee Lewis. In *Last Man Standing*. Compact disc. Artists First AFT-20001–2, 2006. Young sang a verse in a blues-soaked and echoed voice. He also added background vocals and a lead guitar solo.

SELECTED COVER VERSIONS OF NEIL YOUNG COMPOSITIONS

"Nowadays Clancy Can't Even Sing" (Young). fever tree. In *fever tree*. 33-1/3 rpm phonodisc. UNI 73024, 1968. The psychedelic rock combo tried its hand at the first Buffalo Springfield single on fever tree's sophomore effort. The band played it close to the vest in an admirable version. The raspy-voiced lead singer is closer in style to Stephen Stills than Richie Furay (who sang lead on the Buffalo Springfield recording). The arrangement has a Western movie soundtrack flavor with some backwards flute added to spice things up.

"Down to the Wire" (Young). Yellow Hand. In *Yellow Hand*. 33-1/3 rpm phonodisc. Capitol ST-549, 1968. The rock sextet tried to fill the void left by the demise of the Buffalo Springfield with a debut that included four tracks by Stephen Stills and two by Young that had not been previously released. This is the opening track on the band's only album. The combo takes the track at a faster tempo than either of the Buffalo Springfield readings by Young or Stephen Stills. Yellow Hand sings with California rock group harmonies that would later be popularized by Poco and the Eagles. The band leaves out the slow bridge that appears in both Springfield versions. The production includes very good acoustic and electric guitar work plus an excellent lead line at the close that emerges from some gospel-style chorus vocals.

"Sell Out" (Young). Yellow Hand. In *Yellow Hand*. 33-1/3 rpm phonodisc. Capitol ST-549, 1968. The opening Young composition is followed by another by him. The band approaches "Sell Out" with a different style than "Down to the Wire." Rather than a group vocal, Jerry Tawney handles most of the lead effort himself. The track opens with a fuzz guitar and has a bit of rhythm and blues flavor in style and beat.

"The Loner" (Young). Three Dog Night. In *Three Dog Night*. 33-1/3 rpm phonodisc. Dunhill DS-50048, 1969. In their best-selling debut, the trio read this track from Young's debut at a faster tempo. As in Young's take, the organ is prominent. This was the first best-selling version of a Young composition.

"Nowadays Clancy Can't Even Sing" (Young). Carpenters. In *Ticket to Ride*. 33-1/3 rpm phonodisc. A & M SP 4205, 1969. The Carpenter siblings were one of the first recording acts to lay down a Young tune. Richard sang lead and arranged the track that includes horns and keyboards. Karen provided background vocals and added drums to it. The duo recorded the track at a faster tempo than the original and in a jazzier setting. Richard also added a couple of bridges where the twosome sang, "Sing, sing." The outro is an electric piano solo.

"I Believe in You" (Young). Rita Coolidge. In *Rita Coolidge*. 33-1/3 rpm phonodisc. A & M SP 4291, 1970. The singer closes her debut album with Young's composition from the same year. It is a credible interpretation offered at a slower pace than Young's original. Gospel-style background vocals add a nice flavor. Spooner Oldham (who would later collaborate with Young) plays electric piano on the track.

"Helpless" (Young). Buffy Sainte-Marie. In *She Used to Wanna Be a Ballerina*. 33-1/3 rpm phonodisc. Vanguard VSD-79311, 1971. Side 1 closes with the artist's fellow countryman's song. Sainte-Marie does a capable version though the vocal is a tad overwrought. Gospel-influenced background vocals enhance the production. Young and Crazy Horse appear on the album which was co-produced by Sainte-Marie and long-time Young collaborator Jack Nitzsche.

"Birds" (Young). Linda Ronstadt. In *Linda Ronstadt*. 33-1/3 rpm phonodisc. Capitol SMAS-635, 1972. Recorded live at Los Angeles' Troubadour, Ronstadt gives a mournful reading of the two-year-old tune while fronting a country-rock backup band that included future Eagles Randy Meisner, Glenn Frey and Don Henley. This was Ronstadt's first release of a Young composition.

"Birds" (Young). Risa Potters. In *Take Me Away*. 33-1/3 rpm phonodisc. Buddah BDS 5115, 1972. The track is the only cover version on the self-penned sophomore effort by the early 1970s singer-songwriter. Backed only by her acoustic piano accompaniment and several background vocalists, the artist makes the most of her not-too-strong alto in a commendable version of the 1970 song.

"I Believe in You" (Young). Linda Ronstadt. In *Don't Cry Now*. 33-1/3 rpm phonodisc. Asylum SD 5064, 1973. The artist closes her Asylum label debut with Young's song from three years earlier. The arrangement opens with Ronstadt performing a quiet and subtle vocal over understated pedal steel guitar and acoustic piano, before the drums and bass kick in. She then picks up the vocal intensity with vibrato as Asher adds echo to her voice. This marked the beginning of producer Peter Asher's long-time working relationship with Ronstadt. Though John David Souther produced the album, Asher co-produced two tracks including this one.

"Cowgirl in the Sand" (Young). Gene Clark, Chris Hillman, David Crosby, Roger McGuinn, Michael Clarke. In *Byrds*. 33-1/3 rpm phonodisc. Asylum SD 5058, 1973. In the reunion of the five original band members, the group recasts the Crazy Horse jam as a country shuffle in an inspired version that is topped by the signature Byrds harmonies. Gene Clark takes the lead vocal over nice acoustic guitars and an excellent harmonica line.

"(See the Sky) About to Rain" (Young). Gene Clark, Chris Hillman, David Crosby, Roger McGuinn, Michael Clarke. In *Byrds*. 33-1/3 rpm phonodisc. Asylum SD 5058, 1973. Released a year before Young's own version from the *On the Beach* album, the reunited Byrds miss the mark on this track that closes their return. The production does not have the subtleties that the piece requires. The performance is defined by optimistic, acoustic bombast, both in the guitars and mandolin. Again, Gene Clark steps up for the lead vocal. The vocal harmonies cannot save the Byrds' version.

"Love Is a Rose" (Young). Linda Ronstadt. In *Prisoner in Disguise*. 33-1/3 rpm phonodisc. Asylum 7E-1045, 1975. The artist opens her album with the definitive version of this track. Herb Pedersen's banjo playing, as well as the fiddle by David Lindley and harmonica by Jim Connor give the catchy tune its special character. The inside cover of the gatefold album jacket includes reproductions of the handwritten lyrics by each of the composers represented on the album. Young scribbled his words down while in Maui in 1974.

"Lotta Love" (Young). Nicolette Larson. In *Nicolette*. 33-1/3 rpm phonodisc. Warner Bros. BSK 3243, 1978. From the artist's debut album, the performance became a best-selling single, reaching number-8 on the *Billboard* charts, and number-1 on the Adult Contemporary list. The track remains the best-selling cover version of a Young song as a 45 rpm single. The production had the right sound for the late 1970s, with horns and strings, but it was not bombastic. Producer Ted Templeman employed some of the same aural techniques he had been using with the Doobie Brothers for the past few years giving the track a touch of rhythm and blues flavor. Andrew Love adds a nice saxophone line. The tambourine is by Nicolette. The same year Larson contributed harmony vocals on Young's *Comes a Time* album.

"Heart of Gold" (Young). Boney M. In *Nightflight to Venus*. 33-1/3 rpm phonodisc. Sire SRK 6062, 1978. The Eurodisco gang, who popularized the traditional "Rivers of Babylon," offer a rock take on Young's biggest hit in a capable production that closes the album. The song opens and closes with a cappella singing, and includes harmonica and even a pedal steel guitar in the instrumental backing.

"Lotta Love" (Young). Nicolette Larson & the Doobie Brothers. In *No Nukes: From the MUSE Concerts for a Non-Nuclear Future*. 33-1/3 rpm phonodisc. Asylum ML-801, 1979. The artist reworked her hit single from a year earlier. Backed by the full Doobie Brothers band, the track was recorded live during the Musicians United for Safe Energy (MUSE) concerts held at Madison Square Garden in New York City in September 1979. The combo sped up the tempo a bit from Larson's original. Doobies Michael McDonald and Patrick Simmons added background vocals.

"Look Out for My Love" (Young). Linda Ronstadt. In *Mad Love*. 33-1/3 rpm phonodisc. Asylum 5E-510, 1980. In her response to new wave and punk rock, the singer opens side two of her album with a shadowy vocal interpretation of Young's composition. Producer Peter Asher adds echo to Ronstadt's voice to accent the dark side of the tune.

"Long May You Run" (Young). Emmylou Harris. In *Last Date*. 33-1/3 rpm phonodisc. Warner Bros. 9 23740–1, 1982. This live set includes Harris's faithful rendition of Young's ode to Mort, his first hearse. Harris's Hot Band offers a country-rock reading with nice pedal steel and electric guitar lines.

"Only Love Can Break Your Heart" (Young). Stephen Stills. In *Right by You*. 33-1/3 rpm phonodisc. Atlantic 80177–1, 1984. Young's sometimes bandmate has covered a number of Young's tunes. Here he pulls from the *After the Gold Rush* album, as a number of artists have done over the years. Stills turns the rhythm around a bit, transforming the track into a slow reggae. The production has the tell-tale characteristics of the 1980s: synthesizers and big drums. Another of Young's sometimes bandmates, Graham Nash, assists on vocals.

"Like a Hurricane" (Young). The Mission U.K. In *The First Chapter.* Compact disc. Mercury 832732-2, 1987. After a single electric guitar states the theme followed by a spare, lead vocal joining over it, the British band then romps through the song with big drums and synthesizers in a typical 1980s style.

"Winterlong" (Young). Pixies. In *The Bridge: A Tribute to Neil Young.* Compact disc. Caroline CAROL-1374-2, 1989. Frank Black (aka Black Francis) and band present their raucous version of the 1970 Crazy Horse song with jangling rock guitars and Black's high-pitched vocal. The performance is faithful to the original, though a tad faster in tempo. Also available on the 4AD label's Pixies compilation *Wave of Mutilation: Best of Pixies,* 4AD 72406, 2004.

"Powderfinger" (Young). Cowboy Junkies. In *The Caution Horses.* Compact disc. RCA 2058-2-R, 1990. The Canadian group makes the song its own with Margo Timmins's understated, sensual vocal over a parade of acoustic instruments. Also available on the compilation *Studio: Selected Studio Recordings, 1986–1995,* RCA 67412, 1996.

"Cortez the Killer" (Young). Matthew Sweet. In *Girlfriend (Legacy Edition).* Compact disc. Volcano/Legacy 78549, 2006. Originally issued in 1992 on the promotional disc *Goodfriend,* Sweet's cover received its first official release as part of the Legacy edition of *Girlfriend.* Recorded live, with the Indigo Girls adding acoustic guitars and sharing verses with Sweet, the artist offers a greater than six minutes cover flavored with his typically excellent guitar playing.

"Only Love Can Break Your Heart" (Young). Saint Etienne. In *Foxbase Alpha.* Compact disc. Warner Bros. 2-26793, 1992. The trio of British journalists present an electronica reading of the 1970 tune. The recording opens with a long instrumental introduction that subtly introduces the musical theme under electronic percussion and some detached voicing (including a brief spoken recitation). The opening sets the mood as Sarah Cracknell offers the verses and choruses in a sad reading with synthesizer backing.

"Down by the River" (Young). Inner Circle. In *Bad Boys.* Compact disc. Atlantic 7 92261-2 177, 1993. The Jamaican quintet adds soulful harmonies to a reggae rendition of the 1969 Crazy Horse track and performs a commendable job in the process. The lead singer scats toward the end of the recording. This version makes one wonder why more soul and rhythm and blues artists have not tackled the Young catalog.

"Barefoot Floors." (Young). Nicolette Larson. In *Sleep, Baby, Sleep.* Compact disc. Sony 57672, 1994. Included in her album of lullabies.

"Don't Let It Bring You Down" (Young). Annie Lennox. In *Medusa.* Compact disc. Arista 25717, 1995. Like many before (and after), the artist goes to the *After the Gold Rush* well to draw forth this 1970 song that is included in an album of cover material. The performance is subdued and at a bit faster tempo than Young's original. The recording was used in the *American Beauty* film in the late scene with Lester and the cheerleader.

"After the Gold Rush" (Young). Linda Ronstadt. In *Feels like Home.* Compact disc. Elektra 61703-2, 1995. Long-time interpreter of Young's tunes reaches way back to reprise this 1970 composition in a pretty, harmony trio setting with Valerie Carter and Emmylou Harris. The piano accompaniment by Helen Voices and Dennis M. James's contribution on the glass harmonica add much to the track.

"Wrecking Ball" (Young). Emmylou Harris. In *Wrecking Ball*. Compact disc. Elektra 61854, 1995. Producer Daniel Lanois created an atmospheric setting for Harris's weary, fragile and beautiful reading.

"F*ckin' Up" (Young). Pearl Jam. In *Live on Two Legs*. Compact disc. Epic EK 69752, 1998. Ed Vedder and company closed a concert on their 1998 tour with a blistering reading of the 1990 song. The performance features excellent guitar work from Mike McCready and Stone Gossard. The band's workout seems to end before it should have. They could have easily jammed on the song for another ten minutes. Vedder introduces the tune by saying, "This one's for Neil." In the same collection, in the midst of the Pearl Jam song "Daughter," Vedder adds a slow-tempo verse from Young's "Rockin' in the Free World."

"The Needle and the Damage Done" (Young). Our Lady Peace. In *Happiness Is Not a Fish that You Can Catch*. Compact disc. Sony 63707, 1999. In this bonus track, the Canadian rock group took the song through a roller coaster ride of tempo changes over a foundation of keyboard and rock guitar lines.

"After the Gold Rush" (Young). Natalie Merchant. In *Live in Concert New York City June 13, 1999*. Compact disc. Elektra 62444, 1999. The folky chanteuse and her combo give Young's 1970 album title track the Merchant treatment in a mournful, live reading with spare keyboards and a touch of distorted guitar.

"Heart of Gold" (Young). Tori Amos. In *Strange Little Girls*. Compact disc. Atlantic 834862, 2001. The singer-songwriter adds a scary edge in this hard-rocking performance that does not belie the song's origins in country-folk-rock.

"Helpless" (Young). Cowboy Junkies. In *'Neath Your Covers, Part 1*. Compact disc. Zoe/Latent 6–01143–2005–2-6, 2004. The Timmins siblings and friends lay down an achingly beautiful reading of their countryman's composition with appropriately understated harmonica and clavinet from Jeff Bird.

"Old Man" (Young). The Wailin' Jennys. In *40 Days*. Compact disc. Jericho Beach Music/Red House 177, 2004. The trio from the land north of the border put their own stamp on Young's 1972 hit single. In an alt-country style with sweet harmonies and lead vocal exchanges, the threesome recorded the track for their debut, full-length album.

"After the Gold Rush" (Young). k. d. lang. In *Hymns of the 49th Parallel*. Compact disc. Nonesuch 79847, 2004. In a collection of cover versions of songs by fellow Canadians, the silky, smooth-voiced, alt-country pop interpreter offers yet another female take on Young's 1970 track. The performance opens the album with a quiet piano introduction. The electric guitar break borrows from Dick Dale's surf-reverb style.

"Barstool Blues" (Young). Maria McKee. In *Peddlin' Dreams*. Compact disc. Viewfinder/Eleven Thirty 7005, 2005. Backed only by her own acoustic piano accompaniment, McKee voices the 1975 song with a world weariness that makes it sound as though she has been hanging out at the same saloon as Young in a more than capable reading.

"Everybody Knows This Is Nowhere" (Young). Dar Williams. In *My Better Self*. Compact disc. Razor & Tie 182944, 2005. The contemporary folk singer-songwriter offers her take on the title track of the 1969 Crazy Horse LP. Like her mentor Joan Baez before her, Williams does not adjust the gender of the lyric to a female point of view.

"A Man Needs a Maid" (Young). Dala. In *Angels & Thieves*. Compact disc. Universal Music, 2005. The duo from Young's homeland (with a sound reminiscent of the Indigo Girls) present a mellow and pretty version with acoustic instrumental backing of the 1972 track.

"Cinnamon Girl" (Young). Matthew Sweet and Susanna Hoffs. In *Under the Covers, Vol 1*. Compact disc. Shout! Factory 97654, 2006. In the duo's album of covers of 1960s material, Young is the only artist represented with two songs, and both are from his debut with Crazy Horse from 1969. The track offers excellent guitar work by Sweet. It is not a note-for-note reproduction, but it has the same intensity as the original.

"Everybody Knows This Is Nowhere" (Young). Matthew Sweet and Susanna Hoffs. In *Under the Covers, Vol 1*. Compact disc. Shout! Factory 97654, 2006. As with "Cinnamon Girl," both Sweet and Hoffs handle the vocal duties on this track. They basically stick to Young's original arrangement including the "la, la, las".

"Ohio" (Young). Dala. Accessed June 27, 2007, at http://www.myspace.com/dala-girls. The Canadian duo offer a slow, spare guitar and keyboard-backed, ominous version made more so by a sometimes-detached voice reminiscent of the electronica aesthetic. Overall, the harmony vocals are pure and sincere. In the midst of the performance, the women sing a portion of Stephen Stills's "Find the Cost of Freedom," the B-side of the original "Ohio" single by Crosby, Stills, Nash, and Young.

THE FILMOGRAPHY OF NEIL YOUNG

Rock Masters: Neil Young in Concert. BBC. 1971. Film of February, 1971 solo performance at BBC Studio in London. Also known as *In Concert at the BBC*.

Journey through the Past. Produced by Shakey Pictures in conjunction with David Myers, Fred Underhill and L. A. Johnson. Directed by Neil Young. 1974. Combines live performance footage with a series of disparate images. Filmed in 1972.

Rust Never Sleeps. Produced by L. A. Johnson. Directed by Neil Young. Warner Reprise Video 38358. 1979. Film record of concert from 1978 *Rust Never Sleeps* tour.

Human Highway. Directed by Dean Stockwell and Neil Young. Warner Reprise Video 38417. 1982. Surreal musical comedy-drama that includes the band Devo in the cast.

Neil Young in Berlin. Produced by Lorne Michaels. Directed by Michael Lindsay-Hogg. Rhino Home Video. 1983. Video. A concert filmed at the last show of the European *Trans* tour at the Deutschlandhalle in West Berlin. The Trans Band included Nils Lofgren, Ben Keith and Joe Lala. The rhythm section included bassist Bruce Palmer of Buffalo Springfield and drummer Ralph Molina of Crazy Horse. The performance included four songs from *Trans,* plus half a dozen songs from 1969 through 1979. The encore was a Young composition titled "Berlin," which has never had an official release as a recording.

Solo Trans. Directed by Hal Ashby. Pioneer 21320. 1986.

Freedom: A Live Acoustic Concert. Warner Reprise Video 38166. 1990. Culled from two 1989 New York City shows.

Ragged Glory. Warner Reprise Video 38199. 1991. Sound set videos of various tracks from the *Ragged Glory* album.

Weld. Warner Reprise Video 38273. 1991. Visual souvenir of the Winter-Spring 1991 tour with Crazy Horse.

Unplugged. Warner Reprise Video 38354. 1993. Performance from the MTV telecast.

Neil Young and Crazy Horse: The Complex Sessions. Produced by Gary Goetzman. Directed by Jonathan Demme. Warner Reprise Video, 1995. Four live performances of songs from *Sleeps with Angels* filmed October 3, 1994 in Los Angeles. The band is loose and informal. Masking tape indicating where the performers should stand is visible. The tracks included are "My Heart," "Prime of Life," "Change Your Mind" and "Piece of Crap."

Year of the Horse. Executive Producers: Bernard Shakey (Neil Young) and Elliot Rabinowitz (Elliot Roberts). Produced by L. A. Johnson. A film by Jim Jarmusch. October Films/Shakey Pictures. 1997. Video. A documentary of Neil Young and Crazy Horse filmed during the band's 1996 concert tour. Footage from 1976 and 1986 tours is interspersed throughout. Most of the 1996 footage is shot on Super 8 film. Young, Frank Sampedro, Billy Talbot, Ralph Molina, Elliot Roberts, and Scott Young (Neil Young's father) are interviewed.

Silver & Gold. Directed by L. A. Johnson. Warner Bros. 38521. 2000. Filmed at a 1999 solo concert at the University of Texas in Austin.

Red Rocks Live: Neil Young, Friends and Relatives. Directed by L. A. Johnson. 2000. Warner Bros. 38531. Filmed at the Red Rocks Amphitheater in Denver, Colorado.

Live at Vicar St. Produced by Bernard Shakey (Neil Young). Directed by Ned O'Hanlon. Reprise. 2003. DVD. A solo performance of the *Greendale* album recorded at Vicar St., Dublin, Ireland.

Greendale. Sanctuary 88380. 2004. Actors on a high school-style set lip sync to Young's recordings from the concept album.

Neil Young: Heart of Gold. Executive Producers: Bernard Shakey (Neil Young), Elliot Rabinowitz (Elliot Roberts) and Gary Goetzman. Produced by Ilona Herzberg. Produced and directed by Jonathan Demme. A Clinica Estetico/Shakey Pictures Production. 2006. DVD. Jonathan Demme and Young and his musical friends conjure up the ghosts of Nashville's Ryman Auditorium in this warmly lit concert that focuses on the songs from the *Prairie Wind* album. Highlights include a rendition of "Comes a Time" (dedicated to the late Nicolette Larson) performed by eight musicians with acoustic guitars stretched across the front of the stage, and Young alone on the stage with his acoustic guitar (with no audience) performing "The Old Laughing Lady" from his first solo album. Aside from Young's long-time guitar technician Larry Cragg's demonstration of Young's guitar collection and footage of Young performing "The Needle and the Damage Done" on *The Johnny Cash Show*, the extra features seem too self-celebratory.

Notes

INTRODUCTION

1. Gottmann, Jean. *Megalopolis: The Urbanized Northeastern Seaboard of the United States* (Cambridge, MA: MIT Press), 1961.

CHAPTER 1

1. Einarson, John and Richie Furay. *There's Something Happening Here: The Story of Buffalo Springfield: For What It's Worth* (Kingston, Ontario: Quarry Press, 1997), 52.

2. Einarson and Furay, 11.

3. Chart positions are from Whitburn, Joel, *Top Pop Albums, 1955–1996* (Menomonee Falls, WI: Record Research, Inc., 1996) and *Top Pop Singles, 1955–1996* (Menomonee Falls, WI: Record Research, Inc., 1997).

4. McDonough, Jimmy. *Shakey: Neil Young's Biography.* (New York: Random House, 2002), 194.

5. Olsen, Eric, Paul Verna and Carlo Wolff. *The Encyclopedia of Record Producers* (New York: Billboard/Watson-Guptill, 1999), 572–574.

6. Simmons, Sylvie. *Neil Young: Reflections in Broken Glass* (Edinburgh: MOJO/Canongate, 2001), 26.

7. Einarson and Furay explain that Martin's vocal was actually recorded live in the studio and the sounds of the screaming fans came from a recording of a Beatles concert. Einarson and Furay, 226.

8. Young, Neil. *Decade* (Reprise 3RS 2257, 1976), liner notes.

9. Einarson and Furay, 175.

CHAPTER 2

1. McDonough, Jimmy. *Shakey: Neil Young's Biography* (New York: Random House, 2002), 296.
2. McDonough, 160.
3. Einarson, John and Richie Furay. *There's Something Happening Here: The Story of Buffalo Springfield: For What It's Worth* (Kingston, Ontario: Quarry Press, 1997), 257.
4. Einarson, John. *Neil Young: Don't Be Denied: The Canadian Years* (Kingston, Ontario: Quarry Press, 1992), 69.
5. Young, Neil. *Decade* (Reprise 3RS 2257, 1976), liner notes.
6. McDonough, 300.
7. In the *Decade* liner notes, Young says the track was recorded at the Canterbury House in Ann Arbor, Michigan, *Decade* liner notes.
8. Zimmer, Dave (text) and Henry Diltz (photographs). *Crosby, Stills, Nash: The Authorized Biography* (Cambridge, MA: Da Capo/Perseus, 2000), 93.
9. For a good summary of the events at and surrounding the Kent State shootings, see the May 4, 2000 special edition of the Kent State University student magazine *The Burr.*
10. Zimmer, *Crosby, Stills, Nash*, 197.
11. Young, Neil, *After the Gold Rush* (Reprise RS-6383, 1970), liner notes.
12. Young, Neil. *Greatest Hits* (Reprise 48935–2, 2004), liner notes.
13. Crosby, Stills, Nash, and Young. *4 Way Street* (Atlantic SD 2–902, 1971), introduction to album track.
14. Young performed the song at a tribute after several members of Lynyrd Skynyrd died in a plane crash. Accessed March 3, 2008 at http://www.rock-songs.com/songfacts/sweet-home-alabama.html.
15. The feminist healthcare reference book *Our Bodies, Ourselves* by the Boston Women's Health Book Collective (New York: Simon and Schuster, 1973) was published just a year after the release of *Harvest.*
16. Various Artists. *Hard Goods* (Warner Bros. PRO-583, 1974), liner notes.

CHAPTER 3

1. Young, Neil. *Decade* (Reprise 3RS 2257, 1976), liner notes.
2. Joni Mitchell's well-known song "The Circle Game" was written for and about Neil Young.
3. McDonough, Jimmy. *Shakey: Neil Young's Biography* (New York: Random House, 2002), 390.
4. McDonough, 287.
5. The song is found in context in the 2006 release of Young and Crazy Horse's *Live at the Fillmore East* concert.
6. Einarson, John and Richie Furay. *There's Something Happening Here: The Story of Buffalo Springfield: For What It's Worth* (Kingston, Ontario: Quarry Press, 1997), 51.
7. McDonough, 87.
8. Christgau, Robert. *Rock Albums of the '70s: A Critical Guide* (New York: Da Capo, 1981), 437.
9. Flanagan, Bill, *Written in My Soul: Conversations with Rock's Great Songwriters,* 113–129 (Chicago: Contemporary, 1987), 126.

10. *Decade* liner notes.

11. McDonough, 515.

12. Ephesians 5:31, King James Version.

13. Flanagan, 123.

14. Sacheen Littlefeather biography, The Internet Movie Database. Accessed February 25, 2008 at http://www.imdb.com/name/nm0514693/.

CHAPTER 4

1. Doggett, Peter. *Are You Ready for the Country: Elvis, Dylan, Parsons and the Roots of Country Rock* (New York: Penguin, 2001), 421.

2. Goodman, Fred. *The Mansion on the Hill: Dylan, Young, Geffen, Springsteen, and the Head-On Collision of Rock and Commerce* (New York: Random House, 1997), 326.

3. Goodman, 356.

4. McDonough, Jimmy. *Shakey: Neil Young's Biography* (New York: Random House, 2002), 556.

5. Freeman had Top 5 hits with "Do You Wanna Dance" in 1958 and "C'mon and Swim" in 1964.

6. Goodman, 355; McDonough, 580.

7. McDonough, 567.

CHAPTER 5

1. George Bush Inaugural Address, Friday, January 20, 1989. *Bartleby.com*. Accessed February 25, 2008 at http://www.bartleby.com/124/pres63.html.

2. George Bush Inaugural Address.

3. Romans 7:15, King James Version.

4. McDonough, Jimmy. *Shakey: Neil Young's Biography* (New York: Random House, 2002), 107.

5. McDonough, 621.

6. McDonough, 662.

7. Simmons, Sylvie. *Neil Young: Reflections in Broken Glass* (Edinburgh: MOJO/Canongate, 2001), 180.

8. In the *America: A Tribute to Heroes* concert televised several days after September 11, 2001, Young sat at the piano and sang and played Lennon's "Imagine."

9. McDonough, 709.

10. McDonough, 718.

11. Isaiah 2:4.

12. McDonough, 728.

13. The two-disc Elvis Presley set *Memories: The '68 Comeback Special* (RCA 67612-2, 1998) includes five versions of "Baby What You Want Me to Do."

14. Simmons, 193.

CHAPTER 6

1. Simmons, Sylvie. *Neil Young: Reflections in Broken Glass* (Edinburgh: MOJO/Canongate, 2001), 211.

2. McDonough, Jimmy. *Shakey: Neil Young's Biography* (New York: Random House, 2002), 569.

3. Simmons, 211.

4. Simmons, 214.

5. Beamer's words were, "Are you guys ready? Let's roll." McKinnon, Jim. "The Phone Line from Flight 93 Was Still Open When a GTE Operator Heard Todd Beamer say: 'Are You Guys Ready? Let's Roll.'" *Pittsburgh Post-Gazette* (September 16, 2001). Accessed February 25, 2008 at http://www.post-gazette.com/headlines/20010916phonecallnat3p3.asp.

6. Young, Neil. *Greendale* (Reprise 48533-2, 2003), liner notes.

7. Bash, Dana. "White House Pressed on 'Mission Accomplished' Sign." *CNN.com.* Accessed March 22, 2007. http://www.cnn.com/2003/ALLPOLITICS/10/28/mission.accomplished/.

8. Fricke, David. "Neil Young." *Rolling Stone* 1025–1026 (May 3–17, 2007): 138.

9. This excludes the four compilation albums; the seven live-in-concert albums (except for *Time Fades Away* and *Life* and *Rust Never Sleeps,* which count as studio albums, as they included all new unreleased material); the three soundtrack albums; and the four Crosby, Stills, Nash, and Young albums (three studio and one live).

10. Agee, James and Walker Evans. *Let Us Now Praise Famous Men* (New York: Ballantine), 1966.

11. McDonough, 9. While writing her study of Young, Simmons noted an autumn 2000 scheduled release date for the 1963–1972 portion of Young's *Archives* retrospective (Simmons, 216).

Annotated Bibliography

Abel, Judy. "Innocence Found." *Boston Globe* (February 19, 2006): N9. The reporter interviews Jonathan Demme and Young about the *Heart of Gold* film.

Abrahams, Andrew. "*Freedom.*" *People Weekly* (November 27, 1989): 27. A positive review of Young's comeback album.

Abrahams, Andrew. "*Life.*" *People Weekly* (November 23, 1987): 27. A brief review of Young's last album for Geffen in which Abrahams suggests that there are signs of life in Young's music that point to an optimistic future.

Abrahams, Andrew. "*Mirror Ball.*" *People Weekly* (July 10, 1995): 23. Brief, positive review of Young's collaboration with Pearl Jam.

Abrahams, Andrew. "*Ragged Glory.*" *People Weekly* (November 5, 1990): 23. A highly favorable review of the Crazy Horse collaboration.

Abrahams, Andrew. "*Sleeps with Angels.*" *People Weekly* (September 26, 1994): 25. The reviewer gives a thumbs-up to Young's collaboration with Crazy Horse.

Ali, Lorraine. "Still Young at Heart: Neil Young's Sweetly Sentimental Album Sounds Like His Early, Some Say Best, Work." *Newsweek* (May 8, 2000): 76. The journalist interviews Young in Texas after the release of the *Silver & Gold* album. The artist describes the songs on the album as glimpses of his experiences.

Atwood, Brett. "Re-opening Neil Young's *Highway.*" *Billboard* (August 19, 1995): 47. Industry article notes the issue of Young's much-maligned 1982 film *Human Highway* on video. Interview with Young collaborator L. A. Johnson suggests that maybe the film's time has come.

Barr, Brian J. "Neil Young Is Full of Shit but at Least His New Album Is a Gem." *Seattle Weekly* (October 17, 2007). Accessed October 23, 2007, at http://seattleweekly.com/2007–10–17/music/neil-young-is-full-of-shit.php. Complaining that Young has not released a great album since *Broken Arrow*, which Barr asserts was a tribute to David Briggs, the journalist gives a positive review to *Chrome Dreams II*, labeling it *Freedom II*.

Bauder, David. "Pegi Young Makes Some Music of Her Own." *Providence Journal-Bulletin* (July 29, 2007). Accessed August 3, 2007, at http://www.projo.com/music/content/artsun-pegi-young_07–29–07_OU6DHIV.dcee85.html#. Pegi Young is interviewed by the Associated Press music journalist about her husband Neil's contributions to her debut album.

Bienstock, Richard. "The Hawks and Doves Finally Coincide." *Village Voice* (October 16, 2007). Accessed October 23, 2007, at http://www.villagevoice.com/music/0742,bienstock,78080,22.html. The scribe gives *Chrome Dreams II* a favorable review, noting the album's spiritual undercurrents.

Billen, Andrew. "The Godfather of Gruff: 'To Handle Me Is Not Easy'." *The (London) Times* (August 5, 2003): 14. Long interview that took place after Young and Crazy Horse performed their new *Greendale* material at the Red Rocks amphitheater in Denver. Young speaks of his family, the ecological message of Greendale, and the *Shakey* biography.

Bing, Jonathan and Janet Shprintz. "Young Pulls His Support from McDonough Bio." *Variety* (May 8, 2000): 4. Industry note about Young suing his biographer to prevent release of what would become the published *Shakey*.

Birnbach, Lisa. "Despite Anguish and Illness, the Legendary Musician Neil Young says... 'I Just Keep Going'." *Parade* (February 19, 2006), 12–14. Young speaks of the illness and impending surgery that led to the creation of the *Prairie Wind* album.

Blinder, Elliot. "Neil Young: In Conversation." In Fong-Torres, Ben, ed., *The Rolling Stone Rock 'n' Roll Reader,* 773–783. New York: Straight Arrow/Bantam, 1974. Originally published in *Rolling Stone,* April 30, 1970. The author interviews Young during the East Coast swing of the Crazy Horse tour in early 1970. Young speaks of his preference for recording live in the studio and his unhappiness with the sonic quality of his debut album.

Booth, William. "Neil Young's Musical Lifeline." *Washington Post* (January 28, 2006): C1. The writer speaks with Young about the genesis of *Prairie Wind* and how the new songs fit with the old songs in the *Heart of Gold* film.

Borelli, Christopher. "Neil Young and Old Ways: He Shares a Personal Journey in a New Film with Jonathan Demme that Debuted at Sundance." *The (Toledo) Blade* (February 5, 2006), J–1+. The author interviews director Jonathan Demme and Young at the Sundance Film Festival. Young speaks of the torrent of music that came to him for *Prairie Wind*. Demme and Young speak of the mechanics of the film *Neil Young: Heart of Gold.*

Borelli, Christopher. "Picture Perfect: Concert Film Captures the Essence of an Aging Troubadour." *The (Toledo) Blade* (April 28, 2006), D–3+. The film critic grades Jonathan Demme's *Neil Young: Heart of Gold* as "outstanding."

Bowman, Rob. "Exposing His Roots: Young's Exceedingly Personal Album Contains Some of the Finest Music of His Legendary Career." *Time Canada* (October 3, 2005): 54. In a positive review, the reviewer is most impressed that Young wrote a church hymn for the *Prairie Wind* set.

Bream, Jon. "Neil Young & Crazy Horse; Sonic Youth; Social Distortion." *Billboard* (February 16, 1991): 32. The journalist reviews the opening night of the tour in Minneapolis and says it took Young a while to get warmed up. He also noted the show was heavy on new songs, which was a negative to the reviewer.

Breznican, Anthony. "'*Heart of Gold*' Finds Neil Young Mining Tradition." *USA Today* (January 25, 2006): 4D. The author converses with Young and Jonathan Demme at the Sundance Film Festival.

Breznican, Anthony. "Young's Harrowing Journey to '*Heart of Gold*'." *USA Today* (February 10, 2006): 6E. Young speaks of the experiences that led to the making of *Heart of Gold*.

Bronson, Fred. *The Billboard Book of Number One Hits,* 308. New York: Billboard, 1985. The author devotes a full page to the song "Heart of Gold" in his exposition of *Billboard* No. 1 hits from 1955 to 1985.

Browne, David. "Bush Whacker." *Entertainment Weekly* (May 12, 2006): 82. The journalist gives a thumbs-up review to Young's *Living with War*.

Browne, David. "*Dead Man*: Music from and Inspired by the Motion Picture." *Entertainment Weekly* (February 23, 1996): 120. Browne admires Young for continuing to take chances this far into his career, but he finds Young's instrumental soundtrack to be uninspired.

Browne, David. "*Harvest Moon*." *Entertainment Weekly* (November 13, 1992): 78. Browne gives high grades to the album.

Browne, David. "*Mirror Ball*." *Entertainment Weekly* (June 30, 1995): 96. In a creative narrative that embodies his mostly positive review, Browne wonders why Young cheerleader Eddie Vedder was not used more often on the album.

Browne, David. "*Sleeps with Angels*." *Entertainment Weekly* (August 19, 1994): 58. Browne sees potential in some of the album but decides that Young just did not commit enough to it. The critic prefers Crosby, Stills, and Nash's *After the Storm*, released and reviewed at the same time.

Bullock, Scott. "Veteran Rocker Breaks the Rules by Embracing Traditional Values." *Insight on the News* (September 29, 1997): 37. The author discusses Young's varied political stances throughout his career.

Buncombe, Andrew. "Neil Young Sets His Sights on Bush." *The (London) Independent* (April 17, 2006): 22. The journalist writes of the creation of *Living with War* with an eyewitness account from a studio choir member.

Bunte, Jim. "Neil Young's O Gauge Empire Is More than Just Unique—It's a Bond Between Father and Son." *Classic Toy Trains* (March, 1993). Accessed July 27, 2007, at http://www.thrasherswheat.org/tfa/trains-neil-young-1993.htm. The author describes Young's elaborate model train layout and the role of the hobby in Young's relationship with his son Ben Young.

The Burr, Editors of. "Kent State University: May 4, 2000: The Human Side of History." *The (Kent State University, Kent, Ohio) Burr* (May 4, 2000). A special edition of the magazine published by Kent State students commemorating the 30th anniversary of the shootings.

Burr, Ty. "*Dead Man*." *Entertainment Weekly* (January 31, 1997): 65. The noted film critic describes Young's soundtrack work as "growling." But he compares Jarmusch's "debunking of western myths" to Young's "closet-hippie romanticism" in his fair-to-middling review.

Burr, Ty. "From the Stage, A Poignant Portrait of Neil Young." *Boston Globe* (February 17, 2006): E1. An intelligent, favorable review of the *Heart of Gold* film.

Burris, Keith C. "Forever Young." *Commonweal* 131 (August 13, 2004): 38. The author reviews the various ways *Greendale* was presented. The stage show was the critic's favorite medium for Young's musical narrative about the fictional California community.

Carr, Roy. "Crosby, Stills, Nash, Young and Bert." In Zimmer, Dave, ed., *4 Way Street: The Crosby, Stills, Nash & Young Reader*, 125–137. Cambridge, MA: Da Capo/Perseus, 2004. Originally published in *New Musical Express*, August 31, 1974. The author interviewed Crosby, Stills, Nash, and Young during the 1974 reunion tour. He writes of Young's poorly received 1973 solo tour in Great Britain.

Carr, Roy. "Will CSNY Ever Re-Unite and Find True Happiness? This is David Geffen, by Gentleman's Agreement, Manager to the Superstars." In Zimmer, Dave, ed., *4 Way Street: The Crosby, Stills, Nash & Young Reader*, 97–106. Cambridge, MA: Da Capo/Perseus, 2004. Originally published in *New Musical Express*, July 29, 1972. David Geffen offers insights from a manager's perspective about working with and protecting Young.

Cashmere, Paul. "The Pegi Young Interview." *Undercover.com.au* (July 11, 2007). Accessed July 11, 2007 at http://undercover.com.au/News-Story.aspx?id=2430. The author conducts a long interview with Young's spouse who speaks of her husband's influence on the making of her debut album.

Cella, Catherine. "Johnson Helms Neil Young Vid." *Billboard* (May 20, 2000): 100. Interview with Young's videographer L. A. Johnson about the filming of the *Silver & Gold* DVD. Johnson speaks of how Young's songs and performance make the videos he has filmed with Young successful.

Chong, Kevin. *Neil Young Nation*. Vancouver: Greystone, 2005. The author and his buddies took a road trip that approximated Young's legendary 1966 trip in a hearse from Canada to Los Angeles. The book is part memoir, part love letter to Young, and part analysis of Young's music. During the journey, Chong met obsessive fans and people who were part of Young's history.

Christgau, Robert. *Christgau's Record Guide: The '80s*. New York: Da Capo, 1994. The critic wrote capsule reviews of *Hawks and Doves* (A–), *Re*ac*tor* (B+), *Trans* (A–), *Everybody's Rockin'* (C+), *Old Ways* (B), *Landing on Water* (C+), *Life* (B), *This Note's for You* (B–), *Eldorado* (import) (B+), and *Freedom* (A).

Christgau, Robert. *Rock Albums of the '70s: A Critical Guide*, 435–437. New York: Da Capo, 1981. Capsule reviews of *After the Gold Rush* (A+), *Harvest* (B+), *Journey through the Past* (C+), *Time Fades Away* (A), *On the Beach* (A–), *Tonight's the Night* (A), *Zuma* (A–), *American Stars 'n' Bars* (B+), *Comes a Time* (A), *Decade* (A), *Rust Never Sleeps* (A+), and *Live Rust* (A–). Christgau bestows on Young the mantle of the "decade's greatest rock and roller."

Church, Michael. "Gone Way Out, Far Out West." *The (London) Times* (July 3, 1996): 41. The writer's interview with Jim Jarmusch about the *Dead Man* film gives insight into how Young approached the creation of the soundtrack.

Clark, Tom. *Neil Young*. Bolinas, CA: Angel Hair, 1970. This is a limited-edition poetry collection. The title poem is made up of lyrics from 25 of Young's songs. The poem consists of 116 lines printed over 67 pages.

Cocks, Jay. "Dylan and Young on the Road." *Time* (November 6, 1978): 89. On the occasion of Bob Dylan's and Young's separate tours converging on Manhattan during the same week in the autumn of 1978, the author mused on the career trajectory of the two artists. His opinion was that although Young (like countless artists) was heavily influenced by Dylan, Young's body of work and performance style surpassed that of Dylan's. The article unnerved Young because he did not like the journalist tossing off Dylan's long career based on one night's performance.

Cocks, Jay. "*Sleeps with Angels*." *Time* 144.n16 (October 17, 1994): 79. A positive review of the album *Sleeps with Angels*.

Coddon, David L. "Not in His Own Words: Talking Heads' Review of Neil Young's Early Career Not a Must Have for Fans." *(San Diego) Union-Tribune* (March 2, 2007). Accessed March 3, 2007, at http://www.signonsandiego.com/news/features/20070302–9999–1c02neil.html. A lukewarm review of the documentary *Neil Young: Under Review 1966–1975* featuring critics Robert Christgau and Johnny Rogan.

Coleman, Mark. "One Nation Under a Groove: The 70s Era." In "The *Rolling Stone* 200: The Essential Rock Collection." *Rolling Stone* 760 (May 15, 1997): 85. Capsule essays on the significance of Young's *After the Gold Rush, Tonight's the Night*, and *Rust Never Sleeps*.

Collins, Tom. "'Energy Turns Kinetic' at HORDE Festival." *Arizona Summer Wildcat* (July 23, 1997). Accessed December 19, 2007 at http://wc.arizona.edu/papers/90/163/16_1_m.html. Enthusiastic piece about Young and Crazy Horse's performance during their HORDE Festival stop in Arizona.

Collum, Danny Duncan. "A Digital Stage Dive: Neil Young's *Living with War* Reopens the Channel between Artist and Audience." *Sojourners* (August 2006): 40. The author gives an enthusiastic review to Young's album about the Iraq conflict and notes how Young first presented the album for free in a streaming format on his website.

Considine, J. D. "Forever Young." *Rolling Stone* 712–713 (July 13–27, 1995): 107+. A highly favorable review of *Mirror Ball*.

Considine, J. D. "Performance." *Rolling Stone* 664 (September 2, 1993): 29. Positive review of Young concert with Booker T. & the MG's in Stockholm during June, 1993.

Cook, Richard. "Too Much, Man." *New Statesman* (December 13, 1999): 48. The author lambastes the *Looking Forward* reunion album of Crosby, Stills, Nash, and Young, noting that Young has the best songs on the album because unlike his comrades, he does not act as though he is an "indispensable messenger of great thoughts."

Coster, Peter. "Young Days of Gettin' Old." *(Melbourne, Australia) Herald Sun* (June 17, 2006): 84. Using the backdrop of the *Heart of Gold* film as a launching point, the author writes a first-person narrative about being in the hospital operating room with many who first purchased *Harvest* on vinyl.

Crosby, David and Carl Gottlieb. *Long Time Gone: The Autobiography of David Crosby*. New York: Doubleday, 1988. Young's supergroup mate speaks of Young's relationship to Crosby, Stills, Nash, and Young. He also reminisces about the recording of Young's "Ohio."

Crowe, Cameron. "The Actual, Honest-to-God Reunion of Crosby, Stills & Nash." In Zimmer, Dave, ed., *4 Way Street: The Crosby, Stills, Nash & Young Reader*, 177–196. Cambridge, MA: Da Capo/Perseus, 2004. Originally published in *Rolling Stone*, June 2, 1977.

Crowe, Cameron. "Crosby, Stills, Nash & Young: Carry On." In Zimmer, Dave, ed., *4 Way Street: The Crosby, Stills, Nash & Young Reader*, 107–123. Cambridge,

MA: Da Capo/Perseus, 2004. Originally published in *Crawdaddy*, October, 1974. At the time of the 1974 reunion tour of Crosby, Stills, Nash, and Young, Crosby spoke of Young's selfless giving to the group.

Crowe, Cameron. "Heart of Gold." *Rolling Stone* 1000 (May 18, 2006): 90. For the magazine's milestone issue, Crowe reminisces revealingly about his 1975 interview with Young.

Crowe, Cameron. "Neil Young: The Last American Hero." In *Rolling Stone*, Editors of, *Neil Young: The Rolling Stone Files*, 176–195. New York: Hyperion, 1994. Originally published in *Rolling Stone*, February 8, 1979. Long, well-written retrospective and discussion of where Young was career-wise after the *Rust Never Sleeps* tour.

Crowe, Cameron. "Quick End to a Long Run: In which Neil Young and Stephen Stills Find That Old Magic and Lose it All to a Sore Throat." In Zimmer, Dave, ed., *4 Way Street: The Crosby, Stills, Nash & Young Reader*, 169–176. Cambridge, MA: Da Capo/Perseus, 2004. Originally published in *Rolling Stone*, September 9, 1976. Crowe provides the autopsy for the Stills-Young Band.

Crowe, Cameron. "So Hard to Make Arrangements for Yourself: The *Rolling Stone* Interview with Neil Young." In Zimmer, Dave, ed., *4 Way Street: The Crosby, Stills, Nash & Young Reader*, 139–152. Cambridge, MA: Da Capo/Perseus, 2004. Originally published in *Rolling Stone* 193, August 14, 1975. Young was in a talkative mood with the interviewer in a career-spanning article. *Tonight's the Night* was about to be released and he was working on *Zuma* with Crazy Horse.

Dargis, Manohla. "A Weathered Rocker But Still Unbowed." *The New York Times* (February 10, 2006): E1. An enthusiastic review of *Heart of Gold* by the film critic.

Davis, Barry. "Young and Gold." *The Jerusalem Post* (January 18, 2007). Accessed January 19, 2007, at http://www.jpost.com/servlet/Satellite?cid=116746776 4600&pagename=JPost%2FJPArticle%2FShowFull. A positive review of Jonathan Demme's *Heart of Gold* concert film starring Young.

DeCurtis, Anthony. "Let It Bleed: The 60s Era." In "The *Rolling Stone* 200: The Essential Rock Collection." *Rolling Stone* 760 (May 15, 1997): 57. Capsule essays on the significance of Buffalo Springfield's *Again* and Crosby, Stills, Nash, and Young's *Déjà vu*.

DeLuca, Dan. "Making a Concert Film Come Alive: *Neil Young Heart of Gold*." *Philadelphia Inquirer* (February 16, 2006): NA. In an extended piece, the journalist interviews Demme and Young and gives a positive review to the film.

DeLuca, Dan. "Neil Young Gets a Second Wind (Treated for Aneurysm)." *Philadelphia Inquirer* (September 27, 2005): NA. In-depth look at Young at time of filming the Ryman concerts in 2005, with discussion of the *Prairie Wind* songs and Young's ailment.

Denby, David. "Home and Abroad." *The New Yorker* (February 13, 2006): 176. In a trio of film reviews, the critic gives a positive review to *Heart of Gold*.

DeYoung, Bill. "Talk Talk: Graham Nash." In Zimmer, Dave, ed., *4 Way Street: The Crosby, Stills, Nash & Young Reader*, 309–316. Cambridge, MA: Da Capo/Perseus, 2004. Originally published in *Goldmine*, June 19, 1998. Graham Nash complained about not being able to get Young's permission to include Young's "Pushed It over the End" track on the *CSN* box set.

D'Giff, Ian. "Looking Forward: David Crosby Muses on Politics, Life and Music." In Zimmer, Dave, ed., *4 Way Street: The Crosby, Stills, Nash & Young Reader,* 349–358. Cambridge, MA: Da Capo/Perseus, 2004. Originally published on the Musictoday.com website, March, 2002. David Crosby spoke about Young's role in organizing the Crosby, Stills, Nash, and Young Tour of America and Young's place in the group.

Doggett, Peter. *Are You Ready for the Country: Elvis, Dylan, Parsons and the Roots of Country Rock.* New York: Penguin, 2001. The author includes Young in his impressive and expansive history of the emergence of country rock music.

Doherty, Brian. "Neil Young's Quixotic Crusade: A Song Can't Change the World." *Reason* (July 2006): 53. On the occasion of the release of *Living with War,* the cultural observer notes the incongruities in Young's stance on various issues over the years.

Doherty, Mike. "Let's Shake Again." *(Toronto) National Post* (November 28, 2007): AL3. Well-written, observant review of Young's November 26, 2007 concert at Massey Hall in Toronto.

Downing, David. *A Dreamer of Pictures: Neil Young, the Man and His Music.* New York: Da Capo, 1994. A detailed look at Young's life and career through the *Unplugged* album. Downing is not shy about offering his opinions on Young's musical output.

Dufrechou, Carole. *Neil Young.* New York: Quick Fox, 1978. The author writes from a fan's perspective covering the first decade of Young's recording career and primarily using secondary sources.

Dwyer, Michael. "Young All Over Again—And Again." *TheAge.com.au* (April 26, 2007). Accessed April 27, 2007, at http://www.theage.com.au/news/music/young-all-over-again——and-again/2007/04/26/1177459869799.html#. Dwyer reviews both the Fillmore and Massey Hall sets. He finds the Fillmore set wanting, appreciates the Massey Hall set, but is decidedly critical of the way Young is parsing out his backlog.

Echard, William. *Neil Young and the Poetics of Energy.* Bloomington: Indiana University Press, 2005. An erudite analysis relating popular music to culture theory using examples from the work of Young.

Edwards, Mark. "Still Singing His Own Songs." *The (London) Sunday Times* (August 22, 2004): 8. In-depth look at the acted and lip-synched film version of *Greendale.* Young is interviewed about the making of the original album and the original staging of the *Greendale* concert.

Einarson, John. *Neil Young: Don't Be Denied: The Canadian Years.* Kingston, Ontario: Quarry Press, 1992. Excellent, well-researched study of Young's early, prefame musical years including his groups, especially the Squires, and songs. When there is a connection, Einarson ties in Young's early songs, melodies, and experiences with his later releases.

Einarson, John and Richie Furay. *There's Something Happening Here: The Story of Buffalo Springfield: For What It's Worth.* Kingston, Ontario: Quarry Press, 1997. The author, in collaboration with the Springfield's founding rhythm guitarist, gives the full, frustrating story of the band with which Young first found fame.

Ellen, Barbara. "Young's Heart Runs Free." *The (London) Times* (April 21, 2000): 22. In a long, positive review of *Silver & Gold,* the writer notes how the album grows on the listener.

Ellis, Janelle. "Neil Young's First Film Shown: A Docu-Autobio-Musico-Journey." In Rolling Stone, Editors of, *Neil Young: The Rolling Stone Files*, 89–91. New York: Hyperion, 1994. Originally published in *Rolling Stone*, May 24, 1973. A head-scratching, eye witness account of the *Journey through the Past* premiere.

Erwin, Ben. "From Younger Days: Neil Young—*Live at Massey Hall 1971*." *(Southern Illinois University, Carbondale, Illinois) Daily Egyptian* (March 28, 2007). Accessed March 28, 2007, at http://media.www.siude.com/media/storage/paper1096/news/2007/03/28/Music/From-Younger.Days-2808964.shtml. In a positive review, the author focused on the "melancholy" character of the set.

Evans, Paul. "Neil Young." In DeCurtis, Anthony and James Henke with Holly George-Warren, *Rolling Stone Album Guide*, New York: Random House, 1992, 795–797. The tenor of Evans's overview of Young's career is much more positive than the critique provided by Dave Marsh in the *Rolling Stone Record Guide* from a decade earlier. Although Evans notes Young's stumbles along the way, he regards the musician as an important artist.

Everett-Green, Robert. "Neil Young Lets Loose a War Cry." *(Toronto) Globe and Mail* (April 26, 2006): R1. The critic gets a sneak preview of *Living with War* and acclaims it Young's "strongest . . . in years."

Everett-Green, Robert. "One of the Major Discs of the Year." *(Toronto) Globe and Mail* (October 23, 2007). Accessed October 25, 2007, at http://www.theglobeandmail.com/servlet/story/LAC.20071023.CD23/TPStory/TPEntertainment/Music/. Musicologically flavored, positive review of *Chrome Dreams II*, in which the writer notes the "6/4 time" of "Shining Light" and the C major "waltz" of "The Way."

"*Everybody's Rockin'*." *People Weekly* (September 19, 1983): 32. The magazine gives Young's rockabilly album a poor review, suggesting that he has no respect for his rock music forebears.

Farber, Jim. "Neil Young's Latest CD Is No Sequel." *(New York) Daily News* (October 14, 2007). Accessed October 15, 2007 at http://www.nydailynews.com/entertainment/music/2007/10/14/2007-10-14_neil_youngs_latest_cd_is_no_sequel.html. The journalist gives *Chrome Dreams II* a lukewarm review.

"The 500 Greatest Songs of All Time." *Rolling Stone* 963 (December 9, 2004): 130, 138, 144. Capsule stories of Young's entries in *Rolling Stone* magazine's top 500 songs of all time: "Cortez the Killer" (no. 321), "Heart of Gold" (no. 297), and "Rockin' in the Free World" (no. 214).

Flanagan, Bill. "Neil Young." In Flanagan, Bill, *Written in My Soul: Conversations with Rock's Great Songwriters*, 113–129. Chicago: Contemporary, 1987. The editor of *Musician* interviewed Young in 1985, shortly after the release of the *Old Ways* album. The focus is on Young's songwriting and in particular on his mid-1970s albums *On the Beach* and *American Stars 'n' Bars*.

Flea. "Neil Young." In "The Immortals: The Fifty Greatest Artists of Our Time." *Rolling Stone* 946 (April 15, 2004): 122. In a special issue commemorating 50 years of rock music, the Red Hot Chili Peppers bassist writes an appreciation of Young.

Fong-Torres, Ben. "Crosby, Stills, Nash, Young, Taylor and Reeves." In Zimmer, Dave, ed., *4 Way Street: The Crosby, Stills, Nash & Young Reader*, 15–29. Cambridge, MA: Da Capo/Perseus, 2004. Originally published in *Rolling Stone* 49, December 27, 1969. Fong-Torres spoke with Crosby, Stills, Nash, and Young while they were in the process of creating the *Déjà vu* album. Stephen Stills and Graham Nash remark on Young's role in the group. Young speaks about being in two bands at once.

Fong-Torres, Ben. "David Crosby: The *Rolling Stone* Interview." In Zimmer, Dave, ed., *4 Way Street: The Crosby, Stills, Nash & Young Reader,* 39–69. Cambridge, MA: Da Capo/Perseus, 2004. Originally published in *Rolling Stone,* July 23, 1970. David Crosby gives a firsthand account of the creation and recording of "Ohio."

Fong-Torres, Ben. "The Ego Meets the Dove: The Reunion of Crosby, Stills, Nash & Young." *Rolling Stone* 168 (August 29, 1974). After a four-year gap in interviewing the group, Fong-Torres joined the summer stadium tour to find out how Crosby, Stills, Nash, and Young had changed.

Frank, Steven. "Neil Young's Close-Up: A Window into the Softer Side of Canada's Legendary Rocker." *Time Canada* (February 20, 2006): 48. In a positive review of the *Heart of Gold* film, the reviewer notes that the placement of the old songs in the film gives new meaning to the new songs.

Fricke, David. "David Crosby, Stephen Stills, Graham Nash & Neil Young." *Rolling Stone* 838 (April 13, 2000): 92+. Excellent, in-depth article that covers the quartet from rehearsals just before the beginning of their 2000 tour through opening night in Detroit.

Fricke, David. "Forever Young." *Rolling Stone* 689 (August 25, 1994): 87. A far-reaching, well-observed, positive review of *Sleeps with Angels.*

Fricke, David. "Neil's Big Harvest" *Rolling Stone* 839 (April 27, 2000): 36. The author speaks with Young about the upcoming *Silver & Gold* release and the legendary first volume of the *Archives,* which was scheduled to be issued in fall 2000.

Fricke, David. "Neil Young." *Rolling Stone* 930 (September 4, 2003): 98+. Excellent interview with Young about *Greendale* (the album and the stage show) and the state of the Union in 2003.

Fricke, David. "Neil Young." *Rolling Stone* 1025–1026 (May 3–17, 2007): 138+. Young gets the last word in a special 40th anniversary issue of the magazine that features interviews with 20 cultural icons of the past 40 years. Young speaks of the *Living with War* album, of activism in the 1960s, and why the spirit of the age is different in the 2000s. He speaks of musical creativity from the vantage point of an artist in his 60s, and of how it will take someone in her or his 20s to move the younger generation to take a stand for what they believe.

Fricke, David. "Recordings." *Rolling Stone* 840 (May 11, 2000): 127. Highly favorable review of *Silver & Gold.*

Fussman, Cal. "Neil Young (Legend, 60, Woodside, California)." *Esquire* (January 2006): 88. A sort-of interview that includes only answers (without questions) that bounce around a variety of topics. Young gets philosophical.

Gallo, Phil. "Neil Hits Road with Pic." *Daily Variety* (December 11, 2003): 1. Industry announcement about Young going on tour with Crazy Horse and his *Greendale* film.

Gallo, Phil. "Neil Young." *Variety* (September 18, 2000): 42. Gallo positively reviews Young's stop at the Greek Theater in Hollywood on the artist's late summer tour of 2000. The reviewer wishes that Young would dip into the *Sleeps with Angels* album in his repertoire.

Gambaccini, Paul. "Neil Young." In *Track Records,* 31–36. London: Elm Tree, 1985. The British journalist presents a brief overview of Young's career through the *Rust Never Sleeps* release.

Gifford, Barry. "Buffalo Springfield: *Last Time Around.*" In Rolling Stone, Editors of, ed., *The Rolling Stone Record Review,* 343–344. New York: Straight Arrow/ Bantam, 1971. Originally published in *Rolling Stone,* August 24, 1968. A favorable review of the last Buffalo Springfield album.

Gleiberman, Owen. "Old Man Take a Look at This Film, It's a Lot Like a Music Video." *Entertainment Weekly* (April 9, 2004): 66. The journalist gives a lukewarm review to Young's *Greendale* film, saving his praise for the "lo-fi glow" of the Super 8 film.

Goodman, Fred. *The Mansion on the Hill: Dylan, Young, Geffen, Springsteen, and the Head-On Collision of Rock and Commerce.* New York: Random House, 1997. Young is one focus of Goodman's investigation of the rude business realities that face recording artists.

Gordon, Michael. "Staying Young at Heart." *The (Melbourne, Australia) Age* (May 6, 2006): 27. A positive review of Kevin Chong's *Neil Young Nation* in which the journalist provides his own Neil Young fan credentials.

Graff, Gary. "Band of Brothers." In Zimmer, Dave, ed., *4 Way Street: The Crosby, Stills, Nash & Young Reader,* 337–341. Cambridge, MA: Da Capo/Perseus, 2004. Originally published in *The Oakland Press,* February 3, 2002. Graff spoke to Graham Nash and Young just before Crosby, Stills, Nash, and Young began their Tour of America to help heal the nation in the wake of September 11.

Graff, Gary. "Four Play: Crosby, Stills, Nash & Young." In Zimmer, Dave, ed., *4 Way Street: The Crosby, Stills, Nash & Young Reader,* 323–336. Cambridge, MA: Da Capo/Perseus, 2004. Originally published in *Guitar World,* February, 2000. During the CSNY2K tour that followed the release of *Looking Forward,* Stephen Stills and Young speak about the dynamics of playing lead guitar together.

Grant, Steve. *Essential Neil Young.* London: Chameleon, 1998. The author focuses on 43 Young recordings from the days of the Buffalo Springfield through the *Broken Arrow* album in this colorful work.

Greenman, Ben. "Pop Notes." *The New Yorker* (May 15, 2006): 25. In his mixed review of *Living with War,* the reviewer notes what Young compositions the artist borrowed from for the melodies on the antiwar album.

Guarino, Mark. "Young's Latest Casts Wide Musical Net." *(Chicago) Daily Herald* (October 22, 2007). Accessed October 23, 2007, at http://www.dailyherald.com/story/?id=60662. In a positive review, the journalist correctly notes that *Chrome Dreams II* is Young's most musically diverse album since *Freedom.*

Gundersen, Edna. "Neil Young Doesn't Scrap His Old Songs." *USA Today* (November 13, 2007). Accessed November 15, 2007, at http://www.usatoday.com/life/music/news/2007-11-13-neilyoung_N.htm. The writer caught up with Young at a gallery showing of photos of his classic cars. Young speaks of what he wanted to accomplish on *Chrome Dreams II* and of the fall 2007 tour.

Harvey, Dennis. "*Year of the Horse.*" *Variety* (June 2, 1997): 54. Writer gives a mostly positive review to the grainy Jarmusch film of Young and Crazy Horse.

Haworth, Graham. "It's Easy to Get Overlooked When You're Married to Neil Young, but Pegi Young Is a Talented Singer/Songwriter in Her Own Right." *(Santa Cruz) Sentinel* (June 23, 2007). Accessed June 24, 2007 at http://www.santacru

zsentinel.com/archive/2007/June/23/style/stories/08style.htm. The author interviews Young's wife and writes of Young's contributions to her album.

Helm, Levon with Stephen Davis. *This Wheel's on Fire: Levon Helm and the Story of the Band.* New York: William Morrow, 1993. In his reflection, the drummer of the Band notes Young's encounters with Helm's group.

Henke, James. "Back in the Saddle Again." In Rolling Stone, Editors of, *Neil Young: The Rolling Stone Files,* 274–276. New York: Hyperion, 1994. Originally published in *Rolling Stone,* October 4, 1990. Brief interview with Young after the release of *Ragged Glory.* Young talks about the preparations for the long-delayed *Archives.*

Henke, James. "Neil Young: The Rolling Stone Interview." In Rolling Stone, Editors of, *Neil Young: The Rolling Stone Files,* 238–250. New York: Hyperion, 1994. Originally published in *Rolling Stone,* June 2, 1988. The future curator at the Rock and Roll Hall of Fame teases out what was going through Young's head in the 1980s.

Honigmann, David. "Rallying Cries for Instant Download." *The (London) Financial Times* (June 7, 2006): 13. Drawing parallels between Young and another politically aware musician, Zimbabwean Thomas Mapfumo, the writer notes Young's "political wanderings" but is enthusiastic about the *Living with War* album.

Hopkins, Jerry. "The Rise & Fall of a Group." In *The Rock Story,* 189–208. New York: Signet/New American Library, 1970. In his seminal overview of rock music, the author dissects the life and death of the ego-laden Buffalo Springfield. His account is made more credible than others by its proximity in time to the actual events.

Hoskyns, Barney. *Hotel California: The True-Life Adventures of Crosby, Stills, Nash, Young, Mitchell, Taylor, Browne, Ronstadt, Geffen, the Eagles, and Their Many Friends.* New York: John Wiley & Sons, 2006. An illuminating study of the music scene birthed in Topanga Canyon and Laurel Canyon in the late 1960s and early 1970s.

Hoskyns, Barney. *Waiting for the Sun: Strange Days, Weird Scenes and the Sound of Los Angeles.* New York: St. Martin's Press, 1996.

Howell, Peter. "Comes a Time for Young." *Toronto Star* (January 25, 2006): E3. Young speaks of Canadian politics while at the Sundance festival for the premiere of *Heart of Gold.*

Hunt, Dennis. "Crosby, Stills & Nash Bury the Hatchet Again." In Zimmer, Dave, ed., *4 Way Street: The Crosby, Stills, Nash & Young Reader,* 239–245. Cambridge, MA: Da Capo/Perseus, 2004. Originally published in the *Los Angeles Times,* November 27, 1982. Graham Nash tells why Crosby, Stills, and Nash did not ask Young to join them for the *Daylight Again* album.

Hunter-Tilney, Ludovic. "Beery Worship of the Guitar Guru." *The (London) Financial Times* (May 23, 2002): 16. A mostly positive review of Young's tour stop at the Brixton Academy in support of the *Are You Passionate?* album.

Hunter-Tilney, Ludovic. "Mortal Thoughts Enrich the Harvest." *The (London) Financial Times* (September 22, 2005): 15. A long, insightful, positive review of *Prairie Wind.*

Ide, Wendy. "Neil Young Is Cloyingly Nostalgic in Jonathan Demme's Concert Film." *The (London) Times* (October 15, 2006): 17. A lukewarm review of the *Heart of Gold* film.

Inglis, Sam. *Neil Young's Harvest (Thirty Three and a Third Series)*. New York: Continuum, 2003. The author provides the historical, cultural, and musical context for Young's *Harvest* album. The book also includes a song-by-song commentary of the bestseller.

Jackson, David S. "Young, Gifted and Back; He's Got a New Backup Band, Pearl Jam, and a Terrific New Album, But Rock's Ageless Crank Is Still Traveling His Own Road." *Time* (July 3, 1995):56. The author speaks with Young at the Broken Arrow Ranch after the release of *Mirror Ball*, which garners a positive review.

Jenkins, Alan, ed. *Neil Young and Broken Arrow: On a Journey through the Past*. Bridgend, Wales: Neil Young Appreciation Society, 1994.

Jennings, Nicholas. *Before the Gold Rush: Flashbacks to the Dawn of the Canadian Sound*. Toronto: Viking Penguin, 1997. Fascinating, fondly written account of the emergence of the music scene in Canada in the 1960s, with an emphasis on the Yorkville area of Toronto. Jennings notes Young's role in the scene's development.

Johnson, Jeff. "*Living with War*." *CDReviews.com* (no date). Accessed November 30, 2006, at http://cdreviews.com/index.php?option=content&task=view&id=1383. In a positive album review, the Internet scribe focuses on Young's patriotic lyrics.

Johnson, Jeff. "Neil Young & Crazy Horse—*Live at the Fillmore East*." *CDReviews.com* (November 22, 2006). Accessed November 30, 2006, at http://cdreviews.com/index.php?option=content&task=view&id=1642. The Internet reviewer gives a glowing review to the *Live at the Fillmore* archival release.

Johnson, Jeff. "*Prairie Wind*." *CDReviews.com* (no date). Accessed November 30, 2006, at http://cdreviews.com/index.php?option=content&task=view&id=995. The author suggests that this was the best album release of 2005.

Kava, Brad. " '*Shakey: Neil Young's Biography*' by Jimmy McDonough." *San Jose Mercury News* (May 9, 2002): NA. Long, positive review of book telling of its history and of Young's unpredictability in more areas than just music output.

Kaye, Lenny. "Crosby, Stills, Nash & Young: Flying Freely." In Zimmer, Dave, ed., *4 Way Street: The Crosby, Stills, Nash & Young Reader*, 31–38. Cambridge, MA: Da Capo/Perseus, 2004. Originally published in *Circus*, March, 1970. Kaye writes of the "immediacy" that Young brought to the sound of Crosby, Stills, Nash, and Young.

Kelly, Nick. "Long May He Run." *The (London) Times* (June 15, 2001): 13. The author gives a positive review to Young and Crazy Horse's Dublin performance.

Kent, Nick. "Neil Young and the Haphazard Highway that Leads to Unconditional Love." In *The Dark Stuff: Selected Writings on Rock Music*, 295–338. New York: Da Capo, 2002. A long, quick-moving overview of Young's career with some mentions of the author's encounters with the musician.

Kent, Nick. " 'I Build Something Up, I Tear It Right Down': Neil Young at 50." *Mojo* (December 1995). Accessed July 26, 2007 at http://www.thrasherswheat.org/tfa/mojointerview1295pt2.htm. In an extensive interview, the author teases out substantial reflections from Young covering the breadth of his career through the Pearl Jam collaboration.

Koehler, Robert. "*Neil Young: Heart of Gold*." *Variety* (February 6, 2006): 99. In an article that is terse and poetic, the critic labels the Young-Jonathan Demme collaboration as "superbly crafted."

Koltnow, Barry. "Neil Young Gets Personal with CD, New Concert Film." *Orange County (California) Register* (February 15, 2006): NA. A substantial conversation with Young and Demme about the genesis of the *Heart of Gold* film.

Kot, Greg. "Mr. Soul: Neil Young Finds Passion with Booker T. and MG's." *Rolling Stone* 893 (April 11, 2002): 129+. Positive review of *Are You Passionate?*

Lee, Chris. "Neil Young's Harsh Words." *Los Angeles Times* (April 21, 2006): E1. Young speaks of the genesis of *Living with War.*

Lewis, Randy. "Reviews of New Works by Neil Young and Gary Allan." *Los Angeles Times* (October 21, 2007). Accessed October 23, 2007, at http://www.latimes.com/entertainment/news/music/la-ca-spotlight21oct21,1,170527.story?coll=la-entnews-music. In this mostly favorable review of *Chrome Dreams II,* the writer offers a smart, in-depth analysis of "Ordinary People," the centerpiece of the album.

Light, Alan. "Forever Young." In Rolling Stone, Editors of, *Neil Young: The Rolling Stone Files,* 288–296. New York: Hyperion, 1994. Originally published in *Rolling Stone,* March 30, 1972. In the midst of a long period of critically acclaimed creativity, Young reflects on his doings at the time of the release of *Harvest Moon.*

Little, Paul John. "Neil Young: *Living with War.*" *Playback* (May 22, 2006). Accessed August 13, 2007 at http://www.playbackstl.com/content/view/2531/162/. A positive review of Young's antiwar album.

Long, Pete. *Ghosts on the Road: Neil Young in Concert 1961–2006.* Winchester, Hampshire, UK: The Old Homestead Press, 2007. Exhaustive reference work that compiles set lists of almost every performance Young has been involved in. The second edition updates the original 1996 edition through 2006.

MacDonald, Patrick. "Neil Young: Doin' What He Does—and It's Rock Solid." *Seattle Times* (October 24, 2007). Accessed October 25, 2007, at http://seattletimes.nwsource.com/html/musicnightlife/2003971821_neil25.html. Gushing review of Young's fall 2007 tour stop in Seattle.

Mansfield, Brian. "Young's Music Travels into the Past, Future." *USA Today* (September 30, 2005): 10E. The writer had the opportunity to spend a few moments with Young during the Ryman Auditorium filming in Nashville and gives some background to the making of *Prairie Wind* and its closing cut "When God Made Me." In the closing, the journalist mistakenly refers to the album as *Prairie Moon.*

Marcus, Greil "*Comes a Time* Album Review." In Rolling Stone, Editors of, *Neil Young: The Rolling Stone Files,* 172–174. New York: Hyperion, 1994. Originally published in *Rolling Stone,* November 30, 1978. The culture critic writes a mostly unfavorable review of the 1978 release.

Marrone, Mike. "Groundbreakers from Two Originals." *Business Week* (April 16, 2007): 78. The author gives a positive review to the issue of the Massey Hall 1971 concert.

Marsh, Dave. "Neil Young." In Marsh, Dave and John Swenson, eds., *The New Rolling Stone Record Guide,* 563–565. New York: Random House/Rolling Stone, 1983. Marsh's reviews of Young's solo albums (through *Trans*) complement his critical essay in *Rolling Stone*'s 1980 history of rock and roll. Although the critic acknowledges that some of Young's work was brilliant, he chides the musician for a lack of "commitment" to "develop" his compositions.

Marsh, Dave. "Neil Young." In Miller, Jim, ed., *The Rolling Stone Illustrated History of Rock & Roll,* 404–406. New York: Random House/Rolling Stone, 1980. In a well-thought-out essay, the famous critic finds Young's work frustratingly inconsistent. He notes moments of brilliance set up against throwaways. Marsh identifies the problem as a lack of commitment by the artist.

Marsh, Dave. "*Tonight's the Night* Album Review." In Rolling Stone, Editors of, *Neil Young: The Rolling Stone Files,* 135–137. New York: Hyperion, 1994. Originally published in *Rolling Stone,* August 28, 1975. Well-known critic understands where Young was coming from at the time in this favorable review.

Maslin, Janet. "A New Movie and a New Album Signal a Shift in the Career of Neil Young." *New Times* (1973). Accessed July 26, 2007, at http://www.thrashers wheat.org/tfa/groundhog73.htm. The critic reports on the Cambridge, Massachusetts premiere of Young's film *Journey through the Past* and briefly reviews the *Time Fades Away* album, including a comparison with the film.

Maslin, Janet. "Look at My Life: An Enigmatic Rocker." *The New York Times* (May 6, 2002): E6. The *Times* critic rates the McDonough biography high, seeing it as an appropriate way to deal with its subject.

McDonough, Jimmy. *Shakey: Neil Young's Biography.* New York: Random House, 2002. The author delves deep into Young's life, interviewing family members, friends, and acquaintances. Extensive interview segments with Young are interspersed throughout the text, but they could have stood some editing. There are hundreds of four-letter words, many "heh heh heh"s and more than enough uses of the word "innaresting."

McDougall, Allan and Penny Valentine. "The *Sounds* Talk-In: Stephen Stills and Neil Young." In Zimmer, Dave, ed., *4 Way Street: The Crosby, Stills, Nash & Young Reader,* 87–95. Cambridge, MA: Da Capo/Perseus, 2004. Originally published in *Sounds,* November 21, 1970. A short interview with Young during the mixing of the *4 Way Street* live album.

McFadyen, Warwick. "In the US, an Angry Patriot Acts." *The (Melbourne, Australia) Age* (April 29, 2006): 12. Good article about Young's broadside *Living with War* and its context.

McLellan, Joseph. "Rock Plus, in Young's New 'Rust'." *Washington Post* (August 17, 1979): D6. The critic is somewhat confused by it, but ultimately appreciates the *Rust Never Sleeps* film.

Meehan, Ryan. "Neil Young Revisits Glory Days of the Fillmore East." *(Morris County, NJ) Daily Record* (February 23, 2007). Accessed February 24, 2007, at http://www.dailyrecord.com/apps/pbcs.dll/article?AID=/20070223/MCTV/702230370/1128/LIFE. The author, a high school student, presents a well-written and well-researched positive review of the Crazy Horse Fillmore 1970 archive release.

Meltzer, Richard. "Poems in Neil's Suede Pocket." In *A Whore Just Like the Rest: The Music Writings of Richard Meltzer,* 189–191. Cambridge, MA: Da Capo/Perseus, 2000. A somewhat absurd review of Young's early 1970s Carnegie Hall debut, a concert the critic did not attend.

Mendelssohn, John. "*Harvest* Album Review." In Rolling Stone, Editors of, *Neil Young: The Rolling Stone Files,* 80–82. New York: Hyperion, 1994. Originally published in *Rolling Stone,* March 30, 1972. Noted critic infamously skewers the *Harvest* album.

Mengel, Noel. "Neil Young Looks Back." *Brisbane (Australia) Courier-Mail* (November 30, 2006). Accessed November 30, 2006, at http://www.news.com.au/couriermail/story/0,23739,20841794-5003421,00.html#. A rave review of the *Live at the Fillmore* archival release.

Miller, Jeff. "17th Annual Bridge School Benefit." *Daily Variety* (October 29, 2003): 12. Crosby, Stills, Nash, and Young closed the annual benefit concert in 2003.

Mills, Fred. "Neil Young: All My Changes Were There." *Tucson Weekly* (August 1995). Accessed July 26, 2007 at http://www.thrasherswheat.org/tfa/tucsonweekly.htm. The author muses on Young's music, his influence on the author's life, and Young's music as a soundtrack for some of the author's experiences.

Mills, Fred. "New Neil Young *Chrome Dreams II* Album + Tour for October?" *HARP* (August 19, 2007). Accessed August 20, 2007 at http://www.harpmagazine.com/news/detail.cfm?article=11582. The author relays reports of the impending release of a new Young album that was rumored at the time to include three tracks from the legendary *Chrome Dreams* album that was shelved in 1976. The author also reports that the scheduled release of the first set of Young's *Archives* covering 1963 to 1972 has been once again delayed.

Mirkin, Steven. "Crosby, Stills, Nash & Young: Concert Review." *Daily Variety* (August 2, 2006): 19. A mixed review of the group's Hollywood Bowl show that notes a great divide between the continued creativity of Young and the settling of the other three band members in their 1960s and 1970s comfort zone.

Miroff, Bruce. "Neil Young with Crazy Horse: *Everybody Knows This Is Nowhere*." In Rolling Stone, Editors of, ed., *The Rolling Stone Record Review*, 345–347. New York: Straight Arrow/Bantam, 1971. Originally published in *Rolling Stone*, August 9, 1969. A positive review of Young's first collaboration with Crazy Horse. The author focuses on Young's rock and roll voice and notes that the album misses the "beauty" and "lyricism" of Young's debut.

Mitchum, Rob. "Neil Young and Crazy Horse *Live at the Fillmore East*." *Pitchforkmedia.com* (December 6, 2006). Accessed January 19, 2007 at http://www.pitchforkmedia.com/article/record_review/39956/Neil_Young_and_Crazy_Horse_Live_at_the_Fillmore_East. The author gives a positive review to the set although, like many others, he wishes that more of the available Fillmore tracks had been added to the disc.

Moody, Rick. "'It's a Valentine to Country Music'." *The (London) Guardian* (October 13, 2006): 7. The journalist interviews Young and Jonathan Demme in Manhattan about the *Heart of Gold* film.

Moon, Tom. "Neil Young Shows a Passion for Truth on His New Album." *Philadelphia Inquirer.* (April 3, 2002): NA. In a positive review, the journalist offers special praise for Young's sobbing guitar solos on the *Are You Passionate?* release.

Mosier, Oliver. "Filmore (sic) Gives Portrait of the Artist as a Young Man." *(University of) Chicago Maroon* (November 17, 2006). Accessed November 30, 2006, at http://maroon.uchicago.edu/online_edition/voices/2006/11/17/filmore-gives-portrait-of-the-artist-as-a-young-man/. A positive review of the *Live at the Fillmore* set, although the reviewer is disappointed by the omission of "Cinnamon Girl."

Mulvey, John. "Neil Young's *Chrome Dreams II*." *Uncut* (September 14, 2007). Accessed October 15, 2007, at http://www.uncut.co.uk/blog/index.php?blog=6&p=466&more=1&c=1&tb=1&pb=1#more466. Erudite, somewhat favorable review of Young's 2007 release.

Nashawaty, Chris. "Q & A: Neil Young and Jonathan Demme." *Entertainment Weekly* (February 24, 2006): L4. Young lists his favorite films and Demme lists his favorite albums.

"Neil Young." In George-Warren, Holly and Patricia Romanowski, eds., *The Rolling Stone Encyclopedia of Rock & Roll,* 1098–1100. New York: Fireside/Rolling Stone, 2005. A tightly-written entry that covers Young's solo career.

"Neil Young Interview." *Guitare & Clavieres* (April, 1992). Accessed July 27, 2007, at http://www.thrasherswheat.org/ptma/frenchguitar492.htm. Translated from the French by David Ostrosser. Young explains the mystical relationship between his guitars and composing and speaks in technical terms of his guitar-playing style, amplifiers, and guitar sound effects.

"Neil Young Picks Up an Award, and His Rockster Pals Join Him to Pitch in for a Sound Charity." *People Weekly* (December 5, 1988): 62. Short article noting Young's receipt of an award from the Nordoff-Robbins Music Therapy Foundation. At the charity music memorabilia auction that followed, Young purchased the gray suit John Lennon wore on the cover of *With the Beatles.*

Nelson, Paul. "*Rust Never Sleeps* Album Review." In Rolling Stone, Editors of, *Neil Young: The Rolling Stone Files,* 196–200. New York: Hyperion, 1994. Originally published in *Rolling Stone,* October 18, 1979. Enthusiastic, positive review.

Novak, Ralph. "*Landing on Water.*" *People Weekly* (October 13, 1986): 22. A poor review of the album.

Novak, Ralph. "*Old Ways.*" *People Weekly* (September 23, 1985): 22. In his brief, negative review, Novak suggests that Young is making fun of country music.

O'Connor, Rob. "Recordings." *Rolling Stone* 740 (August 8, 1996): 58. Decidedly unfavorable review of *Broken Arrow.*

Olsen, Eric, Paul Verna and Carlo Wolff. *The Encyclopedia of Record Producers.* New York: Billboard/Watson-Guptill, 1999. The authors include essays about producers David Briggs and Jack Nitzsche, important collaborators in the creation of Young's sound.

Orshoski, Wes. "Buffalo Springfield Boxed." *Billboard* (July 7, 2001): 11. The industry scribe allots a lot of space for Stephen Stills and Richie Furay to discuss the creation of their seminal group's box set.

Pachter, Richard. "'*Shakey*': Neil Young's Biography by Jimmy McDonough." *Miami Herald* (January 3. 2003): NA. Sly review that suggests that Young's life story is a good business "textbook" for aspiring musicians.

Paphides, Pete. "Neil Young: *Chrome Dreams II.*" *The (London) Times* (October 19, 2007). Accessed October 23, 2007, at http://entertainment.timesonline.co.uk/tol/arts_and_entertainment/music/cd_reviews/article2687078.ece. Although the review is favorable, Paphides is the rare critic who does not approve of the long "Ordinary People" track on the 2007 release.

Pareles, Jon. "The Latest from Neil Young." *The New York Times* (June 15, 2003). Accessed July 25, 2007, at http://www.thrasherswheat.org/tfa/nyt061503.htm. The critic interviewed Young in Paris about the creation of the *Greendale* album.

Pareles, Jon. "Neil Young in Concert: How to Get to the Point." *The New York Times* (August 21, 1996): NA. An enthusiastic review of Young and Crazy Horse at Madison Square Garden during the tour that was captured on the *Year of the Horse* album and video.

Pareles, Jon. "Neil Young Is Angry About War and Wants Everyone to Know It." *The New York Times* (April 28, 2006): E9. A phone interview with Young about the context and content of *Living with War.*

Pareles, Jon. "Neil Young Proves Himself to Himself." *The New York Times* (August 11, 1997): NA. The music critic spoke with Young while the musician and Crazy Horse were headlining the HORDE tour. Young speaks of having to prove himself to a younger audience.

Pareles, Jon. "Neil Young in Nashville, Pondering Mortality." *The New York Times* (August 20, 2005): B7. Pareles draws out interesting remarks from Young in a conversation that took place during the filming of the Ryman concerts. Young talks about God and the seemingly, always-upcoming archival box sets.

Pareles, Jon. "Vintage Neil Young, Still Working for the Muse." *The New York Times* (October 28, 2007). Accessed October 31, 2007, at http://www.nytimes.com/2007/10/28/arts/music/28pare.html?em&ex=1193889600&en=cbc750af62892f00&ei=5087%0A. The journalist had the opportunity to listen in on two days of rehearsals for Young's fall 2007 tour. He observes Young's impatience with the band and speaks with Young about the spiritual underpinnings of the *Chrome Dreams II* set, Young's 1959 Lincoln Continental, and why projects are dropped.

Pareles, Jon. "With Sept. 11 in Mind, Neil Young Gets Rolling." *The New York Times* (April 7, 2002): AR29. A lukewarm review of the *Are You Passionate?* album.

Parker, James. "North American Idol: Two Sides of Neil Young." *The (Boston) Phoenix* (May 16, 2007). Accessed April 27, 2007, at http://thephoenix.com/article_ektid39809.aspx. An even-handed assessment of the Fillmore and Massey Hall archival releases.

Parr, Geoff. "Buffalo Springfield *Again*: Folk-Rock's Gem Hidden beneath the Shadows." *The (Durham, NH) New Hampshire* (April 13, 2007). Accessed April 15, 2007, at http://media.www.tnhonline.com/media/storage/paper674/news/2007/04/13/ArtsLiving/Buffalo.Springfield.Again-2839404.shtml. Almost 40 years after the release of *Again*, the writer gives a song-by-song defense for why the Springfield's sophomore effort should have received more recognition.

Paul, Alan. "Neil Young." In Graff, Gary, ed. *Rock: The Essential Album Guide,* Detroit: Visible Ink, 1996: 753–754. A consumer guide to the musician's releases. Some of the facts are incorrect, but the writer is generally appreciative of Young's work.

Pearman, Hugh. "On 'Out on the Weekend': Going for a Song." *(London) Sunday Times* (October 29, 2006): 34. The writer reflects back on his teenage years and the place of *Harvest* and its opening track in his life.

Perone, James E. *Music of the Counterculture Era.* Westport, CT: Greenwood, 2005. The author discusses the role of Young's "Ohio" in the antiwar protest movement, and includes a brief encyclopedia entry about Crosby, Stills, Nash, and Young.

Perone, James E. *Woodstock: An Encyclopedia of the Music and Art Fair.* Westport, CT: Greenwood, 2005. The author includes a brief summary of Young's appearance with Crosby, Stills, and Nash at the festival, plus a short encyclopedia entry about Crosby, Stills, Nash, and Young.

Petridis, Alexis. *Neil Young.* New York: Thunder's Mouth, 2000. In this brief, well-written work, part of the publisher's *Kill Your Idols* series, Petridis offers a concise overview of Young's career, a song-by-song commentary through the

Looking Forward release and an assessment of Young's influence on the next musical generations.

Petridis, Alexis. "Neil Young, *Chrome Dreams II*." *The (Manchester) Guardian* (October 12, 2007). Accessed October 15, 2007 at http://arts.guardian. co.uk/filmandmusic/story/0,,2188528,00.html. The author finds the album both confusing and occasionally brilliant. He notes that "Beautiful Bluebird" was rejected for the *Old Ways* disc and that an electrified version of "Boxcar" was to appear on the aborted *Times Square* album.

Powers, Ann. "Neil Young, Burning Castles to Move Out of the Past." *The New York Times* (August 19, 2000): B7. A positive review of Young and his friends and relatives's performance at the Jones Beach Amphitheater.

Puckett, Jeffrey Lee. "Neil Young Floodgates Open: *Live at Massey Hall* Returns to the Roots of a Remarkable Career." *(Louisville) Courier-Journal* (March 24, 2007). Accessed March 24, 2007, at http://www.courier-journal.com/apps/ pbcs.dll/article?AID=/20070324/SCENE04/70324001/1011/SCENE. The author sings the praises of the oft-bootlegged concert that finally has an official release.

Puterbaugh, Parke. "Stephen Stills." In Zimmer, Dave, ed., *4 Way Street: The Crosby, Stills, Nash & Young Reader,* 295–301. Cambridge, MA: Da Capo/Perseus, 2004. Originally published on the Rock and Roll Hall of Fame and Museum Web site, May, 1997. Stephen Stills speaks about Young's role in the induction of Buffalo Springfield into the Rock and Roll Hall of Fame and in putting the Buffalo Springfield box set together.

Rabb, John. "'*Comes a Time*': Young's Wistful Homogenization." *Washington Post* (November 22, 1978): B2. A lukewarm review of the *Comes a Time* album.

Ratliff, Ben. "A Fresh Blast of Yesteryear's Raw, Slobby Sound." *The New York Times* (November 13, 2006): E1. An enthusiastic review of the first archive release of Young and Crazy Horse at the Fillmore East in early 1970. Like many before him, Ratliff reports a release date for the first section of Young's massive archive set, a date that has since passed.

Rayner, Ben. "Keeping Young at Heart." *Toronto Star* (March 17, 2006): D6. Coverage of Young's talk at the South by Southwest music festival. He emphasizes not looking back at the past.

Relic, Peter. "Neil Young's Call to Action." *Rolling Stone* 1000 (May 18, 2006): 41–42. Article about the genesis and recording of *Living with War.*

Rickey, Carrie. "*Neil Young: Heart of Gold*." *Philadelphia Inquirer* (February 13, 2006): NA. A strong, thumbs-up review of the Young-Demme collaboration.

Ridley, Jim. "Neil's Nashville Homecoming." *(Toronto) Globe and Mail* (February 13, 2006): R1. The journalist interviewed Young during the *Heart of Gold* filming in Nashville. Young reminisces about earlier visits to the city.

Robertson, John. *Neil Young: The Visual Documentary.* London: Omnibus Press, 1994. Detailed chronology of Young's career laced with lots of photographs.

Rockwell, John. "Neil Young: As Good as Bob Dylan?" *The New York Times* (June 19, 1977). Accessed July 25, 2007, at http://www.thrasherswheat.org/tfa/ rock well061977.htm. The critic compares two new album releases: *CSN* by Crosby, Stills, and Nash and *American Stars 'n' Bars* by Young. Rockwell favors the latter.

Rockwell, John. "Neil Young: Rock, Populism and Transcendental Primitivism." In Rockwell, John, *All American Music: Composition in the Late Twentieth Century,*

221–233. New York: Vintage, 1984. An erudite essay on Young's composing, singing, and playing styles set in rock music's cultural context.

Rogan, Johnny. *Crosby, Stills, Nash & Young: The Visual Documentary*. London: Omnibus, 1996. Rogan presents a detailed, accurate chronology of the group in a book that is full of color and black-and-white photos.

Rogan, Johnny. *Neil Young: Zero to Sixty: A Critical Biography*. London: Calidore, 2001. Impressive, massive, essential work. Rogan's study goes through the *Looking Forward* collaboration with Crosby, Stills, and Nash.

Rolling Stone, Editors of. *Neil Young: The Rolling Stone Files*. New York: Hyperion, 1994. A collection of short and long pieces from news briefs to album reviews to interviews that span the days of the Buffalo Springfield through the magazine's August 19, 1993 album review of *Unplugged*.

Rosenthal, Andrew. "There Is Silence in the Streets: Where Have All the Protesters Gone?" *The New York Times* (August 31, 2006): A24. Using a Crosby, Stills, Nash, and Young concert as a launch pad, the writer grieves at the disconnection between popular music and a movement against the war in Iraq.

Roznik, Sharon. "Young Again: Neil Young Releases 17-Track Live Album of 1971 Concert." *The (Fond-du-Lac, Wisconsin) Reporter* (April 14, 2007). Accessed April 15, 2007, at http://www.fdlreporter.com/apps/pbcs.dll/article?AID=/20070414/FON05/70411155/1338/FONent. The journalist gushes unabashedly over the Massey Hall concert release.

Ruhlmann, William. "Neil Young." In Erlewine, Michael, Vladimir Bogdanov, Chris Woodstra and Stephen Thomas Erlewine, eds., *All Music Guide: The Experts' Guide to the Best CDs, Albums & Tapes*, 423–425. San Francisco: Miller Freeman, 1997. A brief essay by Ruhlmann and capsule reviews of Young's releases (mostly by Ruhlmann).

Rush, Steve. "A Louisiana Encore for Stephen Stills." In Zimmer, Dave, ed., *4 Way Street: The Crosby, Stills, Nash & Young Reader*, 279–284. Cambridge, MA: Da Capo/Perseus, 2004. Originally published in the *New Orleans Times-Picayune*, June 24, 1988. Stephen Stills speaks about Young's role in Crosby, Stills, Nash, and Young several months before the release of *American Dream*.

Sandall, Robert. "Rebel without a Pause: Interview." *The (London) Sunday Times* (October 30, 2005): 26. Long article and interview with Young conducted during the filming of the *Prairie Wind/Heart of Gold* concerts in Nashville.

Sandall, Robert. "Still Young at Heart." *The (London) Sunday Times* (December 8, 1991): NA. The journalist reports on his extensive interview with Young, including Young's thoughts on working with a wide variety of musicians and his distaste for digital recording.

Santoro, Gene. "American Buffalo." *The Nation* (August 20, 2001): 32. Long, generally positive review of the Buffalo Springfield box set, but more an appreciation of the band that never quite made it to where it should have.

Santoro, Gene. "*Ragged Glory*." *The Nation* (March 11, 1991): 319. In his appreciation of the album, Santoro notes that Young is willing to face aging and not fall into the nostalgia trap. The reviewer also has praise for Young's recent tour.

Santoro, Gene. "Rockin' in the Free World." *The Nation* (March 11, 1991): 318. Santoro singles out Young as someone still making relevant music in a world full of musical nostalgia for the 1960s.

Schneider, John. "Neil Young, Searching for a Heart of Gold." *Exclaim* (August 2003). Accessed October 23, 2007, at http://www.exclaim.ca/articles/multiarticlesub.

aspx?csid1=50&csid2=9&fid1=2117. Breezy, career-spanning, 4,700-word essay about Young's career.

Schreder, John. "The Artists as Young Men." *Georgetown (University) Independent* (March 28, 2007). Accessed March 28, 2007, at http://media.www.thegeorge townindependent.com/media/storage/paper136/news/2007/03/28/ArtsAnd Entertainment/The-Artists.As.Young.Men-2808614.shtml. The author gives a favorable review to the *Live at Massey Hall* release. He suggests that the concert shows Young at the edge of his dark period.

Schwartz, Tony. "How to Stay Young." *Newsweek* (November 13, 1978). Accessed July 26, 2007, at http://www.thrasherswheat.org/tfa/howtostayyoung78.htm. Young speaks to the journalist about the *Rust Never Sleeps* tour and the *Comes a Time* album.

Selvin, Joel. "CSNY: Déjà vu All over Again." In Zimmer, Dave, ed., *4 Way Street: The Crosby, Stills, Nash & Young Reader,* 317–321. Cambridge, MA: Da Capo/Perseus, 2004. Originally published in the *San Francisco Chronicle,* October 9, 1999. Young speaks about recording the *Looking Forward* album.

Selvin, Joel. "Déjà vu for CSNY." In Zimmer, Dave, ed., *4 Way Street: The Crosby, Stills, Nash & Young Reader,* 343–348. Cambridge, MA: Da Capo/Perseus, 2004. Originally published in the *San Francisco Chronicle,* April 2, 2002. During Crosby, Stills, Nash, and Young's Tour of America, Selvin wrote about the band in concert, the *Are You Passionate?* album, and the broadside "Let's Roll."

Selvin, Joel. "Taking Center Stage." *San Francisco Chronicle* (June 24, 2007). Accessed August 13, 2007 at http://sfgate.com/cgi-bin/article.cgi?f=/c/a/2007/06/24/PKGK0QFSA71.DTL. The author speaks at length with Pegi Young about her debut album and her husband's activities related to the album.

Serwer, Andrew E. "An Odd Couple Aims to Put Lionel on the Fast Track." *Fortune* (October 30, 1995): 21. Article about Young's investment in the struggling model train firm. The author reveals Young's "family values" bent, as he desires to wrest youth away from video games and bond with their families at the side of the train layout.

Shapiro, Bill. *The CD Rock & Roll Library: 30 Years of Rock & Roll on Compact Disc.* Kansas City, MO: Andrews and McMeel, 1994. Capsule reviews of *Everybody Knows This Is Nowhere* (B); *After the Gold Rush* (A–); *Tonight's the Night* (A+); *Harvest* (D+); and Crosby, Stills, Nash, and Young's *So Far* (C–). The focus is on the audio quality of the CD versions of the albums.

Sheffield, Rob. "Playlist: The Lost Songs: The Best Neil Young You Never Heard." *Rolling Stone* 992 (January 26, 2006): 38. In a sidebar article, the critic picks 14 favorite Young songs, one each from albums the critic considers weak. His opinion is certainly not universal.

Simmons, Sylvie. *Neil Young: Reflections in Broken Glass.* Edinburgh: MOJO/Canongate, 2001. In colorful, informative prose, the author covers the full range of Young's music career.

Sinclair, David. "A Fine Harvest in Spite of the Rain." *The (London) Times* (July 13, 1993): 35. A highly, favorable review of Young's performance backed by Booker T. and the MGs at London's Finsbury Park.

Sinclair, David. "Still a Young Man's Game: Interview." *The (London) Times* (May 23, 2003): 16. The writer spoke to Young while he was doing a solo tour of Europe performing the *Greendale* songs. Young outlines the creation of *Greendale* and talks about aging.

Smith, Steve. "Young Holds Crowd Spellbound." *(University of Oregon, Eugene, Oregon) Daily Emerald* (January 12, 1971). Accessed July 26, 2007, at http://www.thrasherswheat.org/tfa/uoforegon011071.htm. Days before the 1971 Massey Hall, Toronto concert that was released in 2007, Young performed a similar solo show on the campus of the University of Oregon.

Snow, Mat. "Neil Young and the Buffalo Springfield: Expecting to Fly." *Thrashers wheat.org* (n.d.). Accessed July 27, 2007 at http://www.thrasherswheat.org/tfa/bufspring.htm. The author summarizes the frustrations Young and his bandmates had trying to make the seminal group a success.

Solnit, Rebecca. *Secret Exhibition: Six California Artists of the Cold War Era.* San Francisco: City Lights, 1990. In her study of six visual artists, the author writes of the Topanga Canyon (where Young lived for a while) arts community that emerged in the 1950s and flourished in the 1960s. It was a place where painters were labeled as "lumberjacks after the rugged shirts they affected." Perhaps, this was a direct influence on Young's fashion choices.

Spencer, Charles. "Young Triumphs." *Spectator* (June 3, 2006). A positive review of *Living with War.*

Stevenson, Jane. "Neil Young: Prairie Harvest." *Toronto Sun* (February 10, 2006): E4. A mostly favorable review of the *Heart of Gold* film, although the critic is frustrated by Demme's decision to leave out the audience and the Ryman Auditorium.

Strauss, Neil. "Heart of Gold: Young's Annual Rite of Passage." *The New York Times* (October 19, 1998): NA. An expanded review of the 1998 Bridge School benefit concert hosted by Young and his wife Pegi.

Strauss, Neil. "The Predictably, Unpredictable Neil Young." *The New York Times* (July 2, 1995): NA. The journalist speaks with Young at the Broken Arrow Ranch, while Young muses on his life and music, suggesting that he could have fit in with Led Zeppelin.

Sullivan, Denise. "Pegi Young: Lady in a Canvas Shell." *Crawdaddy* (September 19, 2007). Accessed October 15, 2007, at http://crawdaddy.wolfgangsvault.com/Article.aspx?id=3024. Long, excellent interview in which Pegi Young speaks of her debut album, the time of Young's aneurysm crisis, and being the subject of some of her husband's compositions.

Testa, Bart. "Neil Young: Coming Full Circle." *(Toronto) Globe and Mail* (September 30, 1978): NA. Ruminating on California culture and Winnipeg prairies, the journalist views *Comes a Time* with a sense of closure for Young.

Thompson, Ben. "Neil Young: Out of the Black." *Thrasherswheat.org* (n.d.). Accessed July 26, 2007 at http://www.thrasherswheat.org/tfa/outofblack_thompson.htm. Written in the mid-1990s, the British author reflects on Young's resurgence.

"The Top 100: The Best Albums of the Last Twenty Years: *After the Gold Rush*." *Rolling Stone* 507 (August 27, 1987): 138–139. A brief essay about the *After the Gold Rush* album, ranked number 71 among *Rolling Stone* magazine's best 100 albums of the years 1967–1987.

"The Top 100: The Best Albums of the Last Twenty Years: *Rust Never Sleeps*." *Rolling Stone* 507 (August 27, 1987): 129. A brief essay about the *Rust Never Sleeps* album, ranked number 66 among *Rolling Stone* magazine's best 100 albums of the years 1967–1987.

"The Top 100: The Best Albums of the Last Twenty Years: *Tonight's the Night.*" *Rolling Stone* 507 (August 27, 1987): 84+. A brief essay about the *Tonight's the Night* album, ranked number 26 among *Rolling Stone* magazine's best 100 albums of the years 1967–1987.

Tyrangiel, Josh. "The Resurrection of Neil Young: When The Godfather of Grunge Discovered He Had a Potentially Fatal Aneurysm, He Took a Week, Went to Nashville and Added to His Legacy by Making Another Classic Album." *Time* (October 3, 2005): 68. An extensive interview given while riding in Young's bio-diesel-powered Hummer at the time of the *Prairie Wind* release. Young speaks of his medical crisis, his father, and funk musician Rick James.

Umphred, Neal. *Goldmine's Rock 'n' Roll 45 RPM Record Price Guide.* Iola, WI: Krause Publications, 1992. Comprehensive list of Young's single releases with interesting minutiae.

Vineberg, Steve. "Encore: *Neil Young Heart of Gold.*" *The Christian Century* 123 (May 2, 2006): 43. In his film appreciation, the author notes that the Ryman concert is shadowed by the loss of people Young has known.

Vivanco, Cosme. "Neil Young's Triumphant Homecoming." *Lumino Magazine* (March 22, 2007). Accessed March 22, 2007, at http://www.luminomagazine.com/mw/content/view/1827/27. A favorable review of the Massey Hall concert album.

Von Tersch, Gary. "Neil Young: *Neil Young.*" In Editors of Rolling Stone, ed., *The Rolling Stone Record Review,* 344–345. New York: Straight Arrow/Bantam, 1971. Originally published in *Rolling Stone,* April 5, 1969. A complimentary review of Young's solo debut.

Vruno, Mark. "Green Effect on *Greendale.*" *Graphic Arts Monthly* (April 2005): 64. Young's commitment to the environment is evidenced in his involvement in making an eco-friendly companion book to the *Greendale* album.

Waddell, Ray. "Rockin' in Music City: Young Previews New Album, Films Performance for Movie/DVD." *Billboard* (September 3, 2005): 27. The journalist witnessed the filming of the concerts that resulted in the *Heart of Gold* film and gives a positive review of the performances.

Ward, Ed, Geoffrey Stokes and Ken Tucker. *Rock of Ages: The Rolling Stone History of Rock & Roll.* New York: Rolling Stone/Summit, 1986. Young pops up periodically from the days of the Buffalo Springfield to his appearance at Live Aid in the pages of this chronicle of the music genre.

Wazir, Burhan. "'I Head for the Ditch.'" *The (Manchester) Guardian* (October 4, 2007). Accessed October 15, 2007, at http://music.guardian.co.uk/rock/story/0,,2183160,00.html. The writer interviews Young about *Chrome Dreams II,* aging, politics, and installing an electric engine in an old Lincoln.

Weinstein, Wendy R. "*Neil Young: Heart of Gold.*" *Film Journal International* (March 2006): 37. The critic labels the *Heart of Gold* film "exhilarating."

Wener, Ben. "Neil Young Brilliantly Journeys through His Past." *The Orange County (California) Register* (October 31, 2007). Accessed November 7, 2007, at http://www.ocregister.com/entertainment/young-one-song-1913264-love-springsteen#. A well-written favorable review of Young's Fall 2007 Los Angeles show.

Wener, Ben. "Neil Young Survived the '80s on His Own Terms." *The Orange County (California) Register* (September 1, 2000): NA. The author highlights some of the musical treasure that was issued during what many consider Young's most artistically dismal period, the Geffen years.

Wener, Ben. "A Pair of Live Sets Worth Owning." *The Orange County (California) Register* (May 22, 2000): NA. The writer gives a positive review to Young's *Silver & Gold* DVD, noting that the musician was between albums at the time and, as such, was testing new material, and the performance benefits from this circumstance.

Wener, Ben. "Press-Wary Neil Young Opens Up to Promote His Project 'Greendale'." *The Orange County (California) Register* (March 1, 2004): NA. The author had the opportunity to sit with Young while he promoted the acted *Greendale* film. Young notes that since his music does not get radio airplay, he has to go to the press. The journalist brings some strong questions to the table and wonders whether someone will come forth to carry the torch of concern ignited by Young and his musical peers.

Whitburn, Joel. *Top Pop Albums, 1955–1996.* Menomonee Falls, WI: Record Research, Inc., 1996. The bible of *Billboard* bestseller information for record albums.

Whitburn, Joel. *Top Pop Singles, 1955–1996.* Menomonee Falls, WI: Record Research, Inc., 1997. The ambitious, exhaustively researched compendium of *Billboard* bestseller information for 45 rpm singles.

Wilkinson, Alec. "Neil Young: The Open Man: Inside His Private World." *Rolling Stone* 992 (January 26, 2006): 30–32+. While driving within and around the boundaries of the Broken Arrow Ranch in an ancient Plymouth, Young shares with the reporter his method of songwriting, even revealing his notebook. The interview took place shortly after the release of *Prairie Wind* and just before the film release of *Heart of Gold*.

Williams, Paul. *Love to Burn: Thirty Years of Speaking Out, 1966–1996.* New York: Omnibus Press, 1997. A smorgasbord of what the noted critic has written about Young since the days of Buffalo Springfield. The book is anchored by four long passages about the four-disc bootleg *Rock 'n' Roll Cowboy*.

Williams, Paul. "Buffalo Springfield." In Williams, Paul, *Outlaw Blues,* 46–51. New York: Pocket Books, 1970. Written at the time of the release of the Buffalo Springfield debut album, the author notes the "tightness" of the band and how each member is one part of the whole body. Williams wonders if the band would continue to grow. An interesting read with decades of hindsight.

Williamson, Nigel. "Is This Déjà vu or Are You Just Pleased?" *The (London) Times* (October 15, 1999): 50. In a substantial piece, the author speaks with the optimistic quartet of Crosby, Stills, Nash, and Young just before the release of their *Looking Forward* disc.

Williamson, Nigel. *Journey through the Past: The Stories behind the Classic Songs of Neil Young.* San Francisco: Backbeat, 2002. In this colorful, oversize book, the author lists each Young song from the Buffalo Springfield collection through the *Are You Passionate?* album and comments on each, some more than others.

Willman, Chris. "Chrome at Last." *Entertainment Weekly* 959–960 (October 19, 2007): 125. The author gives a thumbs-up review to *Chrome Dreams II* and explains the title's genesis.

Winner, Langdon. "Crosby, Stills, Nash, Young, Taylor and Reeves: *Déjà vu.*" In Rolling Stone, Editors of, ed., *The Rolling Stone Record Review*, 348–349. New York: Straight Arrow/Bantam, 1971. Originally published in *Rolling Stone*, April 30, 1970. A mostly negative review of the supergroup's first album with Young. Young's composition "Helpless," however, is given special mention for its "merit."

Young, Astrid. *Being Young.* Toronto: Insomniac, 2007. A gentle exploration of life in the family of a rock celebrity. Written by Neil Young's stepsister, the author aims to pick up where her father Scott Young's *Neil and Me* left off.

Young, Scott. *Neil and Me.* Toronto: McClelland & Stewart, 1984, revised 1997. The sportswriter and novelist contributes a unique point of view as he writes about his son. In addition to providing a distinct backstage vantage point, the work illustrates the complicated relationships between fathers and sons.

Zaferos, Bill. "*Live at the Fillmore* Proves We Needed Another Live Young Disc." *OnMilwaukee.com* (November 29, 2006). Accessed January 20, 2006, at http://onmilwaukee.com/music/articles/neilyoungcrazyhorselive.html?10261. A positive review of the *Live at the Fillmore* set.

Zimmer, Dave (text) and Henry Diltz (photographs). *Crosby, Stills, Nash: The Authorized Biography.* Cambridge, MA: Da Capo/Perseus, 2000. An update of the 1984 edition. Zimmer details all the breakups and make-ups of the band (including with Young), the projects that were realized, and those that fell apart.

Zimmer, Dave. "Graham Nash: The Winds of Change." In Zimmer, Dave, ed., *4 Way Street: The Crosby, Stills, Nash & Young Reader*, 215–237. Cambridge, MA: Da Capo/Perseus, 2004. Originally published in *BAM: The California Music Magazine*, February, 1980. Graham Nash gives his recollections about Young joining Crosby, Stills, Nash, and Young and about the recording of "War Song" with Young.

Zimmer, Dave. "Neil Young on CSNY." In Zimmer, Dave, ed., *4 Way Street: The Crosby, Stills, Nash & Young Reader*, 273–278. Cambridge, MA: Da Capo/Perseus, 2004. An excerpt from "Blue Notes from a Restless Loner" originally published in *BAM: The California Music Magazine*, April 22, 1988. Young was interviewed during the sessions for the *American Dream* album. Young speaks of the unrealized "potential" of the group.

Index

About the Author

KEN BIELEN teaches courses in Popular Music at Bowling Green State University. He is the author of *The Lyrics of Civility* (1999) and *The Words and Music of John Lennon* (Praeger, 2007) with Ben Urish.

www.ingramcontent.com/pod-product-compliance
Lightning Source LLC
Chambersburg PA
CBHW062029270326
41929CB00014B/2374